Shakespeare Plain

The Making and Performing of Shakespeare's Plays

William G. Leary

McGraw-Hill Book Company

New York • St. Louis • San Francisco • Auckland • Bogotá • Düsseldorf
Johannesburg • London • Madrid • Montreal • New Delhi • Panama • Paris
São Paulo • Singapore • Sydney • Tokyo • Toronto

COVER ILLUSTRATION: The Globe Playhouse, 1599–1613, A Conjectural Re-
construction by C. Walter Hodges from G. B. Harrison: *Introducing Shakespeare* (3rd ed., 1966), pp. 126–127. Illustration copyright © Penguin Books
Ltd, 1966. Reprinted by permission of Penguin Books Ltd.

123456789   MUMU   7987

Library of Congress Cataloging in Publication Data

Leary, William Gordon.
  Shakespeare plain.

  Includes bibliographical references and index.
  1. Shakespeare, William, 1564–1616—Criticism and
interpretation. I. Title.
PR2976.L38   822.3'3   76-45776
ISBN 0-07-036947-X
ISBN 0-07-036946-1 pbk.

To **CELIA**

I sent thee late a rosy wreath,
   Not so much honoring thee,
As giving it a hope, that there
   It could not withered be.

ACKNOWLEDGMENTS

Every book on Shakespeare is in some sense a celebration: the writer celebrates in yet another way the poet-playwright who confers inexhaustible pleasure on all who seek to understand and interpret him.

Shakespeare Plain had its origins in two literal celebrations—two public observances of the Shakespeare quadricentennial in 1964. One of these observances took the form of twenty television lectures on Shakespearean drama which the California State University, Los Angeles, commissioned me to write and deliver over NBC during the academic year 1964–1965. The other observance took the form of a Shakespeare festival at Stanford University in the summer of 1964, in which I played a part, guiding a group of teachers who had gathered to read, view, and discuss several Shakespearean plays performed by two West Coast repertory companies from Ashland, Oregon, and San Diego, California.

Both of these occasions compelled me to recognize the principal obstructions that stand between most readers and playgoers and a confident understanding of Shakespeare's plays, and encouraged me to seek practical strategies that would help them surmount these obstructions. The strategies I devised, and subsequently tested over several years in both collegiate classrooms and public forums, are set forth in the successive chapters of this book.

Anyone writing at this late date on Shakespeare is indebted—consciously or unconsciously—to everyone who has written about him. Only one's conscious debts can be acknowledged in the time-honored way. But the unconscious ones deserve a general, if unspecified, acknowledgment, and I gratefully offer that here.

My conscious debts are acknowledged in the "Notes" and in Part B of the section called "Further Reading." Nevertheless, five writers have put me under such special obligation that they require special mention. For help in understanding Shakespeare's ways with language, I owe the most to Mark Van Doren. Possibly only a poet can write with steady illumination about the language of another poet. I think Mr. Van Doren has done so in his book, *Shakespeare.* For insights into the workings of Shakespearean dramaturgy, I am most indebted to Harley Granville-Barker and Bernard Beckerman, men equally at home on the stage and in the study. Among the many books on the Elizabethan playhouse and its stage, I find C. Walter Hodges's *The Globe Restored* the most useful as well as the most readable. In the green pastures of Shakespearean criticism, I have played Autolycus, snapping up, however, more than trifles. But I owe the most to the books and articles of the late Alfred Harbage, whose learning, critical sanity, and elegant style I find matchless. The products of his mind show forth—I trust neither vulgarized nor distorted—on many pages of this book. All citations are to the Pelican Shakespeare, for which Mr. Harbage served as general editor.

It gives me particular pleasure to acknowledge the more immediate, and in a sense intimate, assistance of those scholars, critics, theater directors, general readers, and friends who generously and thoughtfully scrutinized the manuscript of *Shakespeare Plain* at various stages in its evolution. My desire to compose an essay that would engage the general reader and playgoer and at the same time command the respect of the specialist accounts for both the number and the variety of these reviewers. Without exception, their suggestions helped to make this a better book whenever I had the wisdom to adopt them; the book's shortcomings must be attributed to my own limitations and obduracies.

In alphabetical order—I despair of finding any more appropriate means to acknowledge human generosity—they are my colleague, Professor Norman Fruman, who made a signal contribution to Chapter 1 and to the book's organization; my sometime collaborator, Professor Wallace Graves of California State University, Northridge, whose critical scalpel cut away some excesses; my friend, Lamont Johnson, theater, motion picture, and television director, who helped muffle the hortatory tone that issues from earnest teachers; my colleague, Professor David Laird, whose demands for specificity provided some sinew that might otherwise be missing; my teacher, Alfred Longueil, Emeritus Professor of English, the University of California at Los Angeles, whose timely encouragement sustained me more than he will ever suspect; Professor Maynard Mack of Yale University, who interrupted a busy schedule of his own important activities to help me with mine; my sometime colleague and longtime friend, Professor Edward Partridge of Tulane University, whose incisive reading spared me errors of emphasis, judgment, and fact; my old schoolmate, Richard Rossiter, whose delicate ear detected some lapses in diction; my longtime co-author, Professor James Steel Smith, who helped me distinguish between explanation and exhortation; Dan Sullivan, drama critic of the Los Angeles *Times*, who checkreined impulses that tugged me in the direction of the academic; my colleague, Professor James Sullivan, who played devil's advocate concerning some notions that needed testing; and Professor Homer Swander, University of California at Santa Barbara, whose knowledge of Shakespeare both on the page and on the boards helped me maintain my equilibrium as I moved back and forth from playscript to platform.

Later in the day, the manuscript was read by my colleagues Peter Brier, David Kubal, Jean Maloney, Fred Marcus, and Paul Zall, all of whom fortified my resolve to see it published. Toward this same end, my friend, Don Pardee Brown, subjected the penultimate version to the kind of scrutiny that attests to his own passion for English undefiled.

My audiences—both students and members of the general public—have also put me in their debt. When they were bold, their questions compelled me to revise statements that seemed unclear and to reexamine arguments that seemed unpersuasive. When they were docile, their silence compelled me to search their faces for the telltale distinctions between quiet gratification and glaze-eyed apathy. To them go my thanks for favors they did not always know they were conferring.

No writer is a hero to his typists, but both Nancy Craven and Lyle Waters performed heroic tasks in transcribing my cursive crawls into straightforward pica type.

For many years I have read Shakespeare's plays aloud to my family. Because I was wise enough to salt my own book with plentiful lines from Shakespeare, they sat still for innumerable readings of bits and pieces from *Shakespeare Plain,* to which they then reacted freely, thus becoming, until this moment of public disclosure, secret sharers in this enterprise.

Note: Although the line citations in this book are to *The Complete Pelican Shakespeare* (Penguin Books Inc., 1969), differences in typesetting produce small differences in the line breaks, and in a few instances in the line counts, of *prose* passages. In every instance, however, the Pelican Shakespeare line numbering has been retained.

CONTENTS

PROLOGUE

> Ah, did you once see Shelley plain,
> And did he stop and speak to you?

When Robert Browning wrote these lines, in a brief lyric called "Memorabilia," Shelley had been dead for only thirty years. But Shakespeare has been dead for well over three hundred years. Can we, then, still see Shakespeare plain? And does he still speak to us? Drama critics and English teachers, who preserve Shakespeare's reputation and interpret his art, assure us that we can, that he still speaks to us today. But, even assuming that he does, do most of us understand him when he speaks?

Well, yes and no. We are almost surely right if we think we readily follow the broad lines of the stories he dramatizes, grasp the moral dilemmas of the characters he creates, feel the large emotions these plays generate. We are just as likely to be right if we suspect that we are missing much. Some of the action puzzles us, some of the characters behave in ways we cannot satisfactorily explain, some of the speeches are difficult to comprehend, and a few are downright unintelligible, some of the stage business seems not only unfamiliar, but more than a little odd, and—rather maddeningly, since no one likes to feel left out—some of the nuances of word and feeling that provoke laughter or sighs

1

among the presumably more sophisticated members of his audiences are lost on us.

Shakespeare Plain was written to help convert these losses into gains.

The *plain* of the title is not intended to suggest simplicity. Plain refers to the *view* of Shakespeare's plays that can be attained by a reader or playgoer who comes to understand Shakespeare's customary ways of composing and performing them. Plain does not refer to the form or content of individual plays or of all of them collectively or to the artistry of the playwright. Most of Shakespeare's plays cannot be made plain—meaning *simple*—without falsifying them. But the ways he worked as he set about composing and then producing these plays can be made clear; and, alerted to these ways, we can gain a plain view of both the plays and their performances.

Shakespeare Plain was written to remove the most common obstructions to this plain view. These removed, readers and playgoers can not only achieve understanding; they may also come to enjoy that which all art seeks to bestow—sheer pleasure.

1
PLAYSCRIPT AND PERFORMANCE

> Where, my lord?
> In my mind's eye, Horatio.
> (*Hamlet, I, ii, 185*)

The ancient quarrel over whether Shakespeare comes off best on the printed page or on the living stage is a needless one: the simple answer is that he comes off brilliantly on both—provided his readers, and his audiences and performers, are up to the mark. Moreover, just as a playgoer who knows the text will see more, so a play reader who knows the stage will read better. This book assumes that the informed reader and the informed spectator of Shakespearean plays should be one and the same person, one who is equally at home reading a playscript and watching a performance. So we begin with what readers and spectators of Shakespearean plays must have in common—what they should be able to see and hear, whether on a live stage or in the mind's eye and the inner ear.

A play *performed* is a series of speaking pictures. What spectators view is intended to illuminate and reinforce what they hear. This reinforcement of the ear by the eye is necessitated by the ruthless economy imposed on all drama.

Of all the larger literary art forms, the drama is the most economical in its means. In approximately two hours of playing time it must say and show all that it has to say and show. Every word, every gesture, every stage grouping, every movement is consequential. There can be no waste motion. And everything must work together. What the players *do* cannot run counter to what the playwright has given them to *say* unless, of course, that is the ironical effect the playwright intends.

Shakespeare, who spent well over half a lifetime as an actor, manager, and owner in the workaday theater of his time, knew this as well as any playwright ever has. You expect, therefore, to *see* Juliet standing on the upper stage of an Elizabethan theater when you *hear* Romeo exclaim, "What light through yonder window breaks? / It is the East and Juliet is the sun!" And it is from this same upper stage that you will *see* Richard II descend as you *hear* his wailing voice intone, "Down, down I come, like glist'ring Phaeton, / Wanting the manage of unruly jades," on the occasion of his surrender to the opportunistic Bolingbroke waiting in "the base court" below.

Like all simple illustrations of a principle, these two examples appear to be self-evident. But the principle they illustrate deeply informs the total stage performance and should remain uppermost in the mind of the reader, as well as the spectator, throughout. In *The Merchant of Venice,* the most significant attribute of Shylock is not that he is a crafty local moneylender, but that he is a foreboding universal alien—the enemy of love, light, and laughter. Therefore on the stage he must be made to stand alone, physically as well as spiritually isolated from the golden people of this romantic comedy. An awareness of this principle will permit the reader properly to stage in his mind's eye the scenes involving yet another isolated figure—the rigidly proud Roman, Coriolanus, a man whose perverse sense of his private worth very nearly cuts him off from all public contact. And it will permit the playgoer to notice the important distinction between the cool, rational detachment of a Brutus, as he stands on the speaker's rostrum above and aloof from the mob gathered in the forum, and the warm, kinetic presence of an Antony as he purposefully descends from the rostrum to mingle with the commoners so as better to inflame their passions with a closeup view of Caesar's ripped and bloody mantle. Numerous examples could be given, but they would all point to the same principle: the play's action is staged to let the eye as well as the ear help readers or playgoers grasp the playwright's intent.

A good test of the sense and sensibility of a director of Shakespearean plays is his awareness of this principle. Some directors, alas, apparently persuaded that Shakespeare did not know his business or, more likely, cynically convinced that modern audiences can never be trusted to understand and enjoy what Shakespeare had in mind, are forever busy distracting the spectator's eye with stage business of their own invention. Too abashed to rewrite the lines of the greatest playwright in the English language, they display no reluctance to cut them. So, by a combination of deleted lines and added business, they mar what they seek to mend.

Playgoers are always the momentary captives of the director whose production they are viewing. If the director is a meddler with Shakespeare and the playgoers know it, they can do little but groan in their chains for the duration of the performance. They may have to endure such a monument of tasteless exhibitionism and ingenuity gone to seed as that production of *The Merchant of Venice* which featured a homosexual Bassanio torn between allegiance to his gay companion, Antonio, and his desire to wive it wealthily with Portia; a stud Lancelot Gobbo who has something going with a giggling Jessica; and a corporation executive Shylock, without either dignity or pathos, who presumably suggests how a man too wrapped up in business contributes to the generation gap by neglecting his family. Conversely, if the director is an imaginative interpreter of Shakespeare, he may be boldly inventive in his stage effects and still be perfectly consistent with both the spirit and the structure of the play he is presenting. We may gratefully recall Peter Brook's inspired production of *A Midsummer Night's Dream,* in which the seeming gimmick of high-flying circus swings and aerial artists reveals itself as a marvelously right way to project the fanciful flights of the fairies, dipping and diving above the earthbound mortals. This device, moreover, enables the director to pictorialize a very subtle structural element of this play: the concurrent actions of three sets of entangled characters—aristocratic lovers, rude mechanicals, and fairies—all caught in the toils of love, that greatest of all forms of midsummer madness, and all "translated" in the same nameless forest outside Athens where they enact their follies before our delighted eyes.

Unlike playgoers, readers operate independently of any director, good or bad. Armed with the knowledge that Shakespeare provides nearly all of the necessary cues for performing his plays in the speeches he gives his players to say, keen readers—even those with no professional training in the theater—can learn to stage in their imaginations a remarkably authentic performance of a Shakespearean play.

They will, however, need some help. They will want to know something of the kinds of stages and playhouses Shakespeare wrote for. And they will need to exercise their imaginations as they costume the players, choreograph their movements, and orchestrate their speaking tempos and their silences.

As choreographers, for example, they will need to visualize figures in motion on the large platform where Shakespeare staged most of the action of his plays, and, occasionally, in those auxiliary playing areas—the upper stage, the curtained area at the rear of the platform sometimes still referred to as the *inner stage,* the stage doors (certainly two, perhaps three) also at the rear, and one or more trapdoors cut in the platform. Using the cues Shakespeare provides in the dialogue, readers can learn to see in these various staging areas a great variety of scenes—the stumbling and lurching movements of the men of the Montague and Capulet households clashing in a street brawl in *Romeo and Juliet*; a fear-frozen trio of Danes watching the eerie progress of a ghost on the ramparts of Elsinore; the slowly swaying funeral train of Henry VI brought to a shuddering halt by the sudden entrance of Richard Crookback; Ferdinand and Miranda "discovered" playing chess in the recesses of Prospero's cave; those "instruments of darkness," the three witches, rising through the platform trapdoors enshrouded in stage fog to invoke the world of dread evil in which Macbeth will lose his soul; the measured tread of the departing "country copulatives" in the marriage ritual that brings *As You Like It* to its foreordained close. And, much like an opera director, they will learn to carefully stage solo arias, duets, trios, quartets, and choruses: Hamlet in soliloquy; Beatrice and Benedick sparring feistily; Richard II attempting to mediate the thundering quarrel of those angry petitioners Bolingbroke and Mowbray; Brutus and Cassius on the one hand, and Antony and Octavius on the other, engaged in an angry shouting match just before the battle of Philippi; and always the excitable, fickle mobs whose restless movements and vocal outbursts punctuate many scenes in Shakespeare's Roman and English history plays.

The director (and hence the reader in his study) needs to do more. To the concerns of the choreographer and musical director, he will add those of the painter and sculptor. He will wish to display the painter's sensitivity to color. Not only will Hamlet be suitably clothed in an "inky cloak," but the chaste Desdemona will wear a nightdress of the purest white; and the actress who plays Portia will appear with golden hair to match Bassanio's eloquent compliment: "her sunny locks / Do hang on her temples like golden fleece." When Shakespeare has not supplied the clue either in the text or in one of his infrequent stage directions ("Enter Richard, and Buckingham, in rotten armor, marvellous ill-favored," *Richard III,* III, v. s.d.), the reader and director will exercise a sympathetic imagination: thus Iago will be clothed in some fashion suitable to his pose as a bluff, no-nonsense soldier, whereas Cassio will be dressed with something of a flair befitting his reputation as a lady's man.

In Shakespeare's day, color was chiefly a matter of costume and properties (banners, flags, shields, and the like). He employed nothing like our modern stage sets or lighting effects. It is true that the permanent fixtures on his stage—a canopy over a portion of the platform, the pillars supporting it, and the walls or drapery at the rear of the stage—made use of color. But the decor was unchanging, not modified to suit the dramatic repertory. So the analogy with the painter runs mainly to costume and makeup.

But what of the sculptor—at least the traditional sculptor—the products of whose art cannot be seen in motion? This permits us to assert the importance of motionlessness in drama. One of the infallible marks of the poor actor, as Hamlet tells us, is that he saws the air too much. The more accomplished player—and especially one playing Shakespearean roles—is often content to let the playwright's words speak for him and to accompany them with a minimum of movement and gesture. Nowhere is this principle better employed than with the Shakespearean soliloquy, and nowhere better there than with the most famous of all soliloquies, "To be or not to be—that is the question." Those who have witnessed the artistry of John Gielgud will understand this at once.

If the theater has moments of nearly motionless eloquence in which words are permitted to convey their meaning and their feeling without the distraction of physical movements, it also has moments of marvelous silence—silence absolute. Silences in plays are, like rests in music, indispensable to the rhythmic pattern of the whole composition. The good director and the good reader alike will have a feeling for these moments—moments such as that when Romeo, learning of Juliet's presumed death, says with heartbreaking understatement, "Is it e'en so?" To rush his next remark, "Then I defy you, stars!" is to mar all. A silence—neither too long nor too short—will punctuate these successive statements if either is to achieve its maximum effect. There are many such moments in Shakespearean plays. The good director unerringly finds them out and compels his actors to observe them; good readers will also learn to discover and observe these pauses and so approximate in the private theater of their minds what the director can ensure in the public theater.

Silence may be contrapuntal as well as total: the silence of a listener, or of an ensemble of listeners, contrasting with the eloquence of a single speaker, can work wonderful theatrical effects. Thus Richard II, though powerless, weak, self-indulgent, and nearly hysterical, can, nonetheless, hold the rough baron Northumberland and the steely king Bolingbroke spellbound by his matchless lyrics; and their silence, in turn, provides a massive iron and stone backdrop against which his small but velvet tenor can be heard celebrating his own downfall.

The analogies with painting and choreography need not conjure up a picture of elaborate stage scaffolding; indeed, as we have said, Shakespeare had nothing like our modern sets at his disposal. What he did instead—something remarkably similar to the task of the traditional sculptor—was to arrange groups of figures in space. Readers and playgoers will add cubits to their pleasure as they come to understand that the disposition of these figures in the space allotted by the stage is of critical importance in transmitting the playwright's intentions and the play's meanings.

Toward the end of *1 Henry IV*, the young scapegrace Prince Hal is standing stage center with the recumbent bodies of Hotspur and Falstaff on either side of him. Hotspur is dead—killed in the climactic duel with Hal that immediately precedes this moment in the play—and Falstaff is feigning death, albeit the prince thinks he is dead. Hal thereupon pronounces a kind of benediction over each, the real significance of which is to repudiate an essential quality of these diametrically opposed characters—Hotspur's excessive sense of his own worth and Falstaff's excessive sense of everyone else's worthlessness—qualities that would be disabling in the king Hal will soon become. This piece of stage sculpture is visually pregnant with the meanings suggested by the playwright's words. Thus, both verbally and visually, Shakespeare's hero-king is made to transcend the fatal deficiencies of his dearest friend and his keenest foe who, appropriately, lie at either foot encasing those attributes the prince has discarded.

As befits the works of a symbolic artist, Shakespeare's

plays are studded with scenes of this kind—scenes that both the reader and the playgoer can learn to interpret fully. And this learning can be made very pleasurable. Alert to the principle we enunciated at the outset—that what the play's spectators *see* is intended to reinforce and illuminate what they are given to *hear*—readers and playgoers can, by becoming active instead of passive spectators in the theater, learn enough of the director's art to stage and direct their own "productions" with nothing but the playscript in hand and their own trained imaginations to assist them. In this way they, as readers, come to supply the tissue that joins playscript to performance and so reap immense rewards of pleasure and insight.

Our previous remarks about silence now invite us to a further consideration of sound. A play, as we have said, is a set of *speaking* pictures. Here we may draw a useful analogy between a playscript (all we have before us when we read) and a musical score. The reader of a musical score quite obviously must hear what he reads. Less obviously, but just as certainly, so must the reader of a playscript. If the former hears musical sounds, the latter hears human voices. If the one hears violins, drums, and horns, the other hears human whispers, grunts, and shouts. If the musical score can be made to yield, alternately, mellifluous chords and dissonant discords, so the playscript can be made to yield pleasing sonorities or harsh stridencies when the speeches call for these effects. Plays, like musical compositions, have very distinct tonal patterns. These patterns, recognized and observed, permit the reader to come closer to the full intention of the playwright. Since Shakespeare wrote his plays as combinations of rimed verse, blank verse, and prose, both the reader and the playgoer will wish to train their ears to respond to a great variety of speech rhythms and tonal patterns. So important is this aspect of Shakespearean drama that we will devote parts of two later chapters to it.

So much for preliminaries. Alerted to the hurdles between you and Shakespeare and given some notion of how to go about clearing them, you are now ready to run the course. Or nearly so. Perhaps a demonstration is in order before you start. What may readers and playgoers, armed with the means of analysis set forth in *Shakespeare Plain,* be expected to do?

An examination of the first scene of *Macbeth* provides an admirable opportunity to illustrate the analytical process. It should serve as a model of what the initiated reader may expect to derive from an informed reading or viewing of Shakespearean drama.

Thunder and lightning. Enter three Witches.

1. *Witch* When shall we three meet again
In thunder, lightning, or in rain?
2. *Witch* When the hurlyburly's done,
When the battle's lost and won.
3. *Witch* That will be ere the set of sun.
1. *Witch* Where the place?
2. *Witch* Upon the heath.
3. *Witch* There to meet with Macbeth.
1. *Witch* I come, Graymalkin!
2. *Witch* Paddock calls.
3. *Witch* Anon!
All Fair is foul, and foul is fair.
Hover through the fog and filthy air. *Exeunt.*

This first scene is only eleven lines long. Exclusive of the stage directions, it contains only sixty-one words. What can it be made to yield to the trained eye and ear?

True to our principle that what greets the eye must support and illuminate what declares itself to the ear, we will first consider this scene as spectacle. Our present knowledge of Elizabethan acting companies and of the stage machinery they had to work with in the public playhouses of the day permits us to visualize a spectacular opening scene. Three male actors dressed as ugly Elizabethan crones emerge, very probably from beneath the platform stage by means of one or more trapdoors, enveloped in a cloud of artificially induced, smoky fog, to the accompaniment of thunder-like sounds, produced by rolling an iron ball down a long sheet of metal in one of the huts in the third-story superstructure above the stage, and simulated lightning, provided by a display of pyrotechnics, probably set off from one of those self-same huts. For a few seconds the audience may very well exclaim over this eye-popping, ear-splitting beginning.

Then the first witch chants a pair of four-beat riming lines that tells the audience by means of a rhetorical question what they are already staring at: namely, that three witches are met in appropriately foul weather. More forebodingly, the wailing voice forecasts a second meeting of this unholy trio under similar circumstances.

That these withered crones are witches will be immediately recognizable to an Elizabethan audience, many of whom, like the early Puritans in America who came along just after them, believed firmly in witchcraft. They will instantly recognize, too, that such a meeting is ominous. No good can come from it. Incidentally, this audience would also know that the *or* in line 2 was equivalent to *and.* Thus it is raining *now* and will be when the witches meet again. The audience's imaginations are now being worked on to supply what even this ingenious Globe Theater property room cannot provide—rain. Unless, of course, the moist London climate is coincidentally supplying that too.

The convention of men playing female roles, like all theatrical conventions of any day, is a "given" that no one questions. (Modern-day spectators of a motion picture accept the fact that music often appears out of nowhere; it's always been that way.) But, in this instance, even a twentieth-century spectator would have no problem with men playing these parts, for in a very few minutes he would hear Banquo say of these witches:

> You should be women,
> And yet your beards forbid me to interpret
> That you are so.   *(I, iii, 45–47)*

If the first witch's chanted couplet is a kind of redundant scene painting, the second witch's reply is intellectually provocative: it asserts a paradox and introduces an element of deliberate ambiguity.

2. *Witch*   When the hurlyburly's done,
            When the battle's lost and won.

How can a battle be both lost *and* won? (Here the *and* is *not* equivalent to *or.*) Perhaps all that is meant is that this battle—like any battle—will be won by one side and lost by the other. We are reminded of the riddling answers of the Delphic oracles. And that association triggers another thought. Are these witches truly prophetic? Elizabethan witches were assumed to have such powers. Clearly, their words had better be attended to. But warily.

One of these words reveals a curious tone and attitude. The second witch refers to what we correctly take to be a military battle with all the normal connotations of that word. But she does so in a curiously slighting way: she calls this battle *the hurlyburly.* Do these representatives of the supernatural have contempt for mortals and their affairs? If so, what does this contempt bode for any mortal they single out for attention, as they do Macbeth?

The third witch echoes the chanting rime of the second and, appropriately enough, converts a double rime into a triple rime.

2. *Witch*   When the hurlyburly's done,
            When the battle's lost and won.
3. *Witch*   That will be ere the set of sun.

In doing so, she mentions the time of day—it is "ere the set of sun." At once we are struck by a foreboding anomaly. No matter what the time of day, where these witches are the sun will not shine! (We will not be surprised when, later on,

Banquo refers to them as *instruments of darkness.*) This symbolism is obvious enough, but not the less effective for its obviousness.

Place, always associated with *time,* is next established in a staccato question-and-answer exchange between the first and second witches.

1 *Witch*	Where the place?
2 *Witch*	Upon the heath.

And then the third witch names the fateful *occasion*: the meeting with Macbeth. The named place is a *heath.* This word conveys two sinister meanings: it signifies a *wasteland* (with all that the term connotes); and it rimes—or very nearly does—with Macbeth. No member of Shakespeare's London audience would wish to exchange places with this luckless mortal. He is a marked man. Marked for what? For some kind of death. (It is uncanny the way sound is at work here: *death* also rimes with Macbeth.)

The next three lines,

1 *Witch*	I come, Graymalkin!
2 *Witch*	Paddock calls.
3 *Witch*	Anon!

require an interpretive footnote in the printed text for the modern reader, but they present no problem for the playgoer if the actors know their business. Graymalkin, a cat, and Paddock, a toad, would instantly be recognized by a Shakespearean Londoner as the witches' "familiars"—that is, creatures, here treated as pets, in whom reside the witches' devil contacts. All this a modern-day reader needs to be told. But a good actor can surely suggest that he is talking to some mysterious "spirit" by the way he delivers these lines. And that is enough to alert the modern playgoer to what is taking place. Still, there is more. A specially attentive reader or playgoer may notice something significantly odd here: these witches' pets summon the witches instead of being called by them, as would be normal. That is precisely the point. This is not a normal world.

Any doubt of that is dispelled by the concluding chorus.

All   Fair is foul, and foul is fair.
       Hover through the fog and filthy air. *Exeunt.*

Surely these are the most ominous lines of all and they are sufficient in themselves to impress the reader or listener who has missed all the foregoing clues and cues. This time Shakespeare makes explicit the moral abnormality of this dark world. In any world evoked by these three evil things, fair *is* foul and foul *is* fair. Moral values are inverted. Anyone over whom these three elect to hover in the fog and filthy air of their own making is already spiritual carrion.

All this is much, and the playwright's achievement is impressive. But there is still more. At the beginning of this chapter, we mentioned the ruthless economy that drama must practice. The brief scene just discussed is a tour de force of dramatic economy. As an opening scene, it seeks to accomplish many things indispensable to the success of a play. One merely has to tick off some of these things to admire Shakespeare's craftsmanship here: (1) He names his most important character. (2) He establishes an atmosphere—dark and stormy—that peculiarly suits the dark action that will be unfolded in this play. (3) He sketches in at least one event—the battle—that precedes the action of the play and that also foreshadows things to come. (4) He combines language and special theatrical effects to establish a governing tone and mood—both fittingly dark and menacing. (5) He plants the seeds of several significant ideas—notably the idea of the equivocal nature of "truth" ("When the battle's lost *and* won. . . . Fair is foul and foul is fair.")—that will germinate in the mind of the reader-playgoer and will finally flower into understanding as the play runs its course. (6) He uses language in a way that exactly fits his speakers: by providing the witches with the deliberately monotonous cadence of riming tetrameters, he establishes the tone and rhythm of an incantation; the witches are permitted to cast a spell—not only later, over Macbeth, but now over the reader and playgoer as well.

These, then, are some of the ways in which a poetic dramatist works. Of course, not just any eleven lines are so richly packed with meanings, nuances, and overtones as these. But the infallible sign of art is the felt presence of the various structures that give it shape and coherence. And these appear, sometimes simply, sometimes complexly, on every page of a Shakespearean playscript and in every sustained movement of a Shakespearean performance. The ability to recognize and trace these structural patterns—the aesthetic with one's eye and ear, the emotional with one's feelings, and the moral with one's mind—ranks very high on the scale of human pleasures. Happily, these are not pleasures reserved for the few; they are accessible to many. It is the purpose of subsequent chapters to put these pleasures within the reader's reach.

In a period that has seen the motion picture develop into a mature art form, a short note on Shakespearean films is mandatory. Most of what has been said in this chapter about Shakespeare on the stage will not—cannot—apply exactly to Shakespeare on film. The differences between the staged play and the motion picture are radical. Perhaps the principal difference—especially as the comparison applies to Shakespeare—lies in the *sense* to which the performance most strongly appeals. The greatest strength of any Shakespearean play rests with its language: it is essentially an appeal to the ear. The greatest strength of a film rests with its pictures: it is essentially an appeal to the eye.

It follows that the film director confronts some very serious problems when he sets about filming a Shakespearean play. He cannot simply supply us with filmed "shots" interspersed with a thin narrative line. And he must not try to make his camera duplicate the mental pictures conjured up by Shakespeare's words: the redundancy would be intolerable. Nor, if he wishes to make a genuine motion picture, will he content himself with photographing a stage play, although this can be a splendid means of making a fine stage performance accessible to audiences who would otherwise be deprived of the experience. (The Olivier version of *Othello* is an example of how this may be done.) Furthermore, since some of Shakespeare's lines are given over to the task of "painting" scenes the Elizabethan theater did not even try to provide, and other passages do not lend themselves to a "motion" picture, the film director must make cuts—sometimes pretty extensive ones. (Franco Zeffirelli's movie version of *Romeo and Juliet* appears to have eliminated about half the text.) Conversely, he must greatly expand the "action" that Shakespeare barely alludes to or puts in the mouths of messengers and other choral figures or simply lets his audience assume to have taken place offstage. (Consider in this connection how much attention a movie director like Peter Brook lavishes on the business of Lear's retinue of knights—something that occupies only a few lines in the Shakespearean text.)

In a word, these two media do not follow parallel artistic courses: the play cannot be transferred to film as a motion picture and still retain its Shakespearean form.

All this is not intended to point up an invidious distinction. And certainly it is not intended to damn films or filmmakers, as some Shakespearean purists have done. We need not conclude that movies based on Shakespearean plays cannot succeed as either art or entertainment. There is ample evidence, ranging from Laurence Olivier's filmed version of *Henry V* through John Houseman's *Julius Caesar* down to the more recent *King Lear* of Peter Brook, that motion pictures *based on* Shakespearean plays may achieve a powerful artistic life of their own. But these are *adaptations* of Shakespeare's plays, not reproductions of them. They have a different grammar—the grammar of film. They neither can nor should be judged by the criteria we apply to stage plays in general or Shakespearean plays in particular. A distinct art form, the serious filmed version of a literary work must be judged by criteria applicable to the medium in which it is made. Such films deserve the most thoughtful analysis, but the means for such an analysis are not those we shall set forth in detail in this book.

2

PERSON AND CHARACTER

My lord, the man I know.
(*1 Henry IV, II, iv, 441*)

If readers and playgoers were asked the question, What is the single most noteworthy accomplishment in Shakespeare's plays? it is predictable that most answers would point to the lifelike quality of his characters. This is, I think, the first response of anyone who comes to admire Shakespeare; and it is a response that, not surprisingly, has endured from Shakespeare's own day to the present time. When we see or read a play, our attention goes first to the people in it. And this primary interest is likely to remain the most enduring one, since telling stories about people is what drama is all about. It may seem perverse, then, if this chapter begins—as its title implies—by making a distinction between actual persons and Shakespeare's dramatic characters. And yet this is a distinction that must be grasped by anyone who aspires to understand—and therefore fully appreciate—the dramatic art of Shakespeare.

Art is ordered action; life is disordered action. Art is selective and exclusive; life is unselective and inclusive. Literary characters (at least the principal ones) are sharply defined and controlled, producing an effect of significant unity, whereas people in real life, as a contemporary writer has observed, "hardly seem definite enough to appear in print."[1] This principle of selectivity is true even of the novel, that literary form that comes to us looking most like everyday experience; it is doubly true of drama, that literary form that often—and notably in Shakespeare—deliberately exploits its differences from everyday experience.

Recall what was said earlier about the radical economy drama must practice. Apply this now to the creation of a dramatic character. It will be seen at once that nothing can be left, as it is in life, to chance. Everything that goes to make up a dramatic character—every detail of his costume, every aspect of his face and figure, every gesture and every physical movement, every action he engages in and everything he says—will be carefully selected and orchestrated so that in the relatively brief time he is on the stage we come to understand his driving motive.

The cliché is intentional. A dramatic character is a character in motion, and he is driven by some motive that evolves and finds renewed expression in how he looks, how he stands and walks, the figure he cuts, how he acts and reacts. Because he is in motion, he has some complexity—much more than do the intellectual stick figures (*homo sapiens, featherless biped, tool-using animal*) with which the philosopher, biologist, or sociologist seeks to sum up some central aspect of man. But precisely because a dramatic character has this complexity, this individuality, his characterization must be ordered and harmonized by art so as to render him comprehensible within the radically limited confines of a story played for only two hours on a stage. Thus his central motive is not only a propelling and evolving one; it is also a unifying one.

The dramatist is limited in the number of ways he can create a character. Unlike the writer of fiction, he may not directly *tell* you what a character is like; he can only *show* you. True, he may sometimes permit one character to describe another and thus appear to be telling you. Readers and playgoers, and even critics, sometimes assume that the speaker of such lines is merely the spokesman for the playwright. This is a dangerous assumption, especially with an impersonal playwright like Shakespeare. From the moment the dramatist has introduced an intermediary character, he has immensely complicated the situation. Is this spokesman reliable? Does he really tell us the truth about another character or only the way he perceives him? We must, I think, acknowledge the limitations placed on a dramatist, as contrasted with a novelist, who, if he chooses, may play the omniscient observer and, from his god's-eye view of things, tell us anything or everything.

The dramatist's limitation may, however, prove to be a gain. An author who tells denies his reader a vital share in the act of imagination. The reader sees and thinks mainly what he is told to see and think and so becomes a passive receptor instead of an active collaborator in the recreative process. Worse yet, the author may grow didactic and so convert something marvelously suggestive into something rather flatly explained. The dramatist invites a double collaboration, first with the actor, who gives individuality to the role the playwright provides, then with the reader, who, using the playwright's verbal and visual cues, discovers the universal significance in the actions of a particular character.

The playwright can reveal (can show) a character in several ways. The chief among these are nearly as well known to readers and playgoers as they are to dramatists: (1) what a character does, (2) what he says, (3) how he says it, and (4) what others say about him. Petruchio establishes himself as a masterful man by taming a shrew. Richard III says he is "determinèd to prove a villain" and then proceeds to support his words with his deeds. Thersites views the world as a dungheap and gives expression to this view in a language whose ugly sounds and obscene images reflect the foulness of its meaning. And everyone, including his mortal enemies, proclaims the nobility of character that Brutus regularly displays.

These are single illustrations, each of a single method,

and they are purposely simple. The task of any good
dramatist is more complex. So, fortunately, are his means.
To start with, he may appear to make his characters incon-
sistent when in fact they are not. He does this not to confuse
the spectators but to enrich and complicate his characters.
He may use any of the four common means of character
development to do this.

What He Does.   Falstaff's conduct during the highway
robbery appears to be cowardly and so does his behavior at
the Battle of Shrewsbury. But he receives the news of the
uprising of the formidable rebels coolly enough even though
he knows he will be assigned a role in helping to suppress
them. And would a coward fall asleep when the king's
sheriff is searching the tavern to arrest him?

What He Says.   Lady Macbeth calls on evil spirits to make
thick her blood against any feeling of remorse and vows
aloud that she would dash her babe's brains out before she
would permit herself to swerve from her murderous purpose. Yet, not much later, she explains that she could not
murder Duncan as he slept because he too closely resembled
her own father. And again, after the murder of Duncan,
Lady Macbeth says confidently to her bloody handed husband,
"A little water clears us of this deed." But later, during her troubled sleepwalking, she laments, "Here's the
smell of blood still. All the perfumes of Arabia will not
sweeten this little hand."

How He Says It.   Hamlet appears to have nearly as many
tones as the occasions that prompt him to speak. He is by
turns graciously courteous, as when he welcomes Horatio to
Elsinore ("Sir, my good friend, I'll change that name with
you."), and unspeakably callous, as when, thinking she lies,
he upbraids the terrified Ophelia ("Get thee to a nun-
nery. . . . Or if thou wilt needs marry, marry a fool, for wise
men know well enough what monsters you make of them.");
again, by turns nearly hysterical, after he has seen the ghost
of his father ("Ha, ha, boy, say'st thou so? Art thou there,

truepenny?"), and wonderfully calm as he contemplates what faces him following his escape from the doomsday ship and his return to Elsinore ("The readiness is all. . . . Let be."); still again, by turns quietly remorseful, in speaking of how he has treated Laertes ("But I am very sorry, Horatio, / That to Laertes I forgot myself. . . ."), and cruelly obscene, in his bitter taunting of Ophelia just before the mousetrap play ("That's a fair thought to lie between maids' legs.").

What Others Say About Him. Cassius is seen by Caesar as a threat ("Yond Cassius has a lean and hungry look. / He thinks too much. Such men are dangerous."), and there is no evidence that Caesar ever saw him otherwise. Brutus, however, although capable of using harsh words to Cassius's face ("Fret till your proud heart break."), pronounces a benediction over the dead Cassius that would have assuaged even his proud heart ("The last of all the Romans, fare thee well! / It is impossible that ever Rome / Should breed thy fellow.").

These seeming inconsistencies, while complicating and enriching a character, do not result in clumsy contradictions. Rather, these apparent contradictions are resolved by our discovery of a central motive, a kind of common denominator that underlies all of a character's words and actions. Any character who is thoroughly realized in his creator's mind has this unity. The manner in which this unity displays itself in all of the means used by the dramatist to create a character is best illustrated by more extended examples, and we will begin with a familiar one.

Romeo is seen at once to be young, virile, brave, and handsome—one of life's lucky ones, the object of admiration and envy. As befits his status as the heir of one of the leading families of Verona, he is, of course, richly costumed. His actions and gestures are those of a promising young man: they are elegant, as suits his social position; they are easy and graceful, as comports with his education; and they can be both swift and impetuous. His language complements these visible attributes: it is alternately polished, graceful, ornate, swift, witty, impetuous, impassioned. But peering more closely at this young paragon, we detect from the very beginning two complications in his character that may undermine him: he is a romantic idealist so far as love is concerned, and he is immature in his expectations of, and reactions to, the somewhat unlovely world of Verona in which he lives. Romeo's central motive—established fairly early in the play—is to achieve with Juliet a form of imperishable love.

Juliet is in every way his female counterpart, as nearly perfect a young woman as he is nearly perfect a young man. The two of them are dangerously perfect young lovers in a very imperfect world. Their unifying motive—what governs, explains, and harmonizes all of their qualities—is to realize an ideal love. And that word *ideal* provides us with a kind of revelation. These two move toward an inevitable tragedy in their attempts to realize a transcendental love in a sublunary world. Of course they fail.

When the play is over and the shock of their death has somehow been absorbed, the reader and playgoer may see in retrospect how unified these characterizations have been. Their physical beauty enhanced by the richness of their dress, their impulsive gestures and posthaste speed, their uncompromising passion—these attributes at once elevate them above all the other characters in their story and disqualify them from succeeding in the real world of compromise and expediency. The Chorus has called them "star-crossed lovers," seeming to imply that their fate was predetermined. But the real determiner was their artistic creator. He made "brave, translunary things" of his lovers. They are determined transcendentalists. Viewed from this perspective, everything about them is now seen to have pointed to their inevitable destiny. How consummately right it all is—and how very different from rough-hewn, disjointed, unpatterned real life.

The character of Harry Percy, called Hotspur, provides an equally clear illustration of this principle of unity at work. Hotspur appears as uncomplicated as Romeo. He is another idealist, although his ideal—to see his name

emblazoned first on the honor roll of England's warriors—
seems at once more self-centered and more achievable. Older
than Romeo and already an established military hero, he is
no wiser in judgment, no more mature in his assessment of
the way the world wags. He is, of course, physically robust,
wears his armor as comfortably as another man wears his
skin, and is a paragon of physical courage. He walks and
moves and gestures with the suggestion of bursting energy
barely constrained that we see in a mettlesome horse. And
he declares himself to be a blunt, straightforward soldier, a
man of deeds, not words, a man easily rankled by those glib
men who can give "the tongue a helpful ornament." And
right here we have a delightful example of irony. In the very
passage in which he scorns "mincing poetry," Hotspur reveals himself to be one of the great poets of the play.

Do we have an inconsistency here? Reviewing the
four principal means by which a dramatist creates his
characters—what a character does, what he says, how he
says it, and what others say about him—we find the first
two and the fourth totally consistent. Hotspur's actions
throughout, what he says, and what others say about him
(including Prince Hal's wicked parody of his excesses) are
all of a piece. Is his poetic eloquence a contradiction? The
chief attribute of his speech is its torrential quality: there is
simply no stopping him. Whether he is railing against an
ungrateful king, rebuking his elders for their past folly in
supporting that king, contemptuously dismissing a potential
ally who has proved too cautious, baiting the humorless and
literal-minded Welsh chieftain, Glendower, or teasing his
wife about her overly nice speech, his words run swiftly and
flashingly and clear. They are equally impetuous and re-
freshing. There is, then, no contradiction. Hotspur's eloquence is consonant with the unstudied simplicity and
directness of all his movements and all his acts.

If Hotspur is still not very complicated, Falstaff indubitably is. He who would come to anything like an understanding of Shakespeare's greatest comic character must be
thoroughly familiar with the workings of paradox. He must
understand on instinct that two seemingly contradictory

statements may be reconciled by a subtler proposition that can contain them both. Through the glass of paradox, we see how many of the seeming inconsistencies that complicate Falstaff's character can be reconciled. We come to see that a very clumsy body can house a very agile mind, that a very rusty cloak and doublet can encase a wit kept clean and shining from constant use, that a corrupter of youth may be at the same time youth's wisest mentor, that a seemingly dirty joke may disclose a healthy sense of humor, that a decaying knight already in the winter of his days may nourish the spirit of spring, that the apparent butt of the laughter of others appears always to have the last laugh, that one often labeled a coward appears frequently in places of danger without going to pieces.

In creating Falstaff, Shakespeare has not laid aside the rather simple instruments used by all dramatists: costume, appearance, gesture, movement, physical action, and—most important—language. It is just that he has used these instruments more adroitly, investing them with irony, enriching them with paradox, enveloping them with conscious ambiguity. But we must not make a mystery of this process. Beneath the paradoxes there is a common denominator. Like all dramatic characters, Falstaff is symbolic. (This is still another way of saying that dramatic characters are not—cannot be—actual persons but are creations of art.) He is, especially in *1 Henry IV*, symbolic of that part of all of us (a part that most of us suppress most of the time) that wants to defy grave authority, that wants to say the emperor has no clothes, that wants—or thinks it wants—to take a moral holiday from gritty responsibility. We respond to him because we recognize and respond to that part of our common humanity he represents—the spirit of comic anarchy. That he represents this spirit with unparalleled eloquence accounts for the degree of our delight but not for the fact of it.

Statements of the kind we have been making about Romeo, Hotspur, and Falstaff can be seriously misleading if they convey the notion that they encapsulate all or even most of what these characters are. We have been attempting to illustrate briefly the process by which the dramatist builds characters and some of the gross means used in the construction. This sort of discussion necessarily results in a severe reduction and produces only a simulacrum of the dramatist's creation. Each dramatic character is the sum total of *all* the evidence supplied by the playwright, and anything less is a distortion. This difficulty is commonly present in discussions of art. It should not, however, be permitted to discourage such discussions. So long as we do not mistake the part for the whole, and so long as the proffered part is truly representative of the whole, we may continue to view dramatic characters in this way without fear of falsification.

Having examined some of the principal means of creating characters, let us now consider the possible consequences of confusing dramatic characters with real persons. We must recognize that dramatic characters possess only those qualities their authors endow them with. We have no license to speculate about other qualities we might presume a character to have. Needless controversy has raged over certain characters simply because this principle has been ignored or forgotten. As Alvin Kernan has pointed out, if we insist on approaching dramatic characters as real persons, we may take other details of the play for granted, thus missing their significance.[2] It is as though we were to focus only on the melody of a Bach fugue, blocking out contrapuntal effects and harmonies as unimportant. The analogy is not farfetched. The distortion resulting from such selective listening is not more radically destructive of the composer's intent than is the selective reading or viewing of only some elements of a play. A controversial issue—the role of Shylock in *The Merchant of Venice*—highlights the dangers of selective reading.

Looked at as a whole, *The Merchant of Venice* is a romantic comedy in which the forces of love, light, laughter, beauty, and concord are marshaled against the forces of hate, darkness, sour sobriety, ugliness, and discord in a struggle which, though unequal and foreordained to be won by the forces of light, is sharply and interestingly contested. Portia is the leader, the focal figure, and the radiant symbol of the forces of love, and Shylock is her formidable opposite. The way the rest of the characters line up in this conflict discloses Shakespeare's design: almost all of them—including Shylock's daughter—are ranged on the side of Portia. Only Arragon, who represents arrogance as his name implies, Morocco, whose sensitivity to outward appearance because of his black complexion ironically does not prevent his selecting the wrong casket because of its gilt exterior, and Tubal, a fellow moneylender, belong—and the first two only distantly—to Shylock's side. Clearly, Shylock is destined to be overwhelmed. He is not designed to be a tragic racial hero but a comic villain.

Shakespeare's handling of the other elements of drama offers further evidence of his intentions. His distribution of plot stuff, scenes, and spoken lines is nearly as one-sided as is his allocation of characters. Portia alone is given more lines than Shylock. The entire fifth act, with its resolution of the comic ring plot, takes place after Shylock leaves the story. And the world of Belmont, which is the fairy-tale world where Portia lives and where all of the important characters except Shylock end up, wins a total victory. Its spiritual and emotional values triumph over those of the world of Venice where Shylock spun his plot against Antonio.

Now if Shylock were identified as a Ruritanian, if, in other words, the question of his Jewishness and our reactions to that question did not come between us and this play, it is highly unlikely that we should ever have failed to see him as the *dramatic character* Shakespeare created: an alien in a world of romantic lovers; a tyrannical father, in the age-old tradition of romance, who deserves to see his lovely young daughter escape his jail-like house; and, most significantly, a hater who attempts to disguise revenge as literal justice while repudiating mercy—in a word, the villain of a romantic comedy.

But two considerations have thrust themselves between a contemporary reader and such an unimpeded view of this character. Shakespeare does make Shylock a Jew, and in doing so he draws the invidious distinctions between Jew and Christian which his age took as a matter of course but which ours can no longer accept. And he does make Shylock so dramatically interesting and so relatively complex that many readers and playgoers since the eighteenth century have been ignoring the rest of the play in their desire to transform a comic scapegoat into a near-tragic figure.

Concerning Shakespeare's decision to make Shylock a Jew, we may say these things. Although Shakespeare took the figure of a wicked Jew from his plot source, he has for the most part universalized his character. Several memorable characteristics that Shakespeare gives to Shylock are not peculiarly "Jewish" but are those we might expect to find in any able member of a proscribed minority: resentment at being classified as inferior, exploitation of money as the only source of power available to him, and an inverted sense of superiority together with an aloofness stemming as much from fear as from pride. Also, Shakespeare may be exonerated from the charge of careless or callous Jew-baiting when it is realized that the moneylenders in the London of his day were all Christians and when one recalls that Shylock is permitted to point out with telling eloquence that all of the evils with which he is being charged he has learned from the conspicuous examples set for him by Christians. Finally, in a period that took seriously the doctrine of damnation, no Christian would view the forced conversion of Shylock after the trial as cruel and inhuman punishment. A work of art is necessarily the product of its times. To impose a specific twentieth-century interpretation of morality on a Renaissance play is hopelessly to confuse life and art: by doing so, we are demanding that sixteenth-century drama mirror twentieth-century codes of behavior.

But what of the argument that Shylock bursts the bonds of a traditional character type and emerges as a towering figure of tragic dimensions? If we accept the premise that "the play's the thing," the rebuttal is clear. The evidence from the play as a whole which we have already marshaled and displayed admits of no real issue: viewed from the perspectives afforded by *all* of the principal elements of the play—plot, world, theme, *and* character—Shylock must be consigned to the role of a frustrated villain so that the

time-honored resolutions of comedy—the matching up of
lovers, the restoration of all losses, the reconciliation of all
differences, the removal of all threats of happiness—may be
achieved. Those readers who confuse dramatic characters
with real people may take their eye off the play and focus it,
as others have done before them, on such extraneous matters as the rules of Venetian law courts, the practice of
usury in the Renaissance period, the relations of Jews and
Gentiles in Shakespeare's day and before, and similar matters whose roots are in history and not in art. If to this
mistake they add a twentieth-century predisposition to look
with disfavor on any manifestations of anti-Semitism, it is
no wonder that they end by substituting for Shakespeare's
Shylock some construct of their own that will be seen to be a
projection of their sentiments.

By a kind of comic irony that he himself might enjoy,
Shakespeare is partly to blame for this confusing of actual
person and dramatic character. He has succeeded too well
in making illusion significant and therefore more believable
than workaday reality. As one critic put it, he knows how to
generate belief in the fabulous.[3] How does he do this with
respect to the creation of character? Critics have sometimes
despaired of finding an adequate explanation and have re-
treated behind such verbal smokescreens as "ineffable
genius" or "the impenetrable mystery of the creative process." But the question is susceptible of an answer or,
rather, of several answers, since these will be discovered to
have their roots in various Shakespearean techniques.

Three of these techniques are intimately connected with
Shakespeare's use of language, which is to say that they are
poetic techniques. Beginning early in his career with such a
minor character as the clown, Launce, in *The Two Gentlemen
of Verona,* or such nameless characters as those in the mob
addressed by the demagogue, Jack Cade, in *2 Henry VI,*
Shakespeare reveals his almost phonographic ear for what
our contemporary linguists call *idiolects*—the unique language or speech patterns of single individuals. The result is
that he endows such characters with a cadence, diction, and
idiom so recognizably their own that they simply talk themselves alive. One immediately thinks of Old Capulet, the

Nurse, and Mercutio in *Romeo and Juliet,* of Falstaff and Mistress Quickly in *1 Henry IV,* of Dogberry in *Much Ado About Nothing,* of Bottom in *A Midsummer Night's Dream,* of Shylock in *The Merchant of Venice,* of Malvolio in *Twelfth Night,* of Polonius in *Hamlet,* of Cleopatra in *Antony and Cleopatra,* and of Justice Shallow in *2 Henry IV,* to name only those who come immediately to mind.

Here is one example—a brief but clear demonstration of Shakespeare's skill in projecting a unique voice. We hear old Capulet's angry response to Juliet after her enigmatic reply to his proposal to marry her speedily to the worthy County Paris. Juliet, of course, is secretly married to Romeo and cannot give her father the clear and unequivocal reply he expects. Never famous for his composure, he explodes:

How, how, how, how, chopped logic? What is this?
"Proud"—and "I thank you"—and "I thank you not"—
And yet "not proud"? Mistress minion you,
Thank me no thankings, nor proud me no prouds,
But fettle your fine joints 'gainst Thursday next
To go with Paris to Saint Peter's Church,
Or I will drag thee on a hurdle thither.
(Romeo and Juliet, III, v, 150–156)

Even such a brief passage displays the technique—a perfect matching of the words and phrases to the rhythms that convey them: the jerky breathless quality of the first two and one-half lines, then the long, sustained torrent of abuse, all in one breath, of the final four and one-half lines. The diction is colloquial, the imagery is homely, the proportion of monosyllables is high, the syntax is nervous and varied, the tempo is swift but varied, the tone is tart, the voice is loud and irascible, the total effect is unique. And, as if this were not accomplishment enough, Shakespeare, making use of two of the oldest devices known to writers—alliteration and repetition—manages to give these devices an idiosyncratic turn in the mouth of this angry man that leaves at least one line impressed forever on the memories of those who have heard him: "Thank me no thankings, nor proud me no prouds." With even this single example before them, readers will understand why I wish to designate this particular means of creating naturalistic characters as the method of *poetic idiom*.

It is not surprising that so many examples of this method are associated in our minds with that long line of minor characters whom someone aptly named "Shakespeare's disreputables." Besides Juliet's Nurse and Mistress Quickly, already mentioned, these would include the Porter in *Macbeth,* the gravediggers in *Hamlet,* Ancient Pistol, who follows Falstaff in *2 Henry IV* and outlives him in *Henry V,* Thersites in *Troilus and Cressida,* and the drunken Stephano and Trinculo in *The Tempest.* Surveying this motley crew, one is reminded of Henry James's observation that it is easier to write novels in a class society. England, where until the most recent times a person's accent both revealed and permanently fixed him in his social class, has provided her greatest writers, including Shakespeare and Dickens, Sheridan and Fielding, with endless opportunities to bring a character to life on the breath of his own language. The accomplishment must not be underestimated. The writer's ear is almost phonographic, but he is not a phonograph. The writer invents; he does not simply record. The parallel with the creation of character is perfect: these inimitable speeches, like the inimitable speakers who give them utterance, are works of art. When we call them lifelike, we think we are conferring on them and their creators our highest praise. It would be more accurate, and the praise would be better directed, if we were to call them masterpieces of illusion.

A second technique I shall designate as the method of *poetic epitome,* the kind of compression Emerson called "the power of few words." We see it at work on those occasions when Shakespeare gratuitously confers on one of his characters his own matchless powers of compression so that character A, the speaker, catches the quintessence of character B, the person he is speaking of, in a brief remark. Examples abound. Perhaps the best known is the description of Cassius by Caesar already cited. One of the briefest is found in one of Shakespeare's earliest plays, *3 Henry VI,* suggesting that this particular talent, like most of Shakespeare's talents, was his for the using from the outset of his career as a playwright. Clarence and Edward, the brothers of the crookbacked villain who will become Richard III, learn that he has ridden furiously off to the Tower of London to murder Henry VI, after a Yorkist victory in one of the bloody battles of the War of the Roses. One says to the other "He's sudden if a thing comes in his head" and in these few words captures the terrifying energy that is central to this character. Rosalind, the heroine of *As You Like It,* can tick off almost anyone in a phrase. She dismisses the self-indulgent sentimentalist, Jaques, who has been cultivating his mannered mordancy, with these words: "And your experience makes you sad. I had rather have a fool to make me merry than experience to make me sad: and to travel for it too." And she impales the foolishly proud country girl, Phebe, who has been cruelly resisting proffers of love from the earnest country boy, Silvius, with "Down on your knees, / And thank heaven, fasting, for a good man's love; / For I must tell you friendly in your ear, / Sell when you can, you are not for all markets."

But my own favorite comes from a somewhat unexpected source, *Love's Labor's Lost.* I say unexpected because this relatively early play of Shakespeare's is a furiously literary, even rather arty, play full of what we today call inside jokes, those that appeal to the special audience of sophisticates for whom such confections are prepared. Here Shakespeare was poking fun, in high-comedy fashion, at some young lovers (recognizably like the young gallants in his Elizabethan audience) who are theorizing about love instead of experiencing it. But he seems to have wanted to ventilate this play with some country air, and in the process he introduces four foolish fellows, including a rural curate, Nathaniel, and a clown, Costard. Like the rude mechanicals in the better known *A Midsummer Night's Dream,* these simples decide to entertain their betters with a little play of their own devising, a kind of review of ancient history and its great men, which they entitle *The Nine Worthies.* Nathaniel elects to play Alexander the Great and makes a great botch of it. He comes on, is struck dumb with shyness, splutters two or three lines, and withdraws in utter confusion. Costard, the clown, who is nimble of tongue and who is acting as the master of ceremonies, then gets off the following statement, which is an entire biography in five lines. Pointing to the departing Nathaniel, he says to the audience of lords and ladies:

> There, an't shall please you, a foolish mild man;
> an honest man, look you, and soon dashed. He is a
> marvellous good neighbor, faith, and a very good
> bowler; but for Alisander—alas, you see how
> 'tis—a little o'erparted.
>
> *(V, ii, 575–578)*

To complement the methods of poetic idiom and poetic epitome, Shakespeare had yet another means of making his fictitious characters seem lifelike—the method of *poetic incongruity*. That phrase needs an explanation. It points to the fact that in some of his great plays, at moments of the highest emotional intensity, Shakespeare introduces a simple utterance—a request or a response—on the part of some central figure which strikes us as being totally unexpected, wildly incongruous, and even dangerously close to being ludicrous. This technique requires the greatest boldness, and Shakespeare is up to it. Two examples, chosen from two of Shakespeare's tragedies, *Othello* and *King Lear,* illustrate the process.

Late in the play to which he gives his name, Othello, reduced by Iago's guile and his own consequent cruel jealousy to a kind of madness, confronts Desdemona in her own bedroom. In one of the most painful scenes in all Shakespeare, Othello treats that innocent bedroom as though it were a brothel, the chaste Desdemona as though she were a whore, and her lady-in-waiting, Emilia, as though she were the madam. He overwhelms Desdemona with a torrent of wild accusations and bewilders Emilia, who is present only at the beginning and end of the interview, with his ugly but cryptic references to her "office" and her "function." On Othello's furious departure, Emilia turns to Desdemona, asking, "How do you, madam? How do you, my good lady?"

Whereupon Shakespeare provides Desdemona with this incredible answer: "Faith, half asleep." Who but Shakespeare would have thought that, after a scene of the kind she has just undergone—the brutal interrogation by the frenzied Othello—that the appropriate reaction is one of complete exhaustion? Who else would have introduced here such a low-keyed, anticlimactic, seemingly incongruous phrase instead of some high-flown purple passage, some eloquently rhetorical protest to which a lesser playwright would have gravitated? The effect astonishes us.

The second illustration is deservedly the most famous of its kind in all of Shakespeare's plays. It comes from *King Lear* and from the very last part of that play. With the death of his loved and loving daughter, Cordelia, Lear has paid the highest price for his arrogance, his wrath, and his moral blindness. In the closing scene, he comes carrying the body of the dead Cordelia before Albany, Kent, and Edgar, who represent the forces of good, and there he bitterly laments her death and begins his second and last slide into the peculiar torment that is prompted by grief, this time to be terminated by his own death. His final lines give poignant expression to his grief, but in the middle of them Shakespeare introduces a reference to—of all things—a button! It is unlikely that any other writer would have conceived of such a dangerous device: to ask his actors to engage in a piece of stage business that borders on the ludicrous. Shakespeare dares and wins! Commentators from Shakespeare's own day down to the present time have used the word *natural* to designate the effect he uniquely achieves. Glancing at the body of the dead girl in his arms, Lear cries out:

>   . . . no, no, no life?
> Why should a dog, a horse, a rat, have life,
> And thou no breath at all? Thou'lt come no more,
> Never, never, never, never, never.
> Pray you undo this button. Thank you, sir.
> Do you see this? Look on her! Look on her lips,
> Look there, look there—
>
>   (*V, iii, 306–312*)

And then Shakespeare, having marvelously brought his most powerful character fully to life in his most powerful play, lets his old king die.

Since, to many readers, Shakespeare is first and foremost a poet, it might appear that the three poetic techniques we have been reviewing provide the fullest and best account of, how he achieves the lifelike qualities of his characters. But this is not so. For one thing, he didn't always write like this. Shakespeare seems to have had as many styles as there are ways of writing well, and some of these styles sound far from lifelike. To complicate matters, some of his characters who occasionally speak in this natural poetic idiom, at other times speak in rhetorical patterns and rhythms that are most unlifelike. Hamlet, because he has so many speaking styles and because he seems to so many readers and playgoers to be as "real as life," is perhaps the best example, but there are many others. Moreover, the Shakespeare whose technique we are analyzing was not just a poet; he was a poetic playwright. Recalling the many ingredients that make up such a composite art form as the drama, we are compelled to recognize how fitting to the dramatist's function is the English word *playwright*, with its denotative meaning of a maker, builder, shaper of plays. Albeit the most important of his materials, language is not for the playwright, as it is for the poet, the exclusive one. So it is, finally, to Shakespeare's skills as a playwright that we must look for a technique that comprehends all of the means we have so far examined and, in so doing, comes closest to the explanation we are seeking.

One of the truthful paradoxes of literary criticism is that the whole is always greater than the sum of its parts. Applied to a Shakespearean play, this means that the total effect produced on the reader or spectator is more than the sum of the effects produced by plot, character, world, theme, and language—the principal elements of any play. This larger effect is produced by the *relationships* of these principal elements, by the interplay of the five operating organically, as if parts of a living thing, not mechanically, as if parts of a machine. Viewed this way, a Shakespearean play appears as a process, not a product; as a fluid, modulating, evolving phenomenon, not as a rigid, unchanging, fixed artifact. The analogy is with a living thing, not a lifeless object.

The same analogy underlies Alfred Harbage's analysis of Shakespeare's method of creating lifelike characters—an analysis that puts the primary emphasis on the *relationship* of the character under observation with all the other characters in the play.[4] Armed with this insight, the reader-playgoer can cut more than one Gordian knot. Knowing that Iago's masterful duplicity renders invalid what he says, how he says it, and what others say about him as indices to his true character, are we reduced to understanding him solely from what he does? What he does is to plot and carry out the destruction of good persons. But other villains do this. What is his distinction? An examination of his relationship with Desdemona provides the answer. Although he announces motives for bringing down Othello (even if the ones he makes explicit have never convinced most readers), he has none at all for destroying Desdemona; she has done him no wrong, real or imagined, and she even turns to him for help. He destroys her for the sheer pleasure of it. Coleridge's flashing epithet, "motiveless malignity," is vindicated. Without needing to draw on the resources of modern psychology, Shakespeare's observation of human behavior permitted him to portray a moral monster. And he did so—and this is the important point—primarily by revealing this monster's relationship with decent human beings.

This insight into the inextricable relationships between one character and all the other characters who inhabit the world of the play of which he is a part will work to resolve other puzzling problems of character as well. Why is it that the shocking list of Hamlet's offenses—manslaughter (the accidental killing of Polonius); an entrapment leading to execution (of Rosencrantz and Guildenstern); a series of savage verbal assaults on a defenseless young girl (Ophelia), which may have contributed to her suicide; a self-exculpating lie (to Laertes)—never render him odious to any reader or playgoer? Indeed, when these offenses are catalogued and displayed, as here, they astonish us. Why? It is because our conception of Hamlet is based not only on what he does and says, how he says it, and what others say about him but also on what others—all, in their different ways, good persons (Horatio, Fortinbras, Marcellus, Bernardo, the players, and, significantly, Ophelia herself)—are prepared to do for him. No one loved and admired by these persons can be truly bad; conversely, anyone feared, distrusted, or abused by such greasy citizens of this world as Claudius, Polonius, Laertes, and Rosencrantz and Guildenstern must be good.

Similar instances will occur to the reader already familiar with Shakespeare's principal plays and characters and will be discovered by those who are now encountering them for the first time. The way a noble soul like Brutus feels about Cassius removes much of the patina of villainy from that often-maligned character; the unqualified love and allegiance Lear can command from Cordelia, Kent, and Edgar enable us to see that his sins are all venial, as opposed to the mortal sins of Goneril, Regan, and Edmund; the very fact that Othello could be truly loved by a woman of such peerless virtues as Desdemona is a sufficient answer to those critics so lacking in sensibility as to find a weak rationalization rather than a poignant truth in his final words: "Then must you speak / Of one that loved not wisely, but too well. . . ." A clear grasp of the technique we have been discussing—penetrating to the essence of a character by carefully focusing on his interrelationships with all the remaining characters in the play—may permit us to solve many seemingly difficult problems of characterization. Better yet, it may prevent such problems from rising to puzzle our minds in the first place.

3

SETTING AND WORLD

> O brave new world
> That has such people in't!
> *(The Tempest, V, i, 183–184*

Because Shakespeare, as playwright, actor, manager, and owner, was so completely immersed in the theater, we are not surprised to discover that his most persistent metaphor for the real world he lived in was the stage; and for his fellow human beings who populated it, the players. Moreover, from what we know of the typical Elizabethan public playhouse and its platform stage, it seems quite likely that his audiences thought that way too. For every time they crossed the Thames to see a play at the Globe, they would be reminded by its name and shape that the "wooden O" they were about to enter was a metaphor for this earth. And once they entered, they saw before them a symbolic representation of their universe: a great platform that, like their earth, occupied the middle ground between heaven above (represented by the star-studded canopy that covered much of the playing area) and hell below (the "cellarage" beneath the stage, with access to it by means of trapdoors cut in the platform). Indeed, given their medieval metaphysical heritage, with its notion of this world as merely a way station, a place for tryouts for ultimate roles in heaven, it may be that this theatrical metaphor appeared to them so natural, so inevitable, as almost to lose its figurative quality.

But if Shakespeare thought of the great world metaphorically as a stage, he did not, like his medieval forerunners, attempt to make his literal stage a platform on which to parade all life and all history from Genesis to the Day of Judgment. Instead, drawing his inspiration from the real world and the people in it, whom he seems to have understood as well as any man who ever wrote, he created for each of his thirty-seven plays a unique world—an imaginative projection of some particular sector of the total human landscape against which some particular action of the total human drama was played out with unforgettable vividness.

Used this way, *world* is likewise a metaphor and is, therefore, susceptible to a range of interpretations. Viewed from the perspective of a theater director, the world of a play might be said to define the space around the actors on a stage. Viewed from the perspective of a playwright with a special vision of human behavior, the world of a play is the total imagined environment that envelopes, permeates, compels, and reflects the actions of the characters he has created. At first these two meanings might appear quite different, but these are differences without a distinction: the world of a play embraces both its physical and its imaginative components. From this it is not difficult to understand that the term world traces a greater circumference of meaning than do any one of three more familiar terms—*setting, mood,* and *atmosphere*—that have traditionally been used as substitutes for it. None of these latter terms is very serviceable to one who seeks to understand Shakespeare's plays. It is important to take a moment to say why.

Setting, for instance, implies a fixed and particular locale, whereas Shakespeare's habitual practice is to make use of unlocalized scenes on a kind of placeless stage in order to achieve the fluidity he needs to move his characters freely in time and space. To be sure, he usually supplies a generalized location: one of his plays takes place in Rome, another in Venice, a third in Verona, and others act themselves out in populated forests in Arden or on blasted heaths in Scotland. But except infrequently—and then for some very good purpose—he resists particularizing the locale. We are *somewhere* in Rome when Caesar is first warned about the ides of March and *somewhere else* when Casca is rendered afraid and Cicero seems curiously unmoved by a "tempest dropping fire." And we are somewhere in Arden when Touchstone complains that his legs are tired and somewhere else in that forest when the melancholy Jaques moralizes on the slaying of a deer.

Thornton Wilder, who later adopted Shakespeare's practice, understood very well what he gained by it. Unencumbered by stage sets and using even stage properties very sparingly, Shakespeare never had to harness time to place at the cost, as Wilder puts it, of having to "thrust the action back into past time, whereas it is precisely the glory of the stage that it is always 'now' there." [1]

Ironically, three centuries of editors, apparently misunderstanding Shakespeare's stagecraft, have gratuitously supplied details of place that he deliberately omitted. This practice, though well intended, is at best needless and at worst misleading, as is anything that distracts the reader's attention from the actions of the characters—always Shakespeare's focus. We see, then, what is wrong with the term setting: it suggests something fixed and particular, whereas Shakespeare's customary practice is to play out his action in some generalized location with its suggestion of the universality of human behavior. A Shakespearean world may be named *Illyria,* but it is a state of mind and not a seaport to which Shakespeare is directing our attention. The tourists who trek annually to Elsinore to view Kronborg Castle will not catch a view of the world of Hamlet; only an informed reading of the playscript or a lucky night in the theater will give them that.

The difficulty with the term *mood* is of a different order. First, mood is a term that normally attaches itself more to the character played by an actor than to the space around him. It seems to suggest more of what is "in here" and less of what is "out there." Moreover, even if one is content to employ personification in order to invest the space around the actor with the same feeling that resides within him, the term remains limiting, designating only one dimension of that more complex environment we are defining by the use of the richly metaphorical term world. Shakespeare's worlds, even the simplest of them, are too complex to represent a single mood.

Atmosphere, with its suggestion of something surrounding, enveloping, even pervading the environment of the characters, at first seems better. But for our purposes it, too, retains a defect: it suggests immobility, stasis. And we need a term that will convey the notion of a governing force. If a principal dramatic character is, by definition, a mover, the environment in which he moves and has his being more often than not shapes and conditions the direction of his movement. Clearly, then, what is wanted is a word that will embrace all the meanings—of place, of feeling, and of envelopment—suggested by the older nomenclature and will add to these other meanings suggesting size, weight, pressure. The word we need will encapsulate the notion of force; and this force may be of any kind: physical, psychological, social, aesthetic, or moral.

A word with such an all-inclusive meaning may appear to be almost synonymous with the play itself—with the entire work of art. And in a way, that is true. Because the world of a play will be internally consistent, an exhaustive exploration of that world will touch all of the play's nerve ends. A play's world may be said to embody that unifying principle that at once holds a play together, permeates all its elements, and renders it unique. Expressed another way, it is the projection of that peculiar vision of the artist that, when it is fully realized, informs every aspect of the play he has composed: the particular human experience he has selected to dramatize, the unique attitude toward that experience he presently holds, the creature life he creates to act out that experience, the significance he attaches to both them and it, the tone in which he expresses his attitude and his insight, and the language that conveys all of this to his audience. Thus conceived, the world of a play may appear as a structure of structures, a skein of relationships, the container *and* its contents.

Assuming, as we will, that each play of Shakespeare possesses its unique world and that each of these unique worlds, like all works of art, is an ordered, shaped, and coherent whole (unlike the disorderly great world of which it is only a partial symbol), then we are ready to survey three representative Shakespearean worlds and some selected aspects of those worlds, confident that by doing so we shall obtain yet another insight into the ways Shakespeare worked and yet another perspective from which to understand and admire his achievement.

We will begin close to where Shakespeare himself did, with one of his earliest plays, *The Comedy of Errors.* This farce turns on a gimmick: the confusions that follow when two sets of identical twins—one pair of masters and one pair of servants, all of the same age—find their paths crossing for the first time since their enforced separation as children. Shakespeare tips his hand when, borrowing the idea of twins and mistaken identity from Plautus, he doubles the formula by thrusting *two* sets of twins upon the stage.

This is more than the natural exuberance of a young playwright who is out to dazzle. It is the wise choice of a youthful artist who doesn't yet have very much to say but who instinctively understands the importance of exploring the possibilities of his chosen medium for all the available means of expressing whatever he does have to say. (When asked by aspiring young poets if he thought there was any hope for them, W. H. Auden said no to the novice who "had something of paramount importance to tell the world," but a cautious yes to the aspirant who confessed that he "just liked to knock words together to hear how they would chime.") But what kind of a world do you create to tell an extended joke involving a complex set of mistaken identities?

Shakespeare was of two minds about this. His conscious, prosaic mind worried a bit about the problem of plausibility.

How do you persuade your audience that Antipholus of Syracuse and his Dromio can wander about the streets of the eastern Mediterranean city, Ephesus, for the better part of twelve hours, being constantly mistaken for Antipholus of Ephesus and his Dromio, without tumbling to the obvious solution to the puzzle? Shakespeare's response to this conscious concern was to scatter throughout his play many references to "cozenage, sorcerers, witches, cheaters, mountebanks, a fairy land, sprites, madness, dreams, conjurers, Circe's cup," and so forth, all calculated to plant the idea that a pair of normal boys from Syracuse have gone astray in the cloud-cuckooland of Ephesus, whose mad citizens appear to be engaged in a conspiracy to deprive them of their wits.

But this is the merest surface stuff, and Shakespeare knew it. The world of this play is not Ephesus "full of cozenage." The true world of any play turns on what excites the imagining mind of its author. What kindled Shakespeare's imagination here was the fascinating technical problem of imposing, as his own Hamlet would later do, method on madness. Shakespeare seems to have known, as have all authors of zany comedy, from Aristophanes to the scriptwriters for the Marx Brothers movies, that to direct and control our laughter he must impose the sanity of form on the insanity of matter. We may call this straitjacket of form which Shakespeare here slipped over the quicksilver of substance, *symmetry*. And by symmetry we shall mean all those combinations of parallels, balances, correspondences, echoings—in short, all those suggestions of conscious matchings—which delight the eye and ear and mind because they satisfy our peculiarly human rage for order. Given the pleasing notion that human twins constitute a special form of symmetry, and reminded that farce is preeminently the dramatic mode that depends most heavily on patterned stage business and technique (the split-second entrance and exit, the double take, the clear view by the audience of what is unseen or unguessed at by the actor, sharply contrasting character types, a bewildering number of confusions that must finally be answered by an equal number of "recognitions"), the reader or playgoer will see that symmetry is the very "life of the design" of farce and that the appropriate world of a farce about the mistaken identity of twins will be one in which the pleasures of symmetry will be exhaustively exploited.

And so it is. Beginning with the "people in't," Shakespeare introduces every conceivable variation on the theme of symmetry, most obviously with his characters but just as insistently with the play's structure and its language. So relentlessly does Shakespeare explore all possibilities that a full catalog of them would certainly be too long and might be tedious as well. We will, therefore, single out only a few instances of symmetry as they reveal themselves in three of the play's elements: character, construction, and language.

We begin with the characters. As everyone who has looked into a mirror knows, the most exquisite pleasure of symmetry is to witness the bringing together of a disunited pair. Obviously, to do this, they must first be separated. In an expository first scene, Shakespeare explains with mathematical precision how this happened to his twins. A merchant and his wife, with twin sons for whom they have purchased twin servant boys, escape a disastrous wreck at sea when, the father and one son and one slave boy lashed to one end of a mast, and the mother and the other two boys lashed to the other, they float free of the sinking ship only to founder on a mighty rock that neatly splits the mast in twain, directing one piece to a rescue ship bound for Corinth, the other to a ship bound for Epidamnum. The separation achieved by this perfectly balanced choreography of the imagination, Shakespeare sets about to preserve it for the nine scenes of "errors" that intervene between the opening scene of exposition and the closing scene of resolution.

To do so, he introduces a fair number of other characters—one almost wants to call them dancers, so balletic is their movement. More frequently than not, these characters appear in pairs or in other symmetrical groupings. One Antipholus (of Ephesus), for example, has a wife; inevitably, she has a sister. The two women operate as a pair: the wife a shrew, the sister her gentle counterpart. There are exactly four merchants who appear from time to time, singly or in combination. They are employed to introduce various stage properties (money, a gold chain, a ring) that Shakespeare uses to assist his audience to identify the twin they are presently looking at. There are also two grotesques: one a pedant, and one a policeman. The pedant, like much else, is borrowed from Shakespeare's source in Roman comedy; but the policeman is Shakespeare's own creation—and, again, this addition provides another pair!

Like one devising a crossword puzzle, Shakespeare makes use of many combinations of ingenious pairings to devise symmetry. First there are *romantic* pairings: Antipholus of Syracuse and the Ephesian sister; the loving parents (separated like their twin sons but destined to be reunited in what must be the longest "boy loses girl, boy gets girl" sequence of all time); and Antipholus of Ephesus and his wife, who are reconciled. Second there are the *antiromantic* pairings: Dromio of Ephesus and his grotesque wife, Luce, whose description constitutes some of the play's funniest lines; and Antipholus of Ephesus and the traditional courtesan, derived again from Roman comedy. Other groupings, which anticipate regular patterns of later Shakespearean comedy, are the *young and the old* (the father, Egeon, and son, Antipholus), and the *high-comedy* and *low-comedy* characters (each Antipholus with his Dromio). Unique to this play is a pattern for which a contemporary sports metaphor—the home team and the visiting team—seems the most apposite phrase: the boys from Syracuse and the boys from Ephesus. Finally, since this is a comedy in which coincidence can be employed shamelessly to restore order, there are *two* examples of the traditional *deus ex machina:* the local abbess, who turns out to be the boys' long-missing mother, and the sympathetic Duke of Ephesus, who has, from the start, sought a happy means to avoid imposing his town's heavy penalty on the old merchant from Syracuse, the boys' father.

This considerable, but by no means complete, list of Shakespeare's character pairings is matched by his symmetries of structure. The opening and closing scenes of the play constitute a *frame* within which the nine scenes detailing the "errors" neatly fit. The opening scene opens up the possibilities for endless error, and the closing scene closes off those possibilities by bringing about a succession of recognitions. These last, of course, come in pairs: the two Antipholi recognize each other; the two Dromios recognize each other; the merchant, old Egeon, and the ancient abbess recognize each other as husband and wife; Antipholus of Syracuse and the sister, Luciana, recognize their love for each other; Antipholus of Ephesus and his wife, Adriana, rediscover their connubial love for each other. (But it is very unlikely that any members of Shakespeare's audiences recognize themselves in these zanies. That kind of awareness is prompted by Shakespeare's later plays, which demonstrated that he had more to think about and more to think with. The world of this early farce, like those of the Roman models on which it is based, is a relatively unfeeling one. The appeal of much comedy—and certainly of farcical comedy—is to the head, not the heart.)

Shakespeare's central picture of errors is as cunningly constructed as is the frame. There are, by my count, some eighteen principal errors scattered through the nine scenes, and these come at intervals that are spaced with remarkable evenness. There are three distinct sets of properties identifying each set of twins—six properties in all. There are evenly spaced speeches recapitulating what has just transpired, designed to keep everything clear to the members of the audience, who must never be permitted to share the confusions of the participants. The few scenes that border on romantic love (between Antipholus of Syracuse and Luciana) are followed hard by mock-romantic scenes or lines to provide the kind of symmetrical contrast that Shakespeare will use in many of his later plays. This is one play of Shakespeare's that rigorously observes the unity of time—mistakenly thought to be a classical heritage. The play takes place in one day; it contains, as well, *two* personifications of Time. In addition, the convention of the false arrest, derived from Roman comedy, is doubled in this play. More fancifully, but in view of all that we have seen not irresponsibly, we may point out that this play is in a sense a "tale of two cities," Syracuse and Ephesus, and that these two cities are at opposite points on the Mediterranean, the only known physical world of the time of the play.

Symmetries of language parallel those of character and structure. *Rime* and *meter* are surely the most obvious components of linguistic symmetry. One-fifth of this play's lines rime—a proportion exceeded in only three of all the rest of Shakespeare's plays. Moreover, since there is scarcely a line in the entire play that has the quality of true poetry (its compression, its suggestiveness, its radical multiplicity of meaning), the meter, instead of being subordinate to meaning, tends to be intrusive in its regularity, calling attention to its symmetry. Patterns of alternating rime, as well as the more familiar riming couplets, appear, illustrating two kinds of symmetry.

In addition to these *sound* effects, symmetry appears in the *sense* of the language as well. The *pun,* which is by definition a wedding of sound and sense in symmetrical pattern, is everywhere in this play. So, too, are such symmetrical rhetorical patterns as question and answer, pro and con arguments, cause and effect statements, and the like. Closely associated with these, and also representing a fusion of both sound and sense, is the device known as *stichomythia*: dialogue presented in single alternate lines that—with or without rime—are perfectly balanced in length and rhythm. Two other language devices should be mentioned, partly because again they are arranged symmetrically in this play (coming in pairs), and partly because they are amusements that Shakespeare never abandoned in his later plays. I refer to the cheerful and primitive pastime of name calling, which tends to pattern as brief and explosive passages of epithets exchanged as rapidly as badminton shuttlecocks, and to passages of greater length and greater art in which a master of eloquence unpacks his heart by describing someone he detests in a cascade of verbal abuse, the cumulative effect of which is in direct proportion to its length.

Such, then, is the world of one play—an early effort in

which the means become the end, form becomes substance, and *how* the play means becomes precisely *what* the play means. The how, in this instance, is almost exclusively a matter of structure. How, Shakespeare seems to have asked himself, can you make a big wheel turn swiftly and smoothly by spinning a number of little wheels within its circumference? *The Comedy of Errors* was his answer.

Having glimpsed a play world created by an artist principally concerned with exploiting form, we are ready now to turn to *Richard II,* a play whose world is largely conditioned by its author's infatuation with language; and, more specifically, with the way language can be manipulated to launch a succession of matchless lyrics that will mourn the passing of a king, a kingdom, and an age. Our inquiry begins, as it did with our first example, with a consideration of the developing powers of our playwright. All of his writings at the time he composed this play—and these include *Romeo and Juliet, A Midsummer Night's Dream,* and at least some of his sonnets—provide the answer: Shakespeare has discovered his lyric voice and is giving nearly unquenchable expression to a steady flow of musical verse whose melodies and harmonies are their own excuse for being. For a dramatic poet, this is at once a great asset and a great danger. On the one hand he finds he can say some things incomparably well; on the other hand, he cannot always be sure these stunning lyrics will serve a dramatic purpose. A memorable instance of this danger is the Queen Mab description uttered by Mercutio in *Romeo and Juliet.* The fanciful imagery and artful music of these forty-two lines may delight the eye and ear but may well puzzle the mind of either reader or spectator; in any case, they come dangerously close to arresting the progress of the play. Even sympathetic commentators have noted that Shakespeare's lyric impulse did not always willingly submit itself to the checkreins imposed by dramatic form. Such, then, was the playwright's potential dilemma at the time he composed this history play: the lyric poet at times threatened to overshadow the dramatist.

In Richard II, Shakespeare found a hero who proved congenial to this lyric bent, but his poet-king is not made up of the stuff of ordinary heroes. Sensitive where they are strong, hesitant where they are bold, vacillating where they are firm, contemplative where they are active, and, above all, a man of words where they are men of deeds, Shakespeare's Richard is better qualified to be a medieval minstrel than a warrior king. Indeed, some commentators have discovered in him qualities remarkably like those of his creator: a keen imagination, a turn for introspection, a love of music and pageantry, an awareness of the dramatic implications of a situation together with an instinct for self-dramatization, a ready flow of feelings, and an irrepressible eloquence. These are not altogether fanciful parallels. Certainly Shakespeare was especially fond of his hero. It is no accident that *Richard II* is one of only two plays that Shakespeare wrote entirely in verse or that he gave Richard more lines to speak than he provided any other figure until he came to delineate the character of an even more remarkably eloquent poet-prince, Hamlet.

But if Richard II should have been a medieval minstrel, he was in fact a medieval king. And therein lies still another significant circumstance that contributed to the world of this play. In more than one sense, the historical Richard may be regarded as one of the last of England's medieval kings. For one reason, he died in 1400, toward the end of the period of decay of many of those institutions—monasticism, the guild system, scholasticism, and Romanesque and Gothic styles of art and architecture—that had marked the height of medieval culture in the twelfth and thirteenth centuries. For another, he was the last of the Plantagenets, the royal line that traced itself back to Henry II nearly 250 years before. For a third, Richard, a lawful and anointed king, was deposed by Henry Bolingbroke, Duke of Hereford, whose claim to rule was thus forever tainted, especially in the eyes of a social order that subscribed to the fiction that one of the King's two "bodies" was divine. That Shakespeare was fully aware of both the political and the symbolic shock of this usurpation is made evident by his treatment of it in the play. However, the foregoing historical considerations are only incidental to our inquiry. It is a work of dramatic art that we are construing.

With characteristic impartiality, Shakespeare seeks to preserve a difficult balance in his interpretation of the complex figure of Richard, who possesses qualities at once sympathetic and repellent. And, viewed from many perspectives, he succeeds in doing so. It is only from the aesthetic perspective that he gives Richard the best of it: no poet hates the sound of his own voice. Richard is endowed with his creator's own lyric eloquence. And this balance in characterization is matched by balance in plot design. Shakespeare's dramatic sense told him that the movement of his story line was as clearly defined as a capital X: the "advancing" of Bolingbroke and the "dejecting" of Richard, to quote his favorite chronicle source, Holinshed. He proceeded in just this way in tracing the dramatic reversal of the fortunes of Richard and Bolingbroke, with the climax coming at the meridian of the play, where their paths fatally cross.

But plot lines were only one of the means to establish this sharp contrast between his two contenders. Another quite remarkable means was to see this transfer of power from a legitimate king to a superior, but unauthorized, successor as the passing of an old order and the emergence of a new one. The old order was traditional and ceremonial. It blurred the modern distinction between reality and ideality. And all of its most glorious monuments—the cathedrals, paintings, code of chivalry, theory of government, literary theme of courtly love—fused (a modern might say *confused*) the symbolic and the literal into one indivisible whole. This was the medieval view of things. In this play, its spokesman is, to be sure, a king, but his days are numbered. The world of *Richard II* is a dying world presided over by a poet-king who provides us with vivid views of its landscape while he pronounces its epitaph.

There is encased in the London National Gallery a two-paneled painting known as the Wilton Diptych. The right-hand panel (left as we face it) shows a lifelike portrait of Richard II in profile, kneeling, with three saints, St. John, St. Edward the Confessor, and St. Edmund, standing on his left (thus behind him, since we view his right side). The other panel, toward which Richard is looking, features a standing Virgin Mary holding the Christ child, the two of them surrounded by standing and kneeling angels all of whom wear the king's badge, a white hart and peascod collar. Richard's three patron saints are interceding for him with the Virgin and presenting him to the Christ child, who is bending forward in his mother's arms with a gesture of blessing. This painting is considered a masterpiece of late medieval art. Concerning its qualities, Sir Kenneth Clark exclaims, "How exquisite it is; and how gross, by comparison, are all subsequent royal portraits." [2] These words perfectly fit the sentiments of many readers of Shakespeare when they compare his "portrait" of Richard II with those of the kings who appear in his other English history plays.

The diptych, moreover, quite marvelously captures the peculiar ambience with which Shakespeare has enhanced the portrait of his minstrel-king, especially in the play's most memorable scenes, in which Richard seeks to insulate himself from ugly reality and, in a succession of lovely lyrics, creates his own illusory world wherein he reigns as king of his griefs and seeks to retain by means of magic words all that he is in the course of losing, by means of his actions, in the more brutal real world.

Even before he loses touch with reality, Richard shows himself to be almost mesmerized by words—a victim, as York observes, of "lascivious metres." We first see him adopting a majestic tone and big voice in a futile effort to resolve a dangerous quarrel between the powerful Henry Bolingbroke and Richard's own faithful lieutenant, Mowbray. Failing in this, he assigns them to trial by combat; but at the crucial moment, he calls off the fight and instead imposes exile on them both, characteristically exacting of them oaths of fealty that reveal his blind faith in the efficacy of mere words and revealing in the process a love of his own language that far exceeds any compassion he can muster for either of the knights whose fates he is determining. Following this, Bolingbroke's father dies, and Richard rashly confiscates his estates to finance foreign wars. Predictably, Bolingbroke seizes the first opportunity (Richard's ill-timed expedition to Ireland) to break his word and return to England at the head of a rebel force, ostensibly to recover his estates but actually to steal a kingdom. Richard's supporters melt away, and he finds himself well nigh defenseless. In this emergency his behavior is astonishing: he alternates between verbal invocations to God to send heavenly hosts to preserve his "anointed king" and the most intricate laments and adjurations, fascinating in their rhetorical convolutions and fanciful figures of speech but of no avail against the relentless pressure exercised by Bolingbroke. (It is revealing that Richard somewhere refers to his mighty opposite as the "silent king.")

And thus the play continues, at least whenever Richard is on the stage, as a series of tableaux or, perhaps, scenes stitched in a medieval tapestry, in which everyone surrounding Richard appears immobile and silent so that we may hear the superb arias "sung" by this poet-prince. Continues, that is, until its penultimate scene, in which the now deposed Richard, faced by assassins who invade his prison cell in Pomfret Castle, uncharacteristically makes a brave and violent end, killing two of his tormentors before he falls victim to the blade of the third. But long before this, Richard has found the means of describing the death of all kings, and indeed of everyman, in lines that perfectly suggest medieval woodcuts of the kind known as *memento mori* because of their theme. At the same time, these lines distill the essence of the medieval world of the play:

> . . . for within the hollow crown
> That rounds the mortal temples of a king
> Keeps Death his court; and there the antic sits,
> Scoffing his state and grinning at his pomp;
> Allowing him a breath, a little scene,
> To monarchize, be feared, and kill with looks;
> Infusing him with self and vain conceit,

As if this flesh which walls about our life
Were brass impregnable; and humored thus,
Comes at the last, and with a little pin
Bores through his castle wall, and farewell king!

(*III, ii, 160–170*)

Richard is by no means the only medieval figure in the play. His gentle queen is depicted in three scenes that might well have found their way into another masterpiece of medieval painting, *The Very Rich Hours* of the Duke of Berry, the great French patron of Gothic art. We first overhear her engaging in a very mannered conversation with her husband's favorites, playing metaphorical variations on the theme of premonitory sadness. These premonitions fatally realized, we last see and hear her taking her final leave of Richard in a dialogue full of smoothly polished rhetoric but devoid of human passion. In between seeing and hearing her in these two scenes, we witness her role in the play's most allegorical scene, one that comes just past the midpoint of the play and serves as a choral comment on the reasons for Richard's downfall. It takes place in the royal garden, which is likened to the world, its unpruned trees and untrimmed grass to an ill-governed kingdom, the "noisome weeds" to the parasitical courtiers, those caterpillars of the commonwealth who have fed on the kingdom and irreparably damaged the reputation of its king; and, by implication, Richard himself is likened to the neglectful gardener, the modern-day Adam who must be turned out of the Eden he did not have the prudence to maintain.

Even some of the scenes involving lesser figures like old John of Gaunt (the father of Bolingbroke) and the Duke and Duchess of York and their erring son Aumerle who plots against Bolingbroke have this painted quality, with the various speakers striking attitudes and speaking in balanced cadences and measured lines as though one were hearing the antiphonal responses of soloists in a church choir. The words that spring to mind to describe these scenes—formal, ritualistic, ceremonial, liturgical—provide a clue to their tone and manner: they appeal less to our deep feelings than to our sensibilities, less to our unconscious instincts than to our acquired tastes, less to nature than to culture. This is another way of saying that the play's poet-king, and perhaps his creator as well, are here self-conscious poets whose lyrics are characterized by a literary diction, an intricate imagery, and a sweet and smooth-flowing melody—splendid qualities, but not those we associate with the powerful, seemingly unconscious utterances that give expression to the suffering of Shakespeare's major tragic heroes.

Not that this is all there is to the play. As everyone knows, conflict is at the center of drama. And so it is here. If Richard's world is traditional, Bolingbroke's is not. If Richard lives in a world of symbols, Bolingbroke inhabits a world of palpable objects. His words relate to realities, not visions; to pragmatics, not wishes; to the new world based on power, not to a dying world based on ceremony. His language, like the man himself, is normally clear, logical, forceful, masculine. The men he attracts to his cause, from the burly Northumberland to the latter's mettlesome son (barely sketched in this play but to emerge as Hotspur in the play that serves as a sequel to Richard's story), are enterprising men of a new stamp. They possess those qualities—energy, self-confidence, boldness, courage, initiative, and ruthlessness—that characterized many of the men Shakespeare saw at the court of Elizabeth, the qualities we associate with that company of explorers, sea dogs, politicians, and entrepeneurs who helped usher in the English Renaissance and made London one of the power centers of the Western world.

It would be rash to say with confident dogmatism that Shakespeare had all this explicitly in mind when he came to write *Richard II* and that the play should be read primarily as an account of the death of one era and the rise of another in England. But it does not seem too much to claim that these ideas may be clearly seen at work in the series of striking contrasts incorporated in the play's principal elements—the sharply contrasting main characters, the contrasting styles of their speech, and the contrast between the moral absolutes intoned by Richard and the pragmatic actions carried out by Bolingbroke. When we discern threads and motifs like these running through several of the play's elements, we are not only entitled, we are even compelled, to assert that we are in touch with the world of that play.

By now we have seen the kind of world that can be created by an ambitious young craftsman anxious to explore the formal resources of his chosen medium—drama. And we have examined the very different kind of world this same playwright can project when he particularly wishes to give vent to his lyrical talents to celebrate the mournful passing of a glittering age and its eloquent monarch. It remains to discover what kind of world will emerge when, gathering all of his powers, he sets about to write about the many faces of evil in a series of tragedies.

Shakespeare drew the bow of Achilles several times— surely with *Hamlet, Othello, Lear,* and *Macbeth*—and the great world has gladly acknowledged that he hit the mark every time. So much has been said and written about these four masterpieces it seems improbable anything new can be added. And yet it is perhaps the chiefest wonder of these plays that, taken singly or in combination, they are susceptible of so many insights that even 350 years after their composition a commentator may still advance a suggestion with some hope that it may illumine and not obscure Shakespeare's achievement.

These four tragedies, as everyone comes to perceive, are all intense studies in evil. What has not, I think, been emphasized is that the first three focus on figures who in some useful sense of that word remain innocents albeit seriously tainted, whereas the fourth fixes our horrified gaze on a corrupted man who steadfastly works evil until he is at last brought down. Hamlet, beginning as "Th' expectancy and rose of the fair state," finds, alas, that state grown rotten; and charged "to set it right," discovers that the only human way to do so is to become "a little soiled i' th' working." Othello, a man of "a free and open nature" at home in a

world of "anters vast and deserts idle," finds himself
"perplexed in the extreme" in the more confining world of
Cyprus and falls easy victim to an artless love that "is too
much of joy" and to a supersubtle Venetian who, for his own
perverse pleasure, ensnares both the soul and body of his
gullible general. And Lear, who, despite his great age and
great power, "hath ever but slenderly known himself," must
waste all of himself, her whom he most dearly loves, and the
world that contains them both before he attains the wisdom
that accords with age.

Nonetheless, as we contemplate the fearful suffering of
these three tragic heroes, we never surrender our sympathy
for them or our conviction of their essential worth. However
foolish or terrible or even horrifying their actions, their essential goodness serves to extenuate. In Melville's words,
"At the Last Assizes it shall acquit."[3] But the same cannot
be said for Macbeth. Of all Shakespeare's tragic heroes, he is
the one irretrievably damned. We can, arguably, sympathize
with his suffering but surely not with his conduct. The
world of the play he occupies therefore will be a hell on
earth.

And that is just what Shakespeare creates in the swiftest
and briefest of his tragedies. Beginning with a masterful
first scene of only eleven lines and sixty-one words, the
playwright sets before our eyes a world of physical darkness, of political civil war, of social discord, of personal
treachery, of psychological confusion, and of moral equivo-
cation. To these he adds murder; assassination; an un-
staunched flow of blood (scarcely two pages of text or two
moments of stage action ensue without the sight or stench or
at least mention of blood); a physical landscape that
suggests a wasteland (the blasted heath of the three witches
is its appropriate central image); a kind of universal sleeplessness (which, if not literal, almost seems so, so "full of
scorpions" are the minds of Macbeth and his wife); those
near-companions of sleeplessness, hallucination and "the
affliction of . . . terrible dreams"; the personal as well as
social divisions of a gestapo-ridden police state; and,
perhaps most subtly horrifying of all, a kind of moral ennui,

a sort of boredom with the effects of evil, that creates the feeling that we are witnessing moral zombies stumbling across a lunar landscape in which evil so permeates the atmosphere that it is an undifferentiated phenomenon. To shift the figure, this hellish world of Macbeth strangely resembles the scarifying world of modern warfare flickering nightly on hundreds of thousands of television screens— and, horrifyingly, with much the same result: the reducing of evil to a banality because the human mind refuses to accommodate so much of it ("I am in blood / Stepped in so far that, should I wade no more, / Returning were as tedious as go o'er.").

To delineate this fearful world of Macbeth, Shakespeare, now at the height of his powers, draws freely on all the resources available to the Elizabethan playwright. He exploits to the full all the stage machinery of the public playhouse. His witches emerge from the "hell" below the platform stage through trapdoors, enveloped in artificially induced fog, to the accompaniment of stage thunder and lightning. Minor members of his repertory company take the roles of strangely made up "apparitions" conjured up by the three witches. Following a stage convention immediately understood by his audiences, the ghost of Banquo appears, seen only by Macbeth and the audience. Drawing on the by no means sparsely equipped property room, Shakespeare produces not only blood-dipped daggers, witches' drums, flickering torches, and the usual crowns, swords, and bucklers of a military state but also marching men carrying tree branches as Birnam Wood comes to Dunsinane—and even, on one occasion, an "armed head" and, on another, the simulated severed "head of Macbeth" himself. As a thoroughgoing man of the theater, Shakespeare knew the power of spectacle and never considered its use beneath him simply because he was also endowed with such a mighty imagination. His artistry lay not in eschewing the trappings of the theater but in using them functionally to advance his play, almost never for their own sakes as mere eye-catching diversions.

Still, as we would expect, Shakespeare's language—which works directly on the imaginations of his audience—is an instrument capable of more varied and more wondrous effects than are all of his theater properties and machines. By means of vivid imagery, he creates successively blasted heaths, castle ramparts on which "heaven's breath smells wooingly," castle gates that serve to remind us of the mouth of hell, rough nights and days as black as night when even the sun is eclipsed, and a nearly prostrate Scotland where each morning "New widows howl, new orphans cry, new sorrows / Strike heaven on the face."

If the imagery is powerful, the metaphors are more powerful still. Their greatest pressure is exerted, appropriately, on Macbeth, whose most humane attribute is the imagination that serves as the true instrument of his punishment. From the first, it gives him no peace: ("Why do I yield to that suggestion / Whose horrid image doth unfix my hair / And make my seated heart knock at my ribs . . .?") No wonder Macbeth's is "a face where men may read strange matters." But there is worse locked up inside: "Methought I heard a voice cry 'Sleep no more' "; "But wherefore could I not pronounce 'Amen'?"; "I am cabined, cribbed, confined, bound in / To saucy doubts and fears"; "Thou canst not say I did it. Never shake / Thy gory locks at me"; "But let the frame of things disjoint, both the worlds suffer / Ere we will eat our meal in fear, and sleep / In the affliction of these terrible dreams / That shake us nightly." The talent that makes him a great poet is, ironically the scourge that makes him a great sufferer: "I am sick at heart"; "My way of life / is fall'n into the sear, the yellow leaf"; ". . . all our yesterdays have lighted fools / The way to dusty death."; "I 'gin to be aweary of the sun. . . ."

There is still another dimension to Shakespeare's achievement in *Macbeth*—one that we have not yet seen. Not only does he exceed the dramaturgical skill he first displayed in *The Comedy of Errors* and the power of language that came to lyric flowering in *Richard II*, but here he also displays intellectual and philosophical resources that are absent from these other plays. As one would expect of an artist, these powers express themselves in Shakespeare through the imagination. Not a systematic and original thinker in the manner of his contemporary, Francis Bacon, Shakespeare thinks feelingly. Thus he comes to understand that the actions of a Macbeth bent on murder are most fittingly depicted as those of a man under a spell; that the atmosphere that should seem to envelop him after the deed is committed is a suffocatingly claustrophobic one; that the condition in which he will remain after the murder is one of *puzzled* fear; that the peculiarly appropriate price he should pay for his crimes is that of complete alienation, even from his wife; and that the moral verdict to be passed on his conduct is best summed up in the single word *unnatural*.

Each of these insights is arresting, and each of them and the sum of them all seem psychologically "right." This is the understanding of human behavior that turned many of Shakespeare's nineteenth-century admirers into uncritical idolators. But even when their excesses are properly discounted, the achievement is impressive. Given the kind of man Macbeth appeared to be before committing his fatal crime—a fearless warrior, a great military captain, an admired patriot, a man endowed with a powerful imagination and a clear-eyed moral sense—we are compelled to conclude that he is that most puzzling of killers, the kind who could not possibly commit a murder. Shakespeare never attempts to answer our question, How could such a man commit such a crime? Nor does he address the larger question lurking behind this more immediate one, Why is there evil to do? Instead he creates the kind of world that envelops a Macbeth from the moment he recognizes his own moral contamination and starts down "the way to dusty death."

The world of *Macbeth* is a tour de force of artistic unity. This physically dark and bloody world is made so by the fact that its principal occupant is morally corrupt. Once embarked on his career of crime, he discovers that there is no turning back. His vain efforts to achieve personal security simply beget further crimes. These, in turn, produce a divided society that must then be ruled by a police state. Such a state can operate only by means of terror. When terror is sufficiently widespread, there is insurrection. The threat of insurrection breeds fear in the tyrant, who thereupon becomes ever more vicious and ever more isolated. A despot grown odious in the eyes of all becomes odious in his own eyes. And so at last the man who has made life a hell for those around him discovers the worst form of hell in his own soul. He despairs, grows reckless, and is finally brought down, really indifferent to the prospect of losing his own life since he has already lost everything that might make life worth living.

These three examples afford reasonably full illustrations of Shakespeare's way with the world of a play. As different as they are, they have one thing in common: each of these worlds reflects whatever it was that at the time of composition most excited the imagination of their creator. This "whatever it was" can be a problem in technique, an impulse to give lyric expression to some universal sentiments, a fascination with the psychology of evil—or many other things. For instance, Shakespeare can pit one world against another—a world of light, laughter, music, concord, and love against a world of darkness, dourness, stridency, discord, and revenge, as he elected to do in *The Merchant of Venice.* Or he may choose to startle us by suggesting the remarkable parallels that underlie two worlds that appear superficially unrelated, like the courtly upper world and the gamy underworld of *1 Henry IV.* (We will have much to say about each of these last-named plays in our chapters on "Story and Plot" and "Theme and Meaning," respectively.) As one might expect, the worlds he designs to project the various conditions of love are nearly as varied as is that inexhaustible subject: a neopastoral world to test the durability of the notion of romantic love in *As You Like It;* a hot and violent world to serve as the cruel adversary to a transcendental notion of love in *Romeo and Juliet;* more marvelous than either of these, in *Antony and Cleopatra* an outsized world of seemingly infinite spaciousness within which oscillate two lovers of mythic proportions who both fuse and transcend the smaller worlds of Rome and Egypt that they emblemize. When John Dryden subtitled his version of this story "The World Well Lost," it was the world of Rome and Egypt he referred to; but it was the larger world that Shakespeare powerfully evokes and which Dryden merely hints at that, arguably, made the lesser worlds worth losing.

By now it will be apparent to the reader that Shakespeare's plays are remarkably all of a piece, that a clear understanding of his principal characters sheds light on the world they occupy, and vice versa. This should not come as a surprise: if a work of art has achieved unity, all of its elements will relate intimately to each other and to the whole. It follows that an understanding of one element will illuminate another, and so on until the entire work of art stands forth in its full radiance.

Alert to some useful means of interpreting a Shakespearean character and able to discern both the structure and the texture of a Shakespearean world, the reader is now ready to examine some of the characteristic plot patterns Shakespeare favored. This procedure will prove cumulative: what we have learned about character and world will serve us well when we examine plot structures, and our study of plot will throw light back on the people of the plays and the landscapes they move through. Thus, happily, the economy that distinguishes a well-made piece of art will also be reflected in our efforts to understand and appreciate it. As we come to recognize artistic structures and their workings, we will cease any critical thrashing about and move with surefooted confidence to the heart of the matter.

It is, then, to the study of plot structures that we turn next. But before we examine those larger structural units to which we normally assign the term *plot,* we must first take into account some relatively smaller structural units, which we will designate as *scenes.* The reasons for this progression— and they are both several and important—will emerge in the discussion of *act* and *scene* advanced in the next chapter.

4

STRUCTURE AND CONVENTION

> . . . scene individable, or poem unlimited.
> (*Hamlet, II, ii, 390*)

Every reader of Shakespeare's plays owes much to the long line of scholarly editors who have labored to establish the most reliable possible text. But the blessings conferred by editors on readers are not unmixed. Beginning with the First Folio of 1623 and continuing to the present day, Shakespearean editors, at first through ignorance and later through necessity, have imposed on the original playscripts a five-act structure that is as ill suited to them as would be the arbitrary division of some masterpiece of painting, like da Vinci's *The Last Supper,* into five separate panels.

This is not to suggest gross carelessness, as though the five parts had been wrenched out of order with the reader left to assemble them like a jigsaw puzzle. Rather it is as though an unnecessary set of division points were imposed on an already unified structure and we were then invited to find these divisions significant. Misled, we are apt to "find" a significance that is not there. This is what happened to those commentators who "discovered" a five-step pyramidal structure that they labeled *exposition, rising action, climax, falling action,* and *catastrophe* and then tried to superimpose on these same five acts thus: Act I—exposition, Act II—rising action, and so forth.

An examination of the actual structure of most Shakespearean plays will reveal some very different and much more fluid patterns. *Exposition* will be found to occur almost anywhere: Where do you learn about the players—let alone the pirates—in *Hamlet? Climaxes* often extend across a broad range of swelling scenes: Is anyone really persuaded that Caesar's assassination has a better claim than Antony's funeral oration to be *the* climax of *Julius Caesar?* And actions *rise* and *fall* variously: in *The Merchant of Venice,* the business with the caskets is already concluded before the business with the rings has even begun. Under the pressure of common sense applied to the text, this pyramidal model simply disappears like a guilty ghost. But it is even more important to see that the five-act structure on which it was presumed to rest is equally a ghost.

This ghostly five-act structure devised by editors was applied to a script (the Elizabethans called it "the book of the play") that was originally a much different thing: a succession of manuscript pages bearing speeches, with speech-prefixes indicating the change of speakers and with some authorial insertions indicating entrances and—less often—exits, since the sense of the dialogue frequently provided the actor with his cue to depart. Stage directions were very few, and, significantly, indications of act or scene divisions appeared nowhere.

The gap between Shakespeare's apparent practices as the author of scripts written for actors and his subsequent editors' practices as shapers of plays for readers is an interesting study in literary consciousness. There is no evidence that Shakespeare wrote his plays for readers or ever considered that these dramas were a sort of legacy for posterity. (Conversely, there is some reason to suppose that he did take considerable pains in preparing his two long narrative poems for publication.) He seems to have regarded the words in his plays as just as perishable as the actors who spoke them—things "melted into air, into thin air."

On the contrary, his editors were very conscious that they were preserving "literature." Conservators of literature are usually keenly aware of tradition, and tradition to the first Renaissance editors of the Folio meant the classics. Classical playwrights, they thought, invariably wrote plays that followed a pattern of five episodes. Anxious to confer on their well-beloved colleague the cachet of classical drama, Heminge and Condell divided many of Shakespeare's fluid and organic playscripts into formal five-act structures, sometimes in the process doing considerable violence to the "poem unlimited" Shakespeare had composed. Later editors followed this practice and sought to improve on it. By the time such important reference books as the Shakespeare concordances (listing every use of every substantive word) and the variorum volumes (containing almost all conceivable readings of disputed passages and interpretations) came to be compiled, the standard practice of referring to a given passage was irrevocably fixed in the influential Globe text thus: act, scene, line—e.g. I, ii, 4 or IV, iii, 66–69. The reference books simply followed suit. So indispensable are these reference books to scholars and readers with special interests that it is now too late to undo this established practice: it would be too costly to bring these books into correspondence with correct structural principles. As a result, even current editors must preserve this often nonfunctional scaffolding around the true building and, somewhat awkwardly, ask their readers to ignore it.

The functional structural unit of the Shakespearean play is not the act but the scene. Even here we must be cautious. A Shakespearean *scene* consists of a segment of talk, usually a dialogue but sometimes a monologue, introduced by entrances and terminated by exits with a cleared stage in between scenes. The cleared stage may signify the passing or shifting of time or a change of place or both. The dialogue in Shakespeare's scripts normally supplies the clues necessary to point up these scene divisions, clues especially necessary since the original playbooks bore no explicit structural labels. To these essential ingredients of a scene, subsequent editors have added stage directions and often gratuitous suggestions about place which are rarely necessary and sometimes misleading. The best contemporary editors have removed some of this editorial bric-a-brac, and current standard editions of the plays, like the *Pelican Shakespeare* (whose general editor is Alfred Harbage), usually provide a reliable guide to the play's scenes.

But, for the reasons already given, even these reliably indicated scenes are numbered to correspond with the arbitrary and quite illogical five-act pattern. Thus *Hamlet* does not come to *readers* as a play in twenty scenes, which it is, but as one with five scenes in Act I, two scenes in Act II, and so forth—a printed pattern that does much to obscure the real structure of the play. *Playgoers* are better off. They see the play performed as a succession of scenes with, usually, only one intermission—chosen by the director with some genuine structural division in mind but again with no authority from Shakespeare. We do not know for certain, and are unlikely ever to learn, whether or not the plays were performed in the public playhouses uninterruptedly from beginning to end like contemporary movies. It is possible. We do know that the indoor theaters (called *private theaters*) used by Shakespeare's company toward the end of his career introduced musical interludes (sometimes as many as four, thus conferring the classical five-act pattern on the performance), but the decision to do this, like the decision of the Folio editors, was an arbitrary one and had nothing to do with the playwright's intent as that can be gleaned from the surviving playbooks or the printed quarto editions based on them.

The plays, then, should be viewed as a succession of scenes, ranging in number from as few as seven (*A Midsummer Night's Dream*) to as many as forty-two (*Antony and Cleopatra*), with the average being nineteen (true of more than one play, including *The Merchant of Venice*). This very considerable range suggests what is an important fact about the design of Shakespearean plays: each play has a unique organization, fitted to its peculiar dramatic requirements. There is, then, no such thing as a typical Shakespearean comedy or tragedy—at least so far as structure is concerned. All attempts to fit Shakespeare's plays into a preconceived structural mold are Procrustean: the stretching or sawing off necessary to force these unique dramas into a single critical bed does hopeless violence to the play.

Shakespeare's scenes display a wide range of both length and complexity. They may be as simple as the 21-line monologue in which Edgar explains his disguise as a Bedlam beggar (*Lear*, II, iii) or as complex as the 301-line opening scene of that play (*Lear*, I, i), in which we meet almost all of the principal characters and witness them set in motion those actions that will irresistibly draw them onto a tragic collision course. It does not follow that a scene's length is a perfect index to its complexity. The opening scene of *The Merchant of Venice* is 185 lines long and introduces us to no fewer than six characters, but its action can be summarized as the demonstrated willingness of the rich merchant Antonio to finance the courtship of Portia by his impecunious friend Bassanio. (It is only fair to add that this scene does much, as well, to establish the sights and sound and feel of the world of Venice.) By contrast, the first scene in *Macbeth* consumes only eleven lines—but how hauntingly suggestive, startlingly complex, teasingly paradoxical, darkly portentous are the sixty-one words uttered by the three witches we meet here.

Long or short, simple or complex, comprising a monologue by a single speaker or the dialogue of several, almost every scene has a significant function in the play in which it is found, and it is imperative that the reader come to recognize that function. Here, again, an understanding of some of Shakespeare's working habits proves helpful.

A playwright whose essential structural unit is the scene must solve two problems of unity: he must see to it that each scene has its own integral unity, and he must arrange his several scenes so that these unified parts become a unified whole. We may illustrate the first kind of unity with two examples from *Hamlet*.

Hamlet's first scene, pervaded by an atmosphere of fear and mystery, has always been accounted a theatrical success. The atmosphere lends unity to the scene. But there is more. We learn that Denmark is on guard against a foe outside its gates; even more chillingly, we are made to understand that it stands in greater danger from some rottenness within. Finally, the country is also seemingly made fearful by some supernatural force. This is a little triumph of thematic unity: Denmark, metaphorically speaking, lies under siege from forces without, within, and above!

Mark Van Doren has called attention to the more complex unity that invests the very long second scene in Act II of *Hamlet.* [1] Not only do its 591 lines make it one of the longest scenes in Shakespeare, but it is chockablock full of incidents that may at first glance appear curiously joined. Claudius and Gertrude greet Rosencrantz and Guildenstern, whom they have summoned to seek the cause of Hamlet's "antic disposition"; Polonius announces the return from Norway of the Danish ambassadors, whom Claudius briskly interviews and dismisses; Polonius confidently tells the king and queen he knows the cause of Hamlet's "madness" and plans with Claudius to spy on the prince; Hamlet enters as Claudius and Gertrude withdraw and pillories Polonius with cruel wit; Rosencrantz and Guildenstern are loosed on Hamlet, who quickly sees their drift and baits them with cryptic utterances; these two mention a company of players, and Polonius reenters to announce that the players have arrived; Hamlet greets the players fondly, commands of one an extempore performance, commissions this player to insert "some dozen or sixteen lines" of Hamlet's own composition into a play to be performed the next day at court, and then dismisses them, together with Polonius and Rosencrantz and Guildenstern; Hamlet concludes the scene with a soliloquy in which he upbraids himself for inaction and then asserts his intention to use the play as a trap to "catch the conscience of the king."

This wilderness of incidents might at first seem to yield no pattern. Certainly it does not have the tonal and atmospheric unity of the play's opening scene. But it does, on examination, prove to have unity of plot and theme. We can follow the movement of the scene as if tracing a figure eight, beginning with the forces that Claudius sets in motion to spy on Hamlet and then turning back with the counterforces Hamlet sets in motion to expose the king. That both the once-pure prince and the criminal king employ the same kind of devious stratagems in their duel of mighty opposites suggests its own thematic significance: everyone, to use Polonius's cynical phrase, becomes "a little soiled i' th' working."

Most of Shakespeare's single scenes will, on examination, disclose a pattern of internal unity, whether that unity stems from tone, atmosphere, imagery, style, character, action, theme, or—most likely—some combination of these. Each scene will also take its place as an integral part in the larger structure that comprises the entire play: normally a scene cannot be eliminated without some real loss to the play as a whole.

The uninitiated reader, however, will not always immediately grasp the function of some scenes. He may be especially puzzled by scenes coming early in the play—scenes that do not have any clear connection with those that have gone before. Why, for example, after a full launching of the tragic story of King Lear in the first scene, are we treated in the second scene to such a detailed revelation of the machinations of Edmund against his father, Gloucester, and brother, Edgar—matters seemingly remote from Lear's affairs?

The answer to this question reveals one of the most important structural patterns used by Shakespeare. We may call this the *pattern of multiple plots.* Shakespeare will at times, and notably in *King Lear,* seek to universalize the significance of his story by telling it in at least two ways and on at least two levels. *King Lear* is, among other things, a story of filial ingratitude. Lear, an old, imperious, and perhaps foolish father, has his feelings mercilessly flayed by two dog-hearted daughters. He has displayed folly, but his punishment is out of all proportions to his offense. He was a mighty king, and he suffers mightily. Gloucester, a lesser man, suffers similarly from the cold cruelty of his bastard son. He, too, pays the supreme price for his folly. By telling this tale of woe twice, once as it affects a great man greatly gifted with the eloquence to give voice to his suffering and once as it affects an average man who can command no poetry to express his sorrow, Shakespeare succeeds in suggesting the universal plight of foolish fathers at the mercy of hateful children. We know that this is not just the fate of kings. It could happen to any of us.

This pattern of multiple plots illustrates the structural principle of plots as reflectors: each plot mirrors and throws light on the other. We shall have more to say about this and related matters in the next chapter, "Story and Plot." For now it is sufficient to indicate that Shakespeare does display recognizable working habits; these habits lead him, in turn, to adopt certain structural patterns; and an awareness of these patterns clarifies for both the reader and and playgoer what might otherwise seem a puzzling arrangement of scenes.

A second example will illustrate another structural pattern that Shakespeare favors. What are we to make, we may ask, of the curious first scene in the second act of *1 Henry IV* —a conversation between two obscure hostlers, a chamberlain, and a thief at an inn the sole purpose of which seems to be to house momentarily the merchants whom Falstaff and his gang will later rob? The merchants are in the play only to be robbed by Falstaff, so that he can be robbed in turn by Prince Hal and Poins. They could have slept anywhere—or nowhere—for all we care. Why, then, did Shakespeare lavish ninety-four lines on this scene?

A close look at this scene at the inn provides our answer: because Shakespeare once again wished to universalize the significance of his story and once again elected to do so by the juxtaposition of scenes that serve as reflectors. Just prior to this tavern scene, we watched three noblemen (Northumberland, Worcester, and the fascinating Harry Hotspur) plot to steal a kingdom, although Hotspur dressed up their enterprise with such magnificent rhetoric as to convert a robbery into a glorious and even chivalric adventure. Shakespeare, well aware of the power of language to affect his audience as well as his characters, now wishes to undercut this high-flown posturing with the acid of humor. So he follows this scene between noble brigands with one between ignoble thieves and commoners in which the true state of affairs is seen: "For they pray continually to their saint, the commonwealth, or rather, not pray to her, but prey on her, for they ride up and down on her and make her their boots." Grammatically, *they* refers to Falstaff, the scapegrace Prince, and their companions; but thematically, the allusion is clearly a reference to all despoilers of the commonwealth, serious as well as comic, lordly as well as ignoble, passionately proud as well as willfully pleasure seeking. Without explicitly telling us, Shakespeare *shows* us what he wants us to understand: that white-collar crime is no different in kind from blue-collar crime; that beneath their very different outer trappings, men's motives and behavior are remarkably alike. What at first appeared to be two utterly disjointed actions, on examination stand revealed as a cunningly joined pair of scenes as tightly hinged as a medieval diptych.

It is only fair to say that we must be acquainted with this structural principle of Shakespeare—this tendency to juxtapose comic-ironic scenes with serious ones so that each echoes and illuminates the other—before we can readily recognize the many illustrations of the principle found in Shakespearean drama. And, especially for the reader, the task is not made easier by the division into acts that sometimes—as here—impose an artificial wall between two tightly integrated scenes. The Hotspur-Northumberland-Worcester episode appears in print as Act I, scene iii, and the scene in the inn as Act II, scene i, clearly illustrating the way in which this unfortunate practice may distract the reader from seeing the true structural pattern of the play or some critical segment of it.

If this nonfunctional five-act scaffolding obtrudes on the reader's attention while not distracting the playgoer, the former has some compensatory advantages. Readers of a Shakespearean playscript may advance their understanding considerably if, as they read, they raise certain questions concerning any puzzling scene: Why does this scene appear just where it does? Why, indeed, does this scene appear at all? Why is this scene so short and that one so long? Why did

Shakespeare divide what appears to be a single episode into two scenes, considerably separated from each other? To ask these questions is to focus attention on Shakespeare's technique. To answer them is to discover *how* Shakespeare means and, therefore, to arrive at a surer and fuller understanding of *what* his plays mean. Our earlier discussion provided examples of answers to the first two questions. We may now more briefly illustrate how the latter two might be answered.

Julius Caesar affords an admirable example of the juxtaposition of two long and two short scenes. Well before the midpoint of the play, we are shown Brutus in his orchard (II, i), first wrestling with himself as he rationalizes his decision to join the assassination plot against Caesar, then discoursing with his fellow conspirators, and later fending off the importunate questions of his distraught wife, Portia. This long scene is followed by its counterpart (II, ii) wherein we see Caesar first attempting to reassure his worried wife by promising her he will not go to the Senate on this day following a night of ominous portents and then succumbing to the blandishments of the conspirators who flatter him into going to the Senate and his death. Shakespeare needs here at least one scene between Caesar's departure from his home and his arrival at the Senate. As a good playwright, he must do more than supply some "filler"; he must turn this necessity to some advantage. He does so by constructing two very brief scenes. One, of sixteen lines, adds measurably to the suspense by disclosing that a citizen named Artemidorus has discovered the plot and has prepared a warning in writing which he proposes to thrust into Caesar's hands as the Roman ruler walks to the Senate. The other, of forty-six lines, not only adds a dimension of reality to Portia—trying to behave like an impassive Roman matron but unable to conceal her frantic fear for Brutus's welfare; it also contributes to the suspense by means of a brief dialogue between Portia and the soothsayer who had earlier warned Caesar to "beware the ides of March" and who proposes to repeat this portentous warning. Finally, one must recognize the importance of rhythm in a staged performance. In no more time than it has taken to write these few words, these two scenes are presented on the boards, and the very speed with which they are played and the contrast between them and the more leisurely pace of the two long preceding scenes serves to emphasize the breathless quality with which Shakespeare wishes to imbue this moment of high suspense that just precedes the assassination.

What about an episode turning on a single action but arbitrarily divided into two rather widely separated scenes? *The Merchant of Venice* provides a clear illustration of both this practice and the probable reasons for it. In the first three scenes of that play, Shakespeare has fairly launched two major plots and sketched two different worlds: the bond plot, with all its lurking threat and strident tones, is appropriately laid in a world of discord, Venice; the casket plot, with its fairy-tale quality and mellifluous tone, is appropriately set forth in a world of concord, Belmont. Shakespeare must keep both of these worlds before us while enough time—three months—elapses for the bond to fall due. The first world provides lots of story stuff: Bassanio's preparations, Lancelot Gobbo's transfer of masters, the Jessica-Lorenzo elopement. But the second, static world turns exclusively on the story of the choice of caskets. There are only three caskets, hence material for only three scenes. But Shakespeare wishes to keep his two worlds (and their two plots) in approximate equilibrium for reasons we will elaborate on in the chapter on "Story and Plot." He solves the problem with bold simplicity. He divides the scene in which the Prince of Morocco chooses the golden casket into two segments. And between them he runs no fewer than five brief scenes that not only contribute considerable story stuff (Gobbo, the elopement, further development of Shylock's character) but also create the impression in playgoers' minds of the passage of time. And although on close examination it becomes apparent that the clock time in one world is wildly different from the clock time in the other, this discrepancy is never noticed by playgoers and, truth to tell, never by readers either, unless they are reading some such dissection of the play's structure as the present one. Let us recall once more that what we are construing here is a script written for a stage performance and not something intended, as a Proustian novel might, to be subjected to the close scrutiny of a patient and curious reader. This brings us, logically enough, to a consideration of a few of the principal conventions of Shakespeare's theater, beginning with one of the most important—the treatment of time.

We have just cited an instance of Shakespeare's elastic handling of time: his use of different amounts of elapsed time for actions presumably taking place concurrently. This elasticity is characteristic of him. Elizabethan audiences expected lots of story in their plays, and Shakespeare, like his fellow playwrights, provided them with it. Lots of story means multiple actions (even multiple plots), and these often necessitate a free and easy way with time. But Shakespeare's elasticity presents no problems to the playgoer, or to any but the most pedantic reader, because he conceals it so skillfully. Normal readers or spectators do not ask themselves if Morocco's suit would occupy only a single hour or a single day or whether Bassanio's preparations to sail to Belmont would occupy a day or a week. Nor do they remind themselves that an actor absent from the stage for only five minutes of clock time could not possibly have conducted an operation that would require a half day in real life. Instead, like their counterparts in ancient Athens, Elizabethan London, or seventeenth-century France, they simply accept this theatrical convention: a departure from probability in the interest of artistic economy.

In a word, wise readers and playgoers place themselves in the hands of the playwright, confident that what is important is not real time but dramatic time. They are, for example, interested in the dramatic confrontation between Richard II and Bolingbroke. What do they care that by calendar time the usurping Bolingbroke is back in England almost before he could have departed to fulfill the terms of his banishment, so long as the illusion of his absence is preserved? Those persons who would worry out the fact that by clock time, Cassio and Desdemona have no real opportunity to commit adultery and therefore that Othello is a fool who cannot do simple arithmetic should ponder Horatio's admonition to Hamlet: " 'Twere to consider too curiously, to consider so." Such people are fit companions to the gallery goers who value a painting for its size and a sculpture for its weight.

This is not to say that Shakespeare is without system or that readers and playgoers are left drifting helplessly on a current of time that has no direction. Like other playwrights of the period, Shakespeare keeps the events of his play *in sequence.* The length of time between successive scenes is seldom specified, but one may safely assume that the later scene is later in time. Past action is almost always treated by references to it in the dialogue. (These references may sometimes take the form of lengthy descriptions—e.g., Hotspur's account of why he denied Henry IV his prisoners, or the bloody sergeant's report of Macbeth's victory over the rebels.) If there are instances of dramatizing the past (the murder of Hamlet's father as depicted in the "mouse-trap" play), these are rare.

A good rule of thumb is to pay no attention to time unless Shakespeare explicitly invites you to, as he does when he repeats the three-month term of Antonio's bond to Shylock. More often, he controls time and tempo for dramatic purposes, creating in his audience a feeling of great speed, for example, as he marshals the events that sweep Othello to his destruction or creating its opposite, stillness, as in the lyrical passages in which Lorenzo invites Jessica—and us—to listen to the music of the spheres. Granville-Barker sums it up neatly: "For Shakespeare time has its dramatic uses, but no rights of its own."[2]

Shakespeare's habitual way with time has a direct bearing on his treatment of place. The two cannot be divorced. Thornton Wilder saw both this intimate connection and one of its most significant results when he complained that the cluttered stages of our box-set theaters, as opposed to the relatively bare stage of Shakespeare's day, have had a deleterious effect on drama. "When you emphasize *place* in the theater," Wilder wrote, "you drag down and limit and harness time to it."[3] Wilder means that the realistic use of time and place suggests a *particular* event (the happenings in a professor's house in a small Norwegian town in the last decade of the nineteenth century), whereas the greatest drama always suggests a *universal* event (Lear discovering in the midst of a dreadful storm in an unstipulated place that could be anywhere and everywhere that "unaccommodated man is no more [than] . . . a poor, bare, forked animal").

Once again we are reminded of the importance of technique in art. It is one thing to recognize with a spasm of feeling what Ben Jonson meant when he said of Shakespeare, "He was not of an age, but for all time!" It is quite another to realize the contribution that the theatrical convention of a certain period can make toward the achievement of this universal quality. In a word, Shakespeare seldom emphasizes a specific place. In the language of theater historians, his scenes are usually *unlocalized.* Readers and spectators, freed from focusing on such irrelevant minutiae, can direct their individual attention to what is always important in drama—the people and their actions. And it is human behavior—alike in Athens, Rome, London, and New York—that is truly universal.

When Shakespeare wishes you to pay attention to place, he will name it: "This is Illyria, Lady" or "This is the Forest of Arden" or "How far is it, my lord, to Berkeley now?" Even then, his place names are apt to be more important for their symbolic signification than for their geographical designation. The Illyria of *Twelfth Night* and the Arden of *As You Like It* are of no significance as pieces of real estate. They are comic arenas where those with sane minds and sound hearts can learn what love is while those with neither are mocked for their folly. Even the isle of Cyprus in *Othello* takes on a sort of allegorical significance as a frontier garrison—far removed from civilized Venice— where the primitive passions that lurk in the noble Othello can be unleashed by the wicked promptings of Iago and "Chaos is come again."

Sometimes, as in the history plays, place names assume a more customary function, and so in *Richard II* we hear of Richard's expedition to Ireland, of Bolingbroke's forced march across the middle of England, and of their meeting at a castle near the Welsh border; and in *Antony and Cleopatra,* we sweep back and forth between Egypt and Rome in a to-and-fro motion remarkably akin to the waxing and waning of feelings that distinguishes all of the principal characters in that richly ambiguous play.

Apart from naming places, Shakespeare may occasionally engage in a little scene painting, as when Horatio breaks up the watch on the parapets of the castle at Elsinore with the observation "But look, the morn in russet mantle clad/ Walks o'er the dew of yon high eastward hill" or when Romeo tells Juliet after their wedding night that "jocund day/ Stands tiptoe on the misty mountain tops." This scene painting is less Watteau-pretty, more powerful, and more necessary where Shakespeare wishes to overwhelm his audience as he does one of his characters in a fearful storm, either of the natural kind, as in *King Lear,* or of the supernatural variety, as is the one reported by Casca in *Julius Caesar*.

The emphasis on unlocalized scenes dovetails perfectly with the nearly bare stage Shakespeare favored. Unencumbered by sets and utilizing stage properties sparingly, he could maintain both great fluidity and great speed. Moreover, he could make use of a convention unique to his kind of theater: not only is the locale determined by the persons on the stage—thus where the king and his council are is the court, where two maidens gather flowers is a garden, where armed soldiers fight is a battlefield—but the locale can actually follow the person. Here is a famous illustration of this unusual convention. We know both from a stage direction and from the internal evidence of the dialogue that, after their wedding night, Romeo and Juliet appear on the upper stage—this time designating a window—from which Romeo descends by means of a rope ladder, after which he below and Juliet above exchange a few more words. But following Romeo's departure, Shakespeare extends the scene for another 180 lines during which Juliet's mother, her father, and her nurse all enter and talk. Such a long scene and so many people demand the larger playing area of the platform stage, so Shakespeare simply has Juliet come down and enter the platform stage with (or just before) her mother. At the moment Juliet does this, the lower stage ceases to be the orchard it was when Romeo descended to it and becomes her bedchamber. In short, the locale (the bedchamber) has followed the person (Juliet) whose presence establishes it as such.

The time it takes to explain one of these instances must not be permitted to obscure the simplicity of the principle they illustrate. Once again you may place your confidence in Shakespeare, secure in the knowledge that you will be told all that you will ever need to know about either time or place. To take your eye off the characters and their actions in order to compile a schedule of time or a gazetter of place is worse than failing to see the forest for the trees; it is to miss both the forest and the trees.

A handful of other stage conventions used by Shakespeare are so intimately connected with the concerns of this chapter that they will be mentioned briefly here. A *convention* might be defined as a piece of stage business that looks odd in the other fellow's theater but which we never notice in our own. On our motion picture screens, we customarily watch a giant face, magnified many times, or even a portion of that face, and wait for a bat of an eye or the flicker of a facial muscle that will telegraph the actor's feelings. An Elizabethan might find this odd. Conversely, the modern reader-playgoer may initially find curious such Elizabethan conventions as the *soliloquy,* the *aside,* and the related conventions of *concealment, invisibility,* and *disguise.* But familiarity with their utility will help remove any feeling of strangeness.

The true *soliloquy* gives expression to the private thoughts of a character who speaks them aloud but does not address himself directly to the audience. Hamlet's well-known soliloquies are of this kind. Although it is often said that such soliloquies truly reflect the character of their speakers, it would be more accurate to say that they sincerely reflect what the speakers think they themselves are like. The distinction is an important one in dramatic literature, where irony is frequently achieved by the author's casting doubt on the speaker's estimate of himself. Thus soliloquies must always be interpreted with caution. Any formula assuming that, because a speaker is standing alone on the stage, his revelations may be taken at face value is simplistic.

It is worth noting, too, that whereas soliloquies are by definition monologues, not all monologues are soliloquies. The speeches delivered by the Choruses that introduce a few of the plays, like *Romeo and Juliet* and *Henry V,* are not soliloquies. Neither are the chorus-like utterances of characters occasionally commandeered by Shakespeare to give information or deliver a commentary on the state of affairs, as do certain "citizens" in *Richard III* or "an Old Man" in *Macbeth.* Neither are those seemingly self-revelatory monologues, like the one at the beginning of *Richard III,* in which a very self-conscious villain brags of his villainy. True, the Richard IIIs, the Iagos, the Edmunds are alone on the stage, but they are very consciously directing their words to the audience, often with great relish, not unconsciously revealing their innermost and private thoughts.

The *aside* displays as many variations as does the soliloquy. A modern audience will have no difficulty recognizing the snide remark spoken out of the side of the mouth, since that is a case of art imitating life. Not at all lifelike, however, is the aside that serves a purpose similar to that of the chorus—putting the audience straight about some matter of fact or opinion. Some asides are like true soliloquies: they reveal their speaker's inner thoughts and feelings as he observes the actions of others. And there is a special category, the long aside delivered from concealment, best illustrated in the famous scenes involving, respectively, Beatrice and Benedick, in *Much Ado About Nothing.*

The *concealment* just mentioned is of the conventional kind: the concealed characters are in plain sight of both the audience and other characters on the stage, but, for the sake of the play, the latter cannot see them. This is nonillusionistic and need not be complicated by having the concealed characters elaborately hidden by properties or marred by having them speak in whispers. Closely related is the convention of *invisibility*. A supernatural character, like Ariel in *The Tempest* or Puck in *A Midsummer Night's Dream,* or a character with supernatural powers, like Prospero, is assumed to be visible or invisible as circumstances require. The dialogue may contain some explicit statement making this clear, or the reader-playgoer may be left to infer it from the fact that the other characters present seem unable to see him. And sometimes he has a magic cloak.

A cloak, hat, or beard is a sufficient property to signal the convention of *disguise*. A relatively serious example of this convention is found in *Measure for Measure,* in which Duke Vincentio, disguised as a holy friar, monitors the behavior of all the principal characters in sinful Vienna; but the device is more often associated with lighter comedy, and nowhere is it employed more successfully and delightfully than when Viola in *Twelfth Night* and Rosalind in *As You Like It* disguise themselves as young men and, thus disguised, spend deliciously anxious moments talking about themselves with the men they love. When to the normal pleasure of this device one adds the recollection that women's roles were played by boys so that you get the double switch of a boy playing a woman who disguises "herself" as a boy, one can easily conceive of the extra measure of delight that an Elizabethan audience received from this form of the convention.

Perhaps the single strongest impression one brings away from a consideration of all the matters examined in this chapter is similar to the feeling we derive from examining a Gothic cathedral: a feeling of the remarkable unity of the entire edifice achieved because of (not despite) the myriad details that make it up. Shakespeare's unity, unlike that of Racine (or the ancients on which he modeled himself), is not one of restricted time, place, and action. It has nothing of the severity of the architecture of those moderns whose

motto is "Less is more." Shakespeare's plays are not examples of *scene individable,* to echo the epigraph to this chapter.
Rather they answer to the contrasting phrase, *poem unlimited,* with their multiple actions; their free handling of
time and bold movement in space; their striking juxtaposition of serious and comic scenes, of high life and low life, of
plangent rhetoric and plain style; and their relatively large
casts that suggest a swarm of people whose activities represent a full slice of life. And yet this poem unlimited, like a
Gothic cathedral, is marvelously all of a piece, held together
by some cast of mind, some attitude, some imaginative vision that informs and invests each of its composite parts. The
precise manifestation of this vision varies with each play, in
the same way that each of the great gothic cathedrals carries
its own distinctive stamp. But just as we observe that all
Gothic cathedrals have in common some expression of a
transcendental faith in God, so all of Shakespeare's plays
bear testimony to what it means to be human.

5
STORY AND PLOT

> ... what I know
> Is ruminated, plotted, and set down. ...
> (*1 Henry IV, I, iii, 270–271*)

Those two nouns, *story* and *plot,* that make up this chapter's
title, suggest cryptically what will here be set forth expansively: the distinction in meaning between these two words
which are often used interchangeably, and some explanation
of Shakespeare's unique ways of balancing, in the structure
of his plays, the claims of these two related but distinctive
forms of narrative art.

To differentiate story from plot is not just an exercise in
pedantry; it is, first, to distinguish a rudimentary form of
art from a more complex one and, second, to clarify some
important differences between Shakespeare's characteristic
plot patterns and those found alike in ancient Greek and
modern realistic drama. These differences are radical, and a
clear grasp of them is necessary to an informed reading or
viewing of Shakespeare's plays.

It is no accident that *story* is closely related to *history:*
both words denote the narration of events arranged in a
sequence of time. A pure story, therefore, might be diagramed thus: A and then B and then C and then D and so on,
with the letters representing distinct events that follow

each other in a sequential pattern determined solely by the passage of time.

Looked at this way, a story is not substantially different from the circumstantial testimony elicited from a court witness, the account of the day's events confided to one's diary, the sequence of shots that make up typical home movies, the dinner-table answer to the question, "What happened at the office today?" Viewed from the perspective of audience appeal, a story may be said to satisfy that most fundamental of audience reactions—curiosity about what happens next. It was just this irresistible compulsion to ask "And then what happened?" that prevented the story-loving king in *The Arabian Nights* from killing Scheherazade. Our own everyday narratives are not without this fundamental interest. But they are apt to be without ordered pattern (which is to say, without art), and they are apt to be without much significance (which is to say, without point).

Previous references to the drastic economy imposed on all drama should be sufficient to suggest why plays cannot normally be the vehicles for such relatively formless stories, although plays may be *based on* stories, or even histories, as most of Shakespeare's plays were. But a dramatist cannot usually afford the leisurely pace and slack structure we associate with these linear narratives. Drama is not characteristically the instrument of slow-paced and flattened-out *evolution;* it is, rather, the vehicle of swift-paced and heightened *revelation.* A play, therefore, may be based on a *story;* but, if it is to be dramatic, it must have a sharper focus—which is to say, it must have a *plot.*

A plot, as one of its dictionary meanings suggests, reveals a plan. That plan will disclose some principle of *selection* at work: a plot does not include all—or even most—of the possible events that might make up a story or a history. A plot represents a discriminating choice from among the total number of those events, a choice made according to plan. This plan will also disclose a careful *arrangement* of the selected events: these will be set down in the order best calculated to achieve the playwright's desired result, and this sequence will not necessarily be in the order of time, although it may be. Moreover, these two principles of selection and arrangement will be invoked in order to achieve a pattern that will yield a *significant meaning:* the play will add up to something; the pattern of its events will contribute to a unique insight into some aspect of human behavior that the playwright finds arresting. The *interrelationship* of these three principles in operation yields something like a useful definition of plot: human experience imaged as human actions that are *concentrated* (because they are selected from among many possibilities), *pleasing* (because they are artfully arranged), and *significant* (because they are focused on some universal human concern).

These three principles may, I think, be discovered operating in most plays. But there is a body of received truths about dramatic plots for which the same claim cannot be made, even though they are often found in conjunction with the foregoing principles. Because these truths have nearly oracular origins and because they apply fittingly to both ancient Greek and modern realistic drama, they have very wide currency with readers and playgoers and exercise immense influence in shaping their notions of a proper dramatic plot. We must, therefore, pause to identify these "truths" clearly, the more especially because we must then set about to distinguish them from the very different structural principles adopted by Elizabethan playwrights, including Shakespeare.

E. M. Forster, a modern oracle writing about the novel but making frequent references to drama, wittily pointed up the distinction we have been making between story and plot. He put it this way. "'The King died and then the Queen died' is a story. 'The Kind died, and then the Queen died *of grief*' is a plot."[1] Forster then proceeded to draw some conclusions from this comparison. He pointed out that plot, while preserving the story's time sequence, introduces the element of *causality:* "The Queen died *of grief.*" He said further that, whereas story provokes only *curiosity*—signaled by the question, And then?—plot places demands on the reader's *memory* and *intelligence* by raising the far more provocative question, Why? According to Forster, good readers use their memory to recall all the relevant facts and then use their intelligence to penetrate to the significance of these facts. For a plot to invite this response—to bring out the best in readers and then reward them for their perseverance—it will need to possess one further attribute, which Forster called "beauty." We may understand by Forster's beauty those aesthetically appealing qualities that derive from the playwright's application of our principles of selection and arrangement: in a word, a fitting design.

Perhaps because he was thinking of the novel, Forster also declared that persons (characters) were more important than plot. Not so Aristotle, certainly the most oracular critic in the entire history of Western culture. He said emphatically that plot is the most important element in drama. He thought so because he truly believed that actions speak louder than words: "It is in actions—what we do—that we are happy and the reverse." (Forster disagreed, arguing that some kinds of happiness and misery, concerning which there is no visible evidence, may exist in the secret lives of individuals. But when Forster said this, he was talking about the novel, whose omniscient author is at liberty to enter the private minds of his characters to display their secret thoughts, a power normally denied the playwright. Forster acknowledged that the latter must depict all human happiness and misery in the form of action; otherwise its existence in a drama would remain unknown.) Returning to Aristotle, we find him anticipating Forster in his insistence that plot must show a cause-and-effect relationship between its events. A well-made plot, Aristotle declared, will "neither begin nor end at haphazard," but will be a unified whole with a logical beginning, middle, and end.

If now we should look once more at our diagram, we discover that a story that could be displayed as A and then B and then C and then D and then E might, following the prescriptions of Aristotle and Forster and being shaped by the hand of a Sophocles or an Ibsen, emerge as a plot that could be diagramed as D *because of* A *leading to* E. From a possible five events, only three have been selected, and these have then been arranged in a causal sequence for dramatic effectiveness. We may say, indeed, that this second diagram does reflect in a general way the plot patterns found in ancient Greek and modern realistic dramas. It does not, however, correspond to the habitual plot patterns of Shakespeare and his Elizabethan contemporaries. Nevertheless, before we can turn to the latter, we must add a few more words concerning the critical dogmas that stemmed from a reading—or a misreading—of the principles of plot construction laid down by Aristotle.

Concerning unity of action Aristotle was firm. "The plot . . . must imitate one action and that a whole, the structural union of the parts being such that, if any one of them is displaced or removed, the whole will be disjointed and disturbed." To these words he added, "A well-constructed plot should, therefore, be single in its issue, rather than double as some maintain." From these statements and others scattered among the many paragraphs of *The Poetics* given over to a discussion of plot, subsequent interpreters created an imposing set of critical dogmas. The most notorious of these concerns the so-called *three unities:* the action must be single, must take place in one locale, and may continue for only a limited time (one day). A second dogma asserts that plots must always be single, never multiple, and that episodic plots—those in which actions succeed one another without probable or necessary sequence—are bad. A third dogma declares that the best plots involve a *reversal*—"a change by which the action veers around to its opposite"—and a *recognition*—"a change from ignorance to knowledge."[2]

So impressive were—and are—Aristotle's credentials that his dicta have sometimes been permitted to obscure the actual practices of playwrights both in his own day and since. We even encounter critical absurdities: if the playwright under scrutiny is thought to be great, his actual practices are sometimes construed to fit Aristotelian precepts even when they do not do so; if he is a lesser figure, his deviation from Aristotelian norms may result in his being consigned to outer darkness.

These critical absurdities are compounded when we recall that Aristotle's observations were based only on tragedies and on a certain mode of Greek tragedy at that. A moment's reflection reveals that comedy, with its foreordained fortunate endings, does not even pretend to follow the iron logic of cause and effect. Instead, with its miraculous returns of long-lost sons and its fortuitous discovery of missing documents, it shamelessly gives support to the premise that the wish is father to the thought. Furthermore, a few of Aristotle's suggestions—notably those concerning the three unities—appear to have been misinterpreted by some of his self-styled disciples. In fact, the dogma of the three unities rigidly applied has seldom been a blueprint for actual practices. In one or two times and places—notably in French tragic theater of the seventeenth century—it was taken seriously. And individual plays of any period (including Shakespeare's *The Comedy of Errors*) may exemplify its working principles. But the practices of most playwrights in most places at most times relegate this doctrine to the realm of curious theory. The collateral dogma of a single plot has been more durable and more influential; but it, too, remains prescriptive, not descriptive of the actual practices of many playwrights, notably Shakespeare.

Concerning any of these critical doctrines, we may say that they can be useful to readers and playgoers seeking to sophisticate their knowledge of the grammar of drama if and when these doctrines correspond to the actual practices of most playwrights at most times; that they are of more limited usefulness when they apply only to certain playwrights staging their productions in certain restricted historical periods; but that all of them—including the most exalted—are downright misleading if they are accepted as imperishable truths arrived at deductively and are thus permitted to screen from view the working habits of playwrights which, examined inductively, would be shown to be quite remarkably different from these theoretical doctrines. Such a towering figure as Voltaire made something of a fool of himself by his attempt to level the even more imposing figure of Shakespeare for the latter's failure to adhere to some of these critical dogmas. And lesser critics of several nationalities, including the British, have alternately scolded or grumbled about or apologized for Shakespeare because he "wanted art."

During the more than 350 years that separate Shakespeare's day from our own, innumerable critics have attempted to illuminate his achievement as a dramatic poet. Each of the elements that make up his (and every dramatist's) plays—character, world, plot, theme, and language—has been scrutinized. Curiously, none of these elements has been so consistently misinterpreted as plot. In Shakespeare's own day, there was relatively little formal criticism of the drama written in English. Except for some passages from Ben Jonson's prefaces, what was written (and Sir Philip Sidney's *Defense of Poetry* constitutes what was best known and is best remembered) had, with respect to structure, no correspondence to what Shakespeare and his fellow Elizabethan playwrights were actually doing. Echoing chiefly Italian and some French neo-Aristotelian critics—who were, in turn, echoing several Roman commentators, chiefly Horace—these British academic writers gave expression to some of the dogmas we have outlined, whereas Shakespeare and his contemporaries worked out instead a pragmatic dramaturgy whose roots were in the centuries-long tradition of English mystery plays, moralities, and interludes and whose branches stemmed from the deeply ingrained practices of the public theaters of the day.

This split between critical theory and actual practice with respect to the structure of Shakespeare's plays continued down to relatively modern times, at a cost to generations of readers and playgoers that can be more easily deplored than calculated. Even Dr. Johnson, who these days seems to be every scholar's favorite Shakespearean critic, went wrong here, at least with respect to *Antony and Cleopatra,* whose "events," he declared, "are produced without any art of connection or care of disposition."[3]

But this is not the place to review instances of critical myopia, nor should the modern reader feel smugly superior to those older generations who saw Shakespearean structures as through a glass darkly. The total history of Shake-

spearean criticism has a way of chastening the pride of anyone who reads it. It is a mirror that reflects a whole succession of critical postures: each century can fairly claim to
have made its unique contributions to our total understanding of Shakespeare. Put more ironically in T. S. Eliot's
words, "About anyone as great as Shakespeare it is probable
that we can never be right; and if we can never be right, it is
better that we should from time to time change our ways of
being wrong."[4]

With respect to the *structure* of his plays, however, the
twentieth century can make a better claim than its prede-
cessors to have seen Shakespeare plain. Those twentieth-
century critics who have been content to let the plays instruct
them instead of seeking to instruct the plays have charted
Shakespeare's habitual ways with a plot, the most important
of which we turn to now.

In examining Shakespeare's way with a dramatic plot, we
would do well to focus on the beginnings. Doing so, we discover that he has a curious trick of starting two or more
story lines in rapid succession in a play's first two or three
scenes. Examples come easily to mind. After a complicated
opening scene in *King Lear* in which we witness an old
king's mishandling of the division of his kingdom and his
fatal misinterpretation of the feelings of his three
daughters, we are immediately confronted in Scene ii with
another story about another father, the Earl of Gloucester,
only this time we see an old courtier fatally misinterpreting
the feelings of his two sons, one of whom is good, the other
evil. Two seemingly separate, although interestingly parallel, plots have been launched in the first two scenes. Again,
in *A Midsummer Night's Dream,* we begin by learning of the
nuptial plans of Duke Theseus and his bride, have our attention diverted to the unsmooth course of love involving a
quartet of young Athenian lords and ladies, are suddenly
switched to the amusing spectacle of an awkward group of
workmen trying to plan the production of a play, and then
are whisked to some sylvan suburb where we overhear a

bitter quarrel between the king and queen of the fairies. Still again, in *1 Henry IV,* we open on a king's council, where plans for a crusade are made and as quickly abandoned as news of rebellion in the kingdom is brought in; switch to a low London tavern, where the Prince of Wales is discovered consorting with an amiable old scapegrace, Falstaff, and agreeing to join the latter in a proposed highway robbery; and from there jump to an angry colloquy between three of the king's enemies who, after traducing their monarch's character, agree to despoil him of his throne.

Although this is not Shakespeare's only method of beginning a play, it is a pattern that he follows so frequently that it demands our attention. How does Shakespeare impose the relatively firm shape of plot on the relatively plastic stuff of story? How does he do so when he appears to be working with two or three or more stories? A metaphor from music may assist us to understand Shakespeare's structural strategy here. The end to be achieved was unity. The means that Shakespeare (and his Elizabethan contemporaries) developed from the tradition of Tudor drama which they inherited was a kind of unity in multiplicity. To turn to our musical metaphor, they composed plays in which the narrative unfolds like variations on a theme; and after the fashion of baroque musicians, these playwrights developed narrative patterns which, like musical point and counterpoint, come together in one harmonious fusion after being ingeniously kept apart for intervals of varying length.

We have already seen in the preceding chapter a very clear instance of this technique in the double plot of *King Lear:* two misguided fathers, and two sets of loyal and disloyal children, play out their sad stories, which, although different in detail, are much alike in point. Shakespeare does not attempt to keep these two plots apart throughout the play, but instead brings them together periodically by means of the characters of Gloucester and Edgar, who figure large in Lear's story as well as in their own. Where the two stories touch, their common themes—which include the ironical recollection that age does not automatically confer wisdom, the disturbing reminder of the inexplicable nature of evil, and the repeated revelation that love is not a commodity to be bought and sold—light up to reveal their unity of meaning, a unity that transcends their more superficial differences of action and event.

A variation of this technique may be discovered in *Twelfth Night,* perhaps as notable an achievement in the genre of romantic comedy as is *King Lear* in tragedy. This time, however, Shakespeare works skillfully to keep his two plots—the high-comedy plot involving the graceful Viola, Orsino, and Olivia and the low-comedy plot involving the graceless Sir Toby, Sir Andrew, and Malvolio—apart for well over half the play. But this deliberate separation of the actors and their actions should not obscure the thematic unity that binds these parallel plots long before their principals are physically brought together in the duel scene between Viola and Sir Andrew. The several principals are victims of several kinds of self-deception, especially as this pertains to love; and it is a central purpose of this play to differentiate among those who remain blinded by some form of self-love and those who become clear-sighted because they grow capable of viewing love, and themselves in love, through the glass of comic sanity. The mechanical difference in technique—in *King Lear* two plots periodically joined, in *Twelfth Night* two plots deliberately held apart for more than half the play—need not obscure the similarity in structural principle: both plays are equally clear examples of superficially disparate actions brought into harmonious concord by means of unifying themes.

If Shakespeare can perform this feat of unity in multiplicity with two plots, can he do it with four? He can and does—interestingly, fairly early in his career with *A Midsummer Night's Dream.* We have already indicated how this play begins with no fewer than four story lines established by the end of the first three scenes. How does Shakespeare go on to handle all this plot stuff? With consummate ease. First he suspends any further mention of Duke Theseus and his bride, Hippolyta, until the play's final scene, thus relegating their plot to the function of a "frame" for the play, in much the same manner as we saw him work with old

Egeon and the Duke in *The Comedy of Errors*. Next, working like a rope maker who entwines the several strands that make up his cord, he interweaves the story of the four Athenian lords and ladies with that of Bully Bottom and the "rude mechanicals" and that of Puck, Oberon, Titania, and the rest of the fairy crew. He does this by placing them all in a single setting—a wood near Athens—for a single period of time—one night—under a single spell—the lunacy of love. It is this last that is thematic; and it is again the theme that holds together all the plots—and all the other elements of this dreamlike play. Even the play's best remembered business—the performance by the simple-minded tradesmen of the interlude, *Pyramus and Thisbe,* which might playfully be called a fifth plot, with its burlesque of love—brings us back to the central theme. Then, as we have come to expect at the end, the Duke and his bride pronounce wisdom's verdict on the madness of this midsummer night. But this pronouncement proves to be subtly ironic. Having permitted Duke Theseus to level the obvious criticism of common sense against the moonstruck lovers and, in the process, to score some hits at the expense of other seekers after fantasy, such as lunatics and poets, Shakespeare, as he so often does in his later romantic comedies, reserves the wisest words for the lady. In her reply to Theseus, Hippolyta gently defends the role of the imagination and, in so doing, obliquely implies to him—and, therefore, to us—that the only form of human madness more foolish than love's lunacy is the rational attempt to get along without it.

> But all the story of the night told over,
> And all their minds transfigured so together,
> More witnesseth than fancy's images
> And grows to something of great constancy;
> But howsoever, strange and admirable.
>
> (*V, i,* 23–27)

We hear this theme struck again more clearly and emphatically in the great romantic comedies, most notably in *As You Like It,* where its "pulpiter" is the incomparable

Rosalind, generally acknowledged to be Shakespeare's greatest romantic heroine. *As You Like It,* however, illustrates a variation on the plot patterns we have been looking at. As we might anticipate, a growth in thematic emphasis is accompanied by a commensurate shift in structural design—a shift, not a total change. In place of the distinctive multiple plots of *Twelfth Night* and *A Midsummer Night's Dream,* we discover in *As You Like It* only the most rudimentary subplots in the Orlando-Oliver rivalry and the Duke Frederick–Rosalind conflict. Both of these subplots have only limited functions. The former helps to get the play started and motivates Orlando's exile to Arden. The latter is instrumental in shipping off Rosalind, Celia, and Touchstone to that same idyllic forest where Shakespeare has already assembled a full cast of noble exiles and both real and literary shepherds so that, with Rosalind's arrival there, he can get down to his main plot—the business that really interests him in this play—the opportunity to work as many variations as his ingenuity will permit on the themes of illusion versus reality, country versus city life, sense versus sensibility, and romantic versus materialistic and skeptical attitudes toward love. Once more the musical metaphor of variations on a theme suggests itself. So, too, do choreographic metaphors, for we watch here a series of *pas de deux, pas de trois,* and *pas de quartre* performed nimbly against an imaginary backdrop of noble oaks whose "antique roots peep out / Upon the brook that brawls along." Here in Arden, Rosalind, Celia, Orlando, Jaques, Touchstone, Corin, Silvius, and others meet and part and meet again in combinations that permit Shakespeare to anatomize romantic love until nothing remains of it except the paradoxical conviction on the part of wise Rosalind—and hence wise reader and wise spectator—that it is as indispensable as it is illusory.

Our focus on theme in the foregoing examples must not be misinterpreted. The principal themes in Shakespearean plays should not be viewed as abstract statements, preachments, messages, or morals that are detached (or detachable) from the persons, actions, and environments that image forth Shakespeare's particular view of the human condition in each of his plays. The preceding chapters describing Shakespeare's methods of developing character and creating a world have already familiarized you with this technique of orchestrating the elements of drama, of coordinating character with world and both with plot and all three with theme, instead of elevating one element while subordinating the others. Expressed otherwise, if there is such a thing as the essence of Shakespeare the dramatist, it lies in the interstices between the elements of his plays and may best be discovered by observing the interplay of these elements— their interrelationships. To employ once more our musical metaphor of variations on a theme, we may say that the actors and their actions are akin to musical notes and phrases; their movements and tonalities *are* the theme and variations. Theme is the means of unifying the actions, but the actions are the indispensable means of expressing the themes.

Although Shakespeare never explicitly says that he shares Aristotle's conviction concerning the supremacy of plot, there is ample evidence in his plays that he knew his audiences liked and expected lots of story. And he and his fellow playwrights gave these audiences what they wanted. The amplitude of story stuff that characterizes his plays invariably produces plot patterns and rhythms designed to ingest this narrative matter and give it point—a point that heightens rather than diminishes the primordial pleasures that are associated with the telling of a story. Having already seen how a love of story determined the beginnings of many Shakespearean plays, let us now examine some typical Shakespearean endings.

Unlike the plays of Sophocles and Ibsen (our prototypes for ancient Greek and modern realistic drama), Shakespeare's plays almost never end dramatically—on a wild and swelling wave of passion, at a moment of the highest pitch of excitement, or in an atmosphere of frenzied release or of crushing despair. One explanation advanced for this—that Shakespeare's curtainless stage required some means of "removing the bodies" and hence some dimunition in the emotional electricity of the final moments—while perhaps amusing is both patronizing and wrong. A playwright of Shakespeare's demonstrable skill would never be defeated in his intentions by a mechanical difficulty—as he demonstrated in *Othello,* where, atypically, he did end his play on such a peak of passion.

The explanation lies elsewhere. It lies in part with the Elizabethan audience's well-cultivated love of story and consequent interest in seeing it rounded off—discovering how it all came out. This love of story had been nourished by over a hundred years of popular drama preceding Shakespeare—a drama that supplied the playgoing audiences of that time what the medieval troubadours earlier provided the story-hungry occupants of court and castle and what the great nineteenth-century novelists later offered to the newly literate mass audiences of emerging democratic societies. Shakespeare inherited both his popular audiences and the dramatic practices that were shaped by their love of story.

One has only to recall the ending of almost any Shakespearean play to see the pattern. Ceremony replaces action; the pace and tempo are slowed; resolutions are spelled out explicitly, in detail, and often at some length. In Shakespeare's comedies, the complexities that earlier stood between the characters and the triumph of love are systematically explained and resolved. In the tragedies, the confusions that earlier stood between the characters and the attainment of justice are dispelled, and order is restored. These finales develop their own conventions. As befits the long tradition that associates comedy with fruitful good fortune, Shakespeare's comedies end with the yoking in marriage of every pair that ingenuity can conceive and credulity can accept; his tragedies close with the studied restoration of social order and the binding up of social wounds. Central to these dispensations stands the ranking figure (as often as not a duke) who serves at once as judge and impresario. At times his pronouncements are detailed, at other times brief. Long or short, they serve to tie up the loose ends of the narrative, as later in nineteenth-century novels, like those of Dickens, everything is explained, all problems are re-solved, and the future is forecast.

Examples abound. Thus in *Macbeth,* Malcolm, the right-ful heir to Scotland's throne, his forces having unseated and killed the tyrant Macbeth, briskly but precisely outlines his program to restore order and to heal that suffering state. In *As You Like It,* Duke Senior rejoices in the forthcoming nuptials of no fewer than four "country copulatives" as well as an entire series of restorations—himself to his dukedom, his daughter to himself, his wicked younger brother to a sense of sin and thence to redemption, two other brothers (Oliver and Orlando) to fraternal love—and all of this as satisfaction of the Elizabethean audience's curiosity about the several stories that have been more or less held in abeyance since the end of the first act. And in *Richard III,* Henry, Earl of Richmond (Henry VII to be) accepts the crown, gives an order for burying the dead, grants pardons to Richard's defeated adherents, confidently declares his in-tention to unite the warring factions of "the White Rose and the Red," and to that end announces his purpose to wed the Yorkist princess, Elizabeth, so that "The true succeeders of each house, / By God's fair ordinance conjoyn together!"

This systematic tying up of all the loose ends of the narra-tive in the closing moments of the play means that we must look elsewhere in the tragedies and tragicomedies for their emotional crescendos and elsewhere in the comedies for their best wit battles or most effective horseplay. Conse-quently, we must now turn from Shakespeare's beginnings and ends to his middles. And when we do so, we discover yet another plot pattern and narrative rhythm. This pattern has at least two distinguishing characteristics: it locates the play's climatic scenes rather closer to the midpoint of the play than we are accustomed to expect in modern drama; and it greatly expands and sustains those climaxes, often over several scenes and for a surprisingly long period of playing time.

We might assign to this pattern a descriptive title: *the expanded climax.* This title points up sharply yet another distinction between Shakespeare's habitual ways of working with story and plot and the patterns we associate with the older Greek and modern realistic drama. Both of the latter emphasize the crisis plot: a carefully ordered plot that builds up to a single moment of crisis or climax when, to use Aristotle's words, "the action veers round to its opposite" and we have a reversal of fortune. Thus, we may recall *Oedipus Rex,* with its awful climactic moment when Oedipus discovers, from the faltering words of the reluctant herdsman, the secret of his birth and sees in a flash all the horrible consequences that flow from this knowledge; or that horrifying turning point in Ibsen's *Ghosts* when Oswald reveals to Mrs. Alving his venereal legacy from his father and she is compelled to give expression for the first time to her own recognized complicity in her son's doom. Written 2,500 years apart, these plays have a similar structure: commencing in an emergency, they reveal, in a succession of ironic scenes, the painful past events that compelled that emergency and then, at the critical moment, explode into a devastating revelation that promotes pity and fear in the stunned audience.

How different is Shakespeare's technique. Readers for whom their teachers once set the task of finding *the* climax in *Hamlet* or *King Lear* will now understand their puzzlement: they were given an impossible assignment. There is no single climactic moment in these plays in the sense that there is one in *Oedipus Rex* and *Ghosts.* What do we find when we turn to the middle portion of *Hamlet?* Like the courtiers of Denmark, we watch the play within the play until King Claudius, his conscience stricken by the pantomiming of the murder he committed, cries out for light and rushes from the stage. Only minutes later, we see Hamlet, flushed with triumph at the success of his "mousetrap" play, his sword poised in the air to dispatch the kneeling king, pause fatally because he fears that the soul of Claudius might fly up to heaven on the wings of the prayer he assumes him to be uttering. From there we rush with Hamlet to his mother's bedroom, where we see him mistakenly slay that "wretched, rash intruding fool," Polonius, cruelly upbraid his mother for her carnal sins, and submit to the rebuke of his ghostly father come to chide "his tardy son." Surely what we have here is a plethora of climaxes, not a single turning point. Similarly, in *King Lear* we trace Lear's painful progress toward a kind of redemption through an entire series of storm-lashed scenes in the course of which we witness the reflection in his face of rage, vengefulness, bewilderment, and helplessness as he delivers mighty monologues addressed to the universal gods and takes part in broken dialogues with his natural fool and with Edgar, who simulates madness. Each of these scenes illuminates Lear's progress, but it would be hard to argue that any one moment is more climactic than the others.

In both of these instances, we are witnesses not to concentrated moments of revelation but, rather, to expanded moments of passion: these are agonies, not epiphanies; the movement of events is not one of sudden reversal but, rather, one of sustained suffering and endurance. (This is not to say that Shakespeare is not also a master of the swift reversal when he wants to be. One has only to recall the final duel in *Hamlet*.)

The counterparts to these scenes of swelling passion at the center of many of the tragedies are scenes of extreme complication at the midpoints of some of the comedies. Act III of *Twelfth Night* consists of a succession of four scenes in which the entanglements of both high-comedy and low-comedy plots are given a special twist by a whole series of events: Olivia reveals her fondness for Cesario (Viola); Sir Andrew consents to pursue his hopeless quest for Olivia; Viola's twin brother, Sebastian, arrives in Illyria with predictable consequences; Malvolio takes the bait—a forged letter persuading him that he has found favor in Olivia's eyes; and an equally unwilling Viola and Sir Andrew are bullied into meeting each other in a duel, which is interrupted by Sebastian's friend, Antonio, who mistakes Viola for her twin brother. These are not, of course, climactic moments but a whole succession of "complications," each representing a peak of complexity in its own story line, the entire ensemble of scenes reflecting the artfulness of a playwright who can handle a skein of story lines which he casts like a net to enmesh several of his principals.

Critics who have in their heads a sort of Aristotelian

model of what a plot should be and resent Shakespeare's free and easy way with story stuff have leveled a specific charge stemming from the kinds of scenes that characterize the meridians of many of his plays. The criticism usually takes the form of the accusation that some of his scenes have an autonomous life of their own, that they are only loosely connected with the rest of the play and contribute little toward the forward progress of the play's principal action. The scene in *1 Henry IV* (III, i) in which Hotspur and his uncle, Worcester, are met with the Welsh chieftain, Owen Glendower, presumably to perfect plans for their concerted rebellion against the king might be instanced; for the ostensible story purpose of the scene is dispensed with in the first 2 lines, and the remaining 263 lines are given over to Hotspur's baiting of Glendower for his vanity and superstition, a proposal for the ultimate division of the kingdom leading to a quarrel whose consequences at once appear no more serious than its causes, a lecture delivered by Worcester to Hotspur chiding the latter for his tactlessness in ruffling their touchy Welsh ally, and a concluding love scene between the Englishman, Mortimer, and his Welsh wife which must be conducted entirely in sighs and music since neither understands the other's tongue, this last parodied by Hotspur and his frolicsome wife. The mere recital of its contents with all this "skimble-skamble stuff" would appear to support the charge of the critics. But readers and players know it for what it is: one of the best scenes in the play.

Still, what are we to say about its structure? Are Shakespeare's critics right? Does he display a kind of self-indulgence here, giving his audience some surefire entertainment at the expense of the play's artistic unity? Before coming to any such conclusion, we would do well to recall Shakespeare's artful use of scenic juxtaposition. An examination of the two scenes adjacent to this one discloses that the lecture delivered by Worcester to Hotspur echoes a lecture in the scene immediately preceding and foreshadows a lecture in the scene immediately following. Alert to Shakespeare's fondness for instructive parallels, we at once suspect significance in these. And we find it. The preceding scene (II, iv) features Falstaff, pretending to be King Henry, giving a kind of parody lecture to Hal, the Prince of Wales. The succeeding scene (III, ii) reveals the real king giving a lecture to his son, Hal, on the follies of a misspent life. An examination of these successive "lectures" reveals the thematic unity that informs all three: the first and second reveal the very real charm and equally real moral deficiencies of Falstaff and Hotspur, the play's polar opposites— men who are disqualified from ruling others because they cannot rule themselves; the third discloses the real (and discards the false) qualities of the play's thematic hero, Hal, who represents the golden mean between the extremes of Falstaff and Hotspur. Hal, despite surface appearances, can govern himself and is preparing, moreover, to become the fit ruler of England when the time comes for him to succeed his father.

This trio of scenes neatly illustrates several aspects of Shakespearean dramaturgy we have been discussing in both this chapter and the one just before it: the principle of artful juxtaposition, the meaninglessness of arbitrary act divisions, the alternating of two or more story lines, and the fondness for climactic expansion in the middle of the play. It is with the last that we are concerned and to which we now return.

Because in *1 Henry IV* we are not in the realm of tragedy, the dilation here is not one of passion and pity but rather one of irony and insight. But the principle remains the same. In a play rich in good scenes, these three are among the best. Shakespeare, fully aware of the dramatic possibilities he has here, appears to suspend the progress of his narrative in order to enrich the elements of character, theme, and language in a series of theatrical tours de force that even a doctrinaire Aristotelian structuralist is compelled to applaud. But these theatrically effective scenes are not just entertainments, nor are they casual narrative detours or plot digressions. They are truly functional— enriching characterizations, illuminating themes, foreshadowing future actions, and all these by means of prose and verse as perfectly adapted to its speakers as any Shakespeare would ever compose. Here, then, is that coordinating of the elements of drama, that orchestrating of all its several parts into a harmonious whole that characterizes Shakespeare's supreme achievements as a dramatist.

This triumphant example of Shakespeare's dramaturgic skill drives home the point: it is foolish to talk of *right* and *wrong* structures and forms; all we really have are successful and unsuccessful structures; and the successes are not necessarily from the same mold nor do they always adhere to the same pattern. The dogmas supposedly laid down by Aristotle do not point out the only true ways to make a play. Even the iron law of causality is not the only acceptable way of linking scenes in a play.

Inseparably linked with causality is the question of character motivation: What is the *cause* of a person's acts? Shakespeare's frequent disregard for character motivation has annoyed some critics and puzzled some readers. Although we can perhaps afford to ignore the critics' irritation, readers should not be needlessly puzzled. A large part of the modern reader's difficulty stems from the contemporary emphasis on motivation—in realistic drama, in most novels and short stories, and in films. All of these literary forms place a high value on their degree of fidelity to real life. A concomitant of such a value is an insistence on explaining human behavior by laying bare its antecedents in the immediate past—in short, in discovering a character's past motives in order to understand his present acts. In drama, as we have seen, a person's motives must be displayed by means of action: if a person's motives are to be spelled out, the playwright must invent an action that will have a causal link with that character's subsequent behavior.

For most moderns, this attention to motivation probably seems so ordinary and so necessary as to preclude any further discussion. But a discussion is precisely what is called for when one confronts literary works in which such explanations of motives are neither present nor sought for. Even a swift glance at some familiar Shakespearean plays reveals how often characters act with no explanation for their behavior; there is, therefore, no need for scenes that would establish the reasons for their actions.

For example, we do not always know the motives of Shakespeare's villains. In *Much Ado About Nothing,* the villainy of Don John is simply asserted; it is never explained. What applies to villainy applies also to folly. In *Romeo and Juliet,* we are never told why the Montagues and the Capulets are feuding. Like the weather of Verona, it is simply a "given." In *1 Henry IV*, we are never given any intimation as to why Sir John Falstaff long ago elected to live a dissolute life. Like the Montague-Capulet feud, Falstaff and his way of life are a given. Given such a man, and given a prince bent on taking a moral holiday, what follows are some of the greatest comic scenes in English drama. But we are never invited to look behind the givens.

One might argue that a story has to begin somewhere and that we cannot forever work our way back to original causes or we would never begin—or, worse, would be able to tell only one massive story that encompassed all human experience from the beginning of time. But this argument hardly explains the absence of any clear reason for Lear's decision to divide his kingdom as he does. Here is a momentous decision on which everything else in the play depends. Surely it demands some explanation.

The answer is that it does only if you are writing a play that attempts to portray human actions with something like photographic fidelity and to explain those actions with something like clinical psychological accuracy. If, instead, you are not concerned with trying to be true *to* life but are content to employ larger-than-life characters engaged in admittedly symbolic actions that are only true *about* life— if, in fine, you are an Elizabethan playwright like Shakespeare—you need supply no such explanation because it has no bearing on your purpose. Your purpose is to depict imaginatively on a massive canvas the sufferings of a king who could make a mistake like Lear's, not to explain how he came to make that mistake. You are aware that this story of an old king and his three daughters on which you are going to base your play is the stuff of fairy tales. It is as much the stuff of fairy tales as is the story of the father who decreed that his daughter must bestow her hand and her fortune on the man who selectes the right casket from among three—a story that you had woven into an earlier play called *The Merchant of Venice*. The purpose of both plays is not to explain why fathers do these things but to dramatize the story of what happens after they do them.

It is easy to cite other instances of scenes in Shakespeare that are not causally linked with preceding scenes and of characters whose actions are either unexplained or insufficiently explained. We never really know why Mark Antony, a seasoned general, defers to the stripling Octavius when the latter insists on commanding the troops on the right hand just before the battle of Philippi; we do not really learn why Cleopatra flees in her ship at Actium drawing Antony "like a doting mallard" after her; we remain puzzled by Northumberland's failure to join his son Hotspur at the battle of Shrewsbury. And to turn to something much more massive and at the same time more complex and subtle, we do not ever really understand why a man like Macbeth could carry out the murder of King Duncan. All the talk about ambition and Lady Macbeth's savage importuning of him has never seemed, to readers of sensibility, to unearth the real answer. There is mystery here.

The same mystery envelops an equally powerful portrait of evil. The most naive reader is well aware of Iago's *explicit* reasons for hating Othello: his failure to be advanced to second in command, his expressed suspicion that Othello and Emilia have cuckolded him. But few readers (or playgoers) are persuaded by these reasons. Witnessing acts of evil out of proportion to normal provocation, including those directed against Desdemona, who is guiltless of any provocation, we are reduced, like Othello at the end, to ask:

> Will you, I pray, demand that demi-devil
> Why he hath thus ensnared my soul and body?
> (*V, ii*, 301–302)

Shakespeare, like Iago, denies us any answers—because, quite simply, there are none. In both *Macbeth* and *Othello*,

Shakespeare has displayed the artistic judgment to direct his efforts toward creating a memorable picture of the terrifying effects of evil deeds, leaving the causes to the realm of speculation, with the result that he has imagined works of art instead of detailing clinical case studies.

This ignoring of motivation gives the playwright greater latitude in developing patterns of narrative structure. Freed from the tyranny of causality, Shakespeare may employ looser and more elastic story lines. He may, as in *Hamlet,* adhere to a pattern that despite Aristotle's strictures is consciously episodic.

It is a distinguishing characteristic of the episodic narrative structure that one incident is rounded off and completed before another begins. If the image of joined links in a chain suggests the tight causal organization, then the image of distinctive beads on a single string will identify the episodic kind. Recall, for instance, almost any scene from *Hamlet*—Laertes' farewell to his father and sister, Hamlet's grim quizzing of Ophelia when he finds her at her orisons, his conversation with the newly arrived players, the painful scene between Hamlet and his mother, Ophelia's mad scene, Hamlet's ironic banter with the gravediggers—and you grasp this episodic quality. And yet, there is a very real unity to the whole structure. If we call this the unity of multiplicity, however, we must be clear about how it is achieved.

The paradox implicit in the phrase *unity in multiplicity* will perhaps become clearer if we translate its meaning by using yet another paradox: unity achieved by expansion rather than by compression. This last is a paradox peculiarly congenial to the Renaissance mind. Elizabethan thought strained toward universality. Predictably, Elizabethan plays reflected this cast of thought by grounding their large central themes in as many varied illustrations as ingenuity suggested and formal limits (time, place, action) permitted. Thus, in a comedy, we must see not only sentimental Orsino in love but also, and in the same play, mannered Olivia, silly Sir Andrew, bawdy Sir Toby, conceited Malvolio, pert Maria, ardent Sebastian, and, of course, clear-eyed Viola. Similarly, in a tragedy, we must see not only old Polonius using "indirections to find directions out" but also Claudius employing a series of spies to penetrate Hamlet's antic pose, Hamlet, in turn, devising a "mousetrap" to catch the conscience of the king, Rosencrantz and Guildenstern trying by subterfuge to pluck out Hamlet's mystery, Hamlet seeking by cryptic interrogation to test Ophelia's "honesty"—all struggling from different motives to distinguish appearance from reality in the rotten state of Denmark.

Our musical metaphor seems serviceable once more. What we find are variations on a theme. But these variations may take many manifestations. They may take the form of characters to whom essentially the same thing happens (Hamlet, Laertes, and Fortinbras all lose fathers) or of characters who are in the same state of mind (Rosalind, Orlando, Oliver, Celia, Silvius, and Touchstone all fall in love). They may take the form of actions that raise similar problems although they may produce different solutions (Antonio mortgages himself to assist Bassanio's quest of Portia and then Bassanio and Portia willingly postpone their own happiness to come to Antonio's rescue; Shylock is given several chances to be magnanimous but refuses them all; yet the Duke and Antonio show mercy to him). They may take the form of speeches whose imagery and cadences reflect the different attitudes of their speakers toward a common subject (cool Brutus, hot Cassius, cold Octavius, and mercurial Antony all deliver themselves of remarks on the nature of political power and authority). In all of these instances the mirror is held up to nature, but nature appears in many different guises. If the variations are many, the theme remains one.

Nevertheless, this tendency to expand the number of variations has its limits. The Elizabethan playwrights might stretch nearly to the breaking point Aristotle's dictum concerning a play's proper magnitude. But the best of them, Shakespeare included, tried never to exceed that breaking point. They understood, as all artists must, the need for unity. Even Elizabethan narrative exuberance had to be circumscribed if it was to achieve the kind of pressure that is indispensable to dramatic power.

Shakespeare and his fellow playwrights did have at their disposal several means of keeping their burgeoning plays within bounds. The most obvious of these means was the story they were telling: to satisfy their audience's desire to know how it all turned out, they had to bring it to an end. Finishing something, rounding it off—this alone both requires and bestows a kind of unity. Equally obvious, and always a unifying force despite Aristotle's subordination of it, is the focus on a central character. Even when, as in *Hamlet* and *King Lear,* the cast of characters is very large, no one has ever doubted where the center of interest is. The old saying, "*Hamlet* without Hamlet," to designate an empty accomplishment or meaningless venture, makes the point simply. In addition, the power of language as it finds expression in certain focal and carefully repeated images—images that take on rich symbolic meanings—operates as a unifying force that is so compelling as to lead some twentieth-century commentators to discover the essential unity of Shakespeare's plays in his poetry. (We will devote portions of a later chapter to this aspect of Shakespearean unity.) And we have already provided a number of examples of the ways in which theme operates to achieve unity. We will, moreover, devote the next chapter to a more extensive treatment of theme, so important is this aspect of Shakespearean drama.

There are, then, several avenues to unity. The rounding off of the narrative, the focus on a principal character, the felt pressure of some pervasive imagery, the presence of some pregnant idea in the play's womb—all of these contribute a oneness to these seemingly discursive plays. But it is, to echo Dr. Johnson's words (while denying his strictures), "the art of connection" and "the care of disposition" of the scenes of Shakespeare's plays wherein we may best see unity achieved by means of multiplicity. It has been the principal purpose of this chapter to demonstrate how Shakespeare resolves this paradox, and it is to this that we return with one extended example taken from a play that has always been acknowledged to be a tour de force of plotting: *The Merchant of Venice.* Better yet, this play permits us to demonstrate Shakespeare's characteristic way of coordinating *all* of the elements of drama, of synthesizing plot with world and character and theme so as to achieve not a mechanical but an organic unity. In the process, by a happy economy, we discover ourselves not only synthesizing the materials of this chapter but reviewing the materials of Chapters 2 and 3 as well.

In *The Merchant of Venice,* we come to know two distinct worlds: Venice and Belmont. The principal activities of the world of Venice are commerce and law; those of the contrasting world of Belmont are music and marriage. Appropriately, the atmosphere of Venice is disclosed as one of tension, anxiety, stridency, suspicion, and severity, whereas Belmont luxuriates in a golden glow of lightness, easiness, mellifluousness, openness, and magnanimity. Belmont's representative character is Portia, who is young, fair, quick, bountiful, and loving. The representative character of Venice is Shylock, who is old, dark, deliberate, parsimonious, and vengeful. Their respective characters are reflected in the tonal qualities of their language: Portia's speech is euphonious, open, ready, and smooth-flowing, whereas Shylock's is harsh, guarded, hesitant, and curiously repetitive.

Fittingly, at the play's outset, each of the principals is central to a different plot. Shylock, like a spider, spins the bond plot as a means of ensnaring his hated enemy, Antonio, the merchant of Venice. Portia possesses a very different kind of centrality: she is the "lady richly left" whose "sunny locks/Hang on her temples like a golden fleece, . . . / And many Jasons come in quest of her." Like her picture, she is at the center of the casket plot, the worthy prize of the suitor who has the wit to distinguish reality from appearance.

As is his wont, Shakespeare begins by giving us scenes that alternate between his two plots: we begin in Venice, where Bassanio receives Antonio's offer to subsidize his suit of Portia even though the merchant must mortgage himself to do so; we switch to Belmont, where we hear Portia review the terms of her father's will involving the choice of the caskets and where we laugh at her witty appraisal of the suitors who have so far appeared to try their luck. We immediately return to Venice to witness Antonio's entering into the lethal contract with Shylock; and we switch back to Belmont in time to be introduced to the Prince of Morocco, the first of the really formidable suitors for Portia's hand. This rhythm of regularly alternating scenes is then interrupted and complicated by the introduction of two subplots—one concerning the efforts of the clownish Lancelot Gobbo to leave the service of Shylock so as to enter the service of Bassanio, the other focusing on the secret plans of Shylock's daughter, Jessica, to elope with Bassanio's friend Lorenzo. These subplots occupy five swift successive scenes during which we catch brief glimpses of both Bassanio and Shylock and learn of the former's imminent departure for Belmont. Besides providing intrinsic interest as entertainment (Gobbo's vaudeville) and plot intensification (Jessica's escape from her ogre father fueling Shylock's hatred of Antonio and his Christian friends), these scenes create the impression of the passage of time—the three months before the bond must be paid or a pound of flesh forfeited. All this attended to, we return once more to the steady rhythmic alternation of a scene in Belmont followed by a scene in Venice—scenes that advance the casket plot swiftly and directly and the bond plot more slowly and indirectly. These scenes include the mistaken choices of Morocco (the gold casket) and Arragon (the silver) and the reactions of Shylock to the unwelcome news of his daughter's elopement and the welcome news of Antonio's reported shipping losses.

Then precisely at the midpoint of his play, Shakespeare stages a scene in which he not only successfully merges all of the stories he has so far set afoot but also boldly lays the foundation for still another plot—the ring plot, which he will use to restore the light, bantering tone appropriate to a romantic comedy after he has darkened the mood in the famous courtroom scene that pits Portia against Shylock. He brings about the merger of the earlier stories and the beginnings of the new plot neatly enough. Bassanio chooses the

right casket; Portia bestows on the victor not only herself
but also a ring "Which when you part from, lose, or give
away, / Let it presage the ruin of your love." Enter the
eloped couple, Lorenzo and Jessica, with a messenger from
Venice who conveys the fateful news of Antonio's shipping
losses, the expiration of the due date on the bond, and
Shylock's dreadful claiming of his forfeit. Thus, in a single
scene we see the termination of two plots (casket and
elopement), the origin of another (ring), and the complication of still another (bond).

As impressive as is this structural carpentry, it is not the
mark of Shakespeare's unique accomplishment. Any skillful
maker of plays, one may be inclined to believe, can maneuver
these large structural units as adroitly as Shakespeare has
here. But a close look at what these seemingly disparate
scenes and stories have in common reveals the poetic imagination at work—the deft mind that thinks in analogies and
correspondences. Consider the common element of disguise
that informs all of these plots. We begin with an example of
literal disguise (Jessica dressed as a boy) in the elopement
plot. It requires only a short metaphoric step to see the
disguise of Portia (literally, her picture) within the dull
lead casket whose threatening outward appearance disguises the radiant reality within. Armed with this insight, it
takes no teacher come from the classroom to tell us that the
"merry bond" is in reality a terrible ambush—hate disguised as a "merry sport." (Perhaps some readers, knowing
Shakespeare's relentless ingenuity, are even willing to
acknowledge the relevancy of the "disguise episode" in the
vaudeville act between Lancelot Gobbo and his "high-
gravel-blind" father, although it is not necessary to press
this point.)

Now, standing back from the entire play, much as one
does from an impressionist painting to see it whole, we come
to see how disguise as a motif and the ancient conundrum of
appearance and reality as a theme run through the play like
a golden thread holding the disparate beads of narrative
together. When, further, we recall that the play's most thrill-
ing scene—the duel in the Venetian court of law between

Shylock, come to claim his pound of flesh, and Portia, posing as a Doctor of Laws asserting the higher claims of mercy— turns precisely on the element of both the literal disguise of Portia and the "disguised" defense ("This bond doth give thee here no jot of blood') and, furthermore, that the entire last act following the courtroom scene depends on this same element of disguise for its humor (Bassanio having surrendered his ring out of gratitude to the Doctor of Laws [Portia] and his man, Gratiano, having surrendered his, in turn, to the lawyer's clerk [Nerissa]), we are compelled to acknowledge that disguise is the very "life of the design" of this play.

As ingenious as all the foregoing may seem, this working out of variations on the motif of disguise, there are still greater subtleties to be discovered. Whereas a lesser artist would be satisfied with this display of metaphoric ingenuity, this brilliant exercise in definition ("How many kinds of disguise do we have here?"), Shakespeare makes all this ingenious plot stuff operate for him on the thematic level as well. Witness: the disguises employed in the casket, elopement, and ring plots are all harmless; that employed in the bond plot is malevolent. This dichotomy in the plots reminds us that the same division runs like an earth fault through all the other elements of the play. The two worlds of *The Merchant of Venice* are more than two places—they are two utterly different visions of life, and they are, to give fresh meaning to a stale phrase, worlds apart! Note that Shylock, the proponent of retributive justice, may not even enter Belmont, the world whose governing value is that undiscriminating mercy that "droppeth as the gentle rain from heaven / Upon the place beneath." Note, too, that this world is precisely where the eloping lovers, Lorenzo and Jessica, do come and find a welcome. Note that the principal property of the bond plot is the knife, an instrument used to cut away something, to sever, whereas the principal property of the ring plot is, of course, the ring, an instrument meant to encircle, enclose, unite. Recall all of the qualities we have associated with Venice, and they add up to—discord. Recall all the qualities we have associated with Belmont, and they add up to—concord.

Cut into the play at any point—character, world, plot, theme, language—and you will discover the same set of oppositions manifesting themselves in appropriate ways. This is what is meant by artistic unity. The playwright is so clear as to his ends and has so mastered his means that no aspect of the play can be examined without discovering his identifying signature. Out of the gossamer stuff of fairy tales and romances he has woven a fabric that is tough enough to encase some elemental truths about the power of love and the nature of reality.

Only a few words remain to be said. Earlier in this chapter, we examined characteristic Shakespearean beginnings, middles, and ends. *The Merchant of Venice* displays all of the patterns we discovered. We have already indicated the alternating of story lines in the opening scenes. These story lines are kept apart until the playwright is ready to bring them together in the scene in which Bassanio chooses the right casket. But however apart they may appear, they comment on each other, either by means of obvious contrasts or by means of more subtle parallels. The climactic plateau that we found in several plays here becomes a two-peaked height in the third and fourth acts—the first bringing the casket plot to its culmination, the second performing the same office for the bond plot. What we said about dilating the emotional moments of the play has never been made clearer than here: the scene that features the winning of Portia runs to 326 lines, and the scene that features the overthrow of Shylock swells to 455 lines. Having given the emotions their head, Shakespeare turns, as we have repeatedly seen him do, to the business of rounding off the narrative stuff of his play. Aware of the need for some transition between the thundering theatrics of his courtroom scene and the light high-comedy banter of his final scene in Belmont, he employs his minor lovers, Lorenzo and Jessica, to intone some of the loveliest lyrics he ever wrote ("How sweet the moonlight sleeps upon this bank! / Here will we sit and let the sounds of music / Creep in our ears."). Again, everything is functional. Even this set piece of unabashed lyricism makes its contribution to the play's theme and vision, for it is to the world of concord and music and the harmony of loving hearts that we are being returned after our exposure to the harsh and bitter atmosphere of a Venetian law court.

Once safely back in Belmont, the conventions of comedy will be observed. We are ready for the by now familiar ceremonial ending with three pairs of lovers—Bassanio and Portia, Lorenzo and Jessica, Gratiano and Nerissa—united in connubial bliss, all debts canceled or paid, Antonio restored to prosperity, Shylock defanged but not totally despoiled (mercy has seasoned justice), and everything done that an Elizabethan playwright could think to do in order to send his audience back home across the Thames pleased because they had just been treated to a comedy served up as they liked it.

6

THEME AND MEANING

> It is a theme as fluent as the sea.
> (*Henry V, III, vii*, 32)

Several chapters in this book begin by focusing attention on the definition of critical terms. Chapter 2 starts out by distinguishing between actual *persons* and *dramatic characters*, Chapter 3 opens with a detailed definition of the metaphorical term *world*, and Chapter 5 commences with a careful distinction between *story* and *plot*. In similar fashion, we will begin this chapter by examining several definitions of *theme*, demonstrating in the process how each has been applied—or misapplied—to a Shakespearean play. We will conclude by demonstrating how one of the definitions of theme best illuminates Shakespeare's dramatic craftsmanship and thus affords us the surest understanding of how his plays convey their meanings.

Theme is sometimes simply and loosely equated with *subject*. For example, we may be told that the "themes" of *Troilus and Cressida* are love and war, those of *The Winter's Tale* loss and restoration, and those of *The Merchant of Venice* pagan justice versus Christian charity. Readers familiar with these plays will recognize easily enough the incidents

to which these very general terms refer: they will recall that
the love affair between faithful Troilus and faithless Cressida is played out against the background of the Greek and
Trojan war; that King Leontes's jealous wrath results in the
loss of both his daughter, Perdita, and his wife, Hermione,
but that both are restored to him in seeming recognition of
his genuine contrition, in a manner that closely resembles
the Christian pattern of redemption; and that Portia's gos-
pel of mercy triumphs over Shylock's doctrine of retributive
justice in an exciting courtroom duel of hearts and heads.

But to name something, which is all we do when we designate a play's subject, is not to explain it: we can identify
many experiences without understanding their significance. Worse yet, sometimes the naming of a play's subject
is not only inadequate, because it falls well short of understanding, but also positively misleading, because it directs
our attention to surfaces and blinds us to depths. Some
common misunderstandings of two of Shakespeare's best
known plays will serve to illustrate this kind of misinterpretation.

No one would deny that *Othello* is about jealousy, among
other things, and that jealousy is so central to the play's
principal actions that it may fairly be called the subject of
the play. But having said so much, we may discover that we
have in fact raised questions, not provided answers. The
play may be about jealousy, but so may the headlines on
today's scandal sheet. What gives the play permanent interest? Jealousy, in the sense of Iago's envy of Cassio's good
fortune at the expense of his own, hardly accounts for the
ferocity of his hatred of Othello and does not account at all
for the "motiveless malignity" he displays toward the innocent Desdemona. And sexual jealousy is surely an inadequate term to define and explain the extraordinary behavior of Othello, who calls a *sacrifice* what any other would
call a *murder* and who convinces himself that he can kill
now only to love the more hereafter. There is complexity
here. And mystery.

If *jealousy* proves to be a gross and misleading response to
the question, What is *Othello* significantly about? then *am-*

bition is a similarly clumsy and misleading response to the same question concerning *Macbeth*. Nothing that can be said about ambition throws any revealing light on the haunting hallucinatory trance in which the hero-villain of that play appears to move—from crime to crime and from punishment to punishment. Nor does it weaken our argument that the very word is in the mouth of his dreadful lady as she responds to Macbeth's letter telling her of his first fateful meeting with the three witches ("Thou wouldst be great, / Art not without ambition . . ."). Lady Macbeth, although she speaks with fierce confidence, only slenderly knows her husband; indeed, the remainder of the play makes unmistakably clear that she never really understands herself: this woman who thought she could become a monster by an exercise of will ("unsex me here") is reduced before our eyes to the stricken somnambulist who tries in vain to wash the guilty stains of blood from her hands ("Here's the smell of blood still. All the perfumes of Arabia will not sweeten this little hand.") Again, there is complexity. And mystery.

Those persons who read (or witness) these two plays thoughtfully and feelingly become aware that *Othello* and *Macbeth* are not simply case studies in jealousy and ambition but are instead disturbing and provocative glimpses of the shifting faces of evil. Any adequate statement of their themes, therefore, cannot take the form of tidy answers to simple questions. Like the plays that embody them, these themes will be tentative, not pat, shot full of darkly suggestive ambiguities, not circumscribed by too neat resolutions.

To equate a play's theme with its subject, then, is both to oversimplify and to distort. It is fatally easy to do this. Most of us can recall how brutally we disfigure a work of literary art when we are asked to respond too quickly to the question, What's it all about? Or how we distort a subtle performance when we must hastily improvise an answer to the question, What was it like? Our responses do not necessarily lack sincerity or conviction, but they lack art—the very quality that gives distinction to the work we are presumably construing. It is not enough, though, that we are made aware that our responses are too crude. That is only the lesser

shortcoming; there is a more serious one. Lacking refine-
ment, these responses are only too apt to miss the point as
well. Failing to reveal the work's true distinction, they may
also fail to discern its meaning.

But equating theme with subject is not the only instance
in which this term is loosely applied. The term themes is
sometimes assigned to the *moral maxims* with which
Elizabethan plays, including Shakespeare's, are so plentifully stuffed. An audience raised on a tradition that included morality plays and accustomed to hear even the
common criminal preparing to be hanged on Tyburn Hill
deliver himself of some moral homily expected its popular
plays to be full of "wise saws and modern instances." As a
writer for the popular public theater, Shakespeare obliged.
And because almost everything he touched became memorable, some apothegms out of this mass ("Who steals my
purse steals trash. . .") or some longer moral reflections in
the form of a soliloquy ("What is a man, / If his chief good
and market of his time / Be but to sleep and feed?") have
taken on a life of their own independent of the play in which
they originally appeared and in this fashion have found
their way into classrooms as set pieces for oral interpretation or onto rostrums as adornments for speeches desper-
ately in need of borrowed glitter since they give off no light
of their own. More than this: they have become a part of
everyday conversation. Persons who would be hard put to
identify the precise source will repeat "All that glisters
(they almost invariably say *glitters*) is not gold" or "It is a
wise father that knows his own child" or will comment on a
particular piece of human folly by reminding their listeners,
"What fools these mortals be!" So insidious is the habit and
so inveterate the practice of salting our conversation with
these familiar lines that jokes concerning them have grown
up, including the story about the ancient one who declared
peevishly: "I can't understand why Shakespeare is so highly
rated. He's just full of quotations!"

Although we should not equate these maxims and moral
tags with the central themes or principal ideas of the plays
in which they appear, we may recognize that because they

are generalizations about significant aspects of human behavior they are such stuff as themes are made on. For that
reason, they call for a few explanatory remarks.

If we remain sharply aware of the character of the speaker
and of the situation in which he is speaking, we will not
detach these moral speeches from their dramatic contexts.
And alert to the dramatic contexts, we will be struck by the
number of times favorite maxims are found in the mouths of
villains, cynics, or expedient politicians. It is Iago who reminds us that the loss of money is nothing compared to the
loss of one's good name; it is Polonius who concludes a cascade of sententious wisdom to a departing son with the unforgettable "to thine ownself be true"; and it is the wily
Ulysses who, for the purpose of resolving a petty quarrel
between two foolish Greek commanders, gives eloquent expression to one of the period's favorite doctrines—the notion of the virtue of established order. All this should not be
interpreted as Shakespearean cynicism. On the contrary, it
is evidence of Shakespearean art. He was a moral artist but
not a moralizer; thus his moral maxims are often undercut
or complicated by the ironic circumstances in which they
are delivered, one more reminder of his balanced rather
than one-sided view of human behavior.

Still, even if we guard against the naive error of assuming
these worthy sentiments to be Shakespeare's own "messages" to his readers or auditors, we need to recognize the
significance of their frequent appearance in his plays. A
part of the explanation has already been offered: the
Elizabethan audiences and the writers who served them
were alike agreed that the double purpose of art is to instruct and delight. This echo of Horace's famous prescription was not confined to literary theorists; persons who did
not know or guess its origins in Horace's dictum endorsed
its purport. Another part of the explanation is related to the
first: As a popular artist writing for the members of a popular audience, Shakespeare gave them what they wanted. But
there is far more to it than this bald statement would seem
to imply. Shakespeare was not just pleasing his audience; he
was pleasing himself. Which is to say once more that

Shakespeare was radically a moral artist. As Alfred Harbage has told us, ". . . there are not thirty consecutive lines in Shakespeare that do not levy upon the vocabulary of ethics, or relate in some way to standards of conduct, to choices between right and wrong."[1]

Once again, we must carefully distinguish between this conclusion and a false corollary that has proven fatally easy to attach to it: Shakespeare's constant concern is with problems of good and evil, but he is never concerned with prescribing how people should behave or teaching ethical lessons or playing the preacher. If we were to ask Shakespeare the question Macbeth asked the Doctor:

> Canst thou not minister to the mind diseased,
> Pluck from the memory a rooted sorrow,
> Raze out the written troubles of the brain,
> And with some sweet oblivious antidote
> Cleanse the stuffed bosom of that perilous stuff
> Which weighs upon the heart?   *(V, iii, 40–45)*

we should receive the reply Macbeth received:

> > Therein the patient
> Must minister to himself.
> > > *(V, iii, 45–46)*

This is not to say that Shakespeare was without moral opinions of his own. He is not a writer idiot pure, devoid of attitudes and the values these attitudes reflect.

The mention of attitudes and values at once brings us closer to a more useful definition of theme. All writers have what we may call a *vision* of the world. This vision is the sum total of the writer's experiences as a human being and an artist, and these experiences are brought into focus by the play of his imagination. His vision, or, more exactly, aspects of his vision, are found projected in his art. Some writers—a minority, but a writer as great as Tolstoy is among them—so wish to persuade their readers to share a particular insight that they spell it out explicitly in the form of a *thesis,* and their story then becomes an example of proof of the truth of this thesis. However, the majority of storytellers (dramatists, fictionists) know that the strength of their persuasion lies not in any statement of thesis but in the story itself. Even if they are conscious of some purpose to persuade, they discover no reason to reveal their purpose openly but are satisfied that if the members of their audience temporarily experience the world as seen through the eyes of the artist, they will come to share the artist's vision. Such a gentle and unobtrusive persuasion is their way of commenting on what it means to be human. This comment is *implicit:* fused with the action, resting at the center of all the play's elements like a hub in a wheel, this implicit comment becomes part of the reader's or spectator's experience of the play. In this meeting of the minds and spirits of the artist and his audience we may trace the movement of the play's theme.

Applying this definition of theme, one would be right to conclude that at the center of each individual work of literary art one may discover a unique theme. (A combination of common sense and modesty might also suggest that with a complex work of art, this central theme might well be accompanied by a constellation of companion themes and that the task of charting this web of meanings would not be a simple one.) But before tracing such a pattern, we must touch on one or two other matters that have a direct bearing on the process by which themes evolve.

Literary themes, of necessity, have their origins in the underlying assumptions about humanity that artists share with other men who live in the same period they do. This is not the place for a full and systematic review of the common assumptions about humanity and the universe that were widely held during Shakespeare's lifetime. (These will be given a fuller, though still cursory, treatment in this book's final chapter.) But one pervasive set of assumptions that left their mark on both the life and the literature of the period during which Shakespeare wrote must be mentioned before we turn to examine in detail the workings of theme in one of his dramatic masterpieces, *1 Henry IV.*

A great legacy of medieval thought that finds both implicit and explicit expression in many of the plays of
Shakespeare is the notion of a preordained *order*—a fixed
pattern governing the relationships of man to God (hence to
his future), of man to nature (hence to his universe), of man
to man (hence to his society), and of man to himself (hence
to his identity as a moral creature). This notion of a preestablished order (Shakespeare calls it *degree*) was one of the
great myths of the Elizabethan world, and like all myths it is
characterized by the unconsciousness with which its assumptions were held and acted on and the pervasiveness of
its influence on almost every aspect of human behavior—
from political allegiance to the king, through firmly rooted
laws relating to marriage and inheritance, to personal codes
of conduct. It finds expression, both literal and figurative, in
countless remains of Elizabethan writing but nowhere more
eloquently—or famously—than in the words of Ulysses on
degree, the speech in *Troilus and Cressida* with which he at
once upbraids the Greek leaders for their failure to take
Troy and sets down the reason and the remedy for their
failure.

> The specialty of rule hath been neglected;
> ....
> The heavens themselves, the planets, and this centre
> Observe degree, priority, and place,
> Insisture, course, proportion, season, form,
> Office, and custom, in all line of order.
> And therefore is the glorious planet Sol
> In noble eminence enthroned and sphered
> Amidst the other; whose med'cinable eye
> Corrects the influence of evil planets,
> And posts, like the commandment of a king,
> Sans check to good and bad. But when the planets
> In evil mixture to disorder wander,
> What plagues, and what portents, what mutiny,
> What raging of the sea, shaking of earth,
> Commotion in the winds, frights, changes, horrors,
> Divert and crack, rend and deracinate

The unity and married calm of states
Quite from their fixure? O, when degree is shaked,
Which is the ladder of all high designs,
The enterprise is sick. How could communities,
Degrees in schools, and brotherhoods in cities,
Peaceful commerce from dividable shores,
The primogenity and due of birth,
Prerogative of age, crowns, sceptres, laurels,
But by degree, stand in authentic place?
Take but degree away, untune that string,
And hark what discord follows. Each thing meets
In mere oppugnancy. The bounded waters
Should lift their bosoms higher than the shores
And make a sop of all this solid globe;
Strength should be lord of imbecility,
And the rude son should strike his father dead;
Force should be right, or rather right and wrong,
Between whose endless jar justice resides,
Should lose their names, and so should justice too;
Then everything include itself in power,
Power into will, will into appetite.
And appetite, an universal wolf,
So doubly seconded with will and power,
Must make perforce an universal prey
And last eat up himself.   *(I, iii, 78, 85–124)*

Ulysses' speech, it will be seen, contains an important corollary of this doctrine of the efficacy of preordained order: the notion of what Emerson called *correspondences* between a person's internal self (in which order was ensured when reason, operating by free will, governed the passions), the social and political community (in which order was ensured when both family and nation deferred to the authority of father and king), and the universe (whose stars and planets march rank on rank around the ancient track of heaven as though they were indeed the army of unalterable law). Everywhere in Shakespearean drama, but most notably in the tragedies and histories, these correspondences are made explicit: readers of *Julius Caesar, Macbeth,* and *King*

Lear will recall how the "little insurrections" in man are invariably accompanied by the "to-and-fro conflicting" storms of wind and rain that engulf these suffering mortals and symbolize their agonies.

We have already suggested that this medieval notion is peculiarly congenial to a literary artist since it provides a tight metaphysical framework within which to construct a unified work of art. The doctrine of correspondences, resting as it must on the processes of metaphor, analogy, symbol, and allusion whereby a poet seeks and finds his parallels, becomes not only a pervasive idea that infuses these plays but also the very vehicle by means of which this idea is conveyed to the artist's audience. Thus, Macbeth's hideous murder of King Duncan is accompanied not only by a profound inner disturbance ("Methought I heard a voice cry, 'Sleep no more!' ") but also by a cosmic clamor ("Thou seest the heavens, as troubled with man's act, / Threatens his bloody stage."). The macrocosm throbs with the same tremor that invests the microcosm.

Nonetheless, everything we have been asserting about Shakespeare's working habits of mind and artistry suggests that he never settled down into the easy harness of dogma or uncritical orthodoxy. Content to make use of orthodox doctrines when these suited his artistic purposes, he was just as sensitive a barometer to the felt pressures of unorthodoxy. When we recall that Shakespeare's period as a productive playwright coincided with that period of intellectual turmoil at the end of the sixteenth century which saw the breaking up of this medieval vision of a concordant universe, we are prepared to discover in his plays reflections of the conflicts that mark any period of history during which one world is dying and another is struggling to be born.

The great ax blows that struck at the roots of the medieval doctrine of a preestablished order were delivered, as Theodore Spencer has pointed out, by Copernicus, whose stunning hypothesis that we live in a heliocentric universe finally removed the earth forever from its central position in the cosmos; by Montaigne, whose relentlessly honest introspections (notably in the *Apologie de Raimond Sebond*) made impossible any easy complacency about man's self-established superiority in the hierarchy of creature life; and by Machiavelli, whose cold-eyed examination of political behavior eroded, if it did not at once remove, the notion of some ineluctable unity between politics and metaphysics.[2] From what we have so far discovered about Shakespeare's cast of mind and practice as a working artist, we should expect to find, then, as much of Renaissance skepticism as of medieval faith in his plays. And we do. But we find still more.

Readers of the literature of our own age of seemingly endless anxiety will not need to be told that contemporary art often appears to operate like a medical chart to plot the rise and fall of the fevers of the moment. But this simile is not an accurate way of describing the greatest art of any period. Great art, while it indubitably reflects the times in which it was composed, transcends these times. It takes note of the human fevers of its day, but it does not "take notes" on them. Its eye is on the "ever-fixèd mark" of universal humanity and is not confined to the particularity of the moment. Thus Shakespeare, as a major artist, could move freely in both the atmospheres of medieval faith and of Renaissance agnosticism without himself asserting, or asking his audience to subscribe to, any specific doctrine. And at the same time, he could employ these doctrines of his day as emblems of human behavior whose commonality elevates the local and particular to the universal and general. Specifically, he could create a suffering sinner in Macbeth whose hell would be instantly recognizable to a Sophocles, a Dante, and a Sartre. These writers, like Shakespeare, would unhesitatingly fix Macbeth's position; and although their maps would seem quaintly dissimilar in superficial ways, all good readers could navigate by them and find themselves on the same course.

This universal quality in a poet represents a great gain for modern readers and playgoers: they are not really in totally unfamiliar territory, for even though the play they are considering is particularly Greek or medieval or Elizabethan, it is also universally human. But with Shakespeare they must pay a price for that gain. If emphasis on the universal makes a Shakespearean play easier for twentieth-century readers and playgoers to recognize, the playwright's refusal to think in predictable mental patterns makes the play's meaning more subtle. Shakespeare seems to have consistently thought of human behavior as a series of questions to be raised rather than of answers to be supplied. Precisely because he follows no dogmas, adheres to no doctrines, and subscribes to no programs, his meanings will never be easy even while, paradoxically, they appear to be familiar. To knit the paradox in a phrase, his will be a complex simplicity.

There is yet one more meaning of the word theme which we must discuss and illustrate before turning to examine the workings of a central theme as it gathers up and unifies all the dramatic elements—character, world, plot—that operate together in any Shakespearean play. And here our foregoing remarks about Shakespeare's universality have a bearing, for we are now concerned with truly universal themes; indeed, they are so deeply rooted in human behavior that no writer can long avoid them. Appropriately, these universal themes may best be identified by declaring the problems they pose—as, for example, the age-old problem of determining if human actions are the result of free choice or of some iron rule of necessity over which human beings have no control; or the equally ancient problem of distinguishing appearance from reality; or the problem posed by conflicting loyalties between human laws and some form of "higher law"; or the paradoxical problem implicit in the recognition that one comes to comprehend happiness only by experiencing pain, is able to receive love only when one is capable of giving it, and comes, finally, to something approximating an understanding of life only when one has looked upon the fact of death.

Even this bald listing of a few such themes discloses some of their principal characteristics: first, they appear as problems with no certain solutions, as questions with no firm answers; second, they are rooted in humanity's deepest philosophical, moral, and psychological concerns; third, they appear in a nearly inexhaustible variety of human situations. Is it any wonder that all serious writers find themselves irresistibly drawn to them? The uncertainty attending their resolution means that they will be both dramatic and complexly (and thus interestingly) so. The depths they sound in all thoughtful persons are a clear indication to the literary artist of the magnitude of his undertaking. And the limitless variety of forms in which they appear gives the writer the kind of latitude he needs to pursue his genius where it leads him.

Instances from Shakespeare's best known play spring easily to mind. Hamlet, summoned by the ghost of his father to avenge his foul murder, finds the time out of joint and is made desperate by the realization that he, alas, seems to have been born to set it right. Is he acting as a free agent, or is he fortune's fool? And in this rotten state of Denmark, what is real and what only seems? Is it an honest ghost? Is his mother guilty of more than adultery? Is Ophelia to be trusted? Can he trust himself? If it is true that Hamlet's inner struggles do not take the form of agonizing over a violation of any statutory prohibition against murder (he feels justified in pursuing revenge), he certainly puts himself above the law in an astonishing fashion when he dispatches Polonius (by accident, to be sure) and, later, Rosencrantz and Guildenstern, with no sign of remorse. This is a kind of transcendental attitude, surely, albeit its manifestations run counter to what we usually connote by that term. Finally, we recall the transformation of Hamlet toward the end of the play—best demonstrated in the tone of his conversations with Horatio during and after the graveyard scene and by his quiet acceptance of the terms of the fatal fencing match even though he is acutely aware of "how ill all's here about my heart." By accepting the fact of his death, he seems for the first time to have come to terms with his life.

We have seen that to commentators, a play's theme sometimes means simply its subject; sometimes they use the word to refer to one or more of the moral maxims or statements of proverbial wisdom that issue frequently from the mouths of Shakespeare's characters, often in unexpected and, hence, ironic ways; at still other times, the word is applied to instances in which Shakespeare may be found to be relying on the intellectual legacies of his day, the unarticulated assumptions that, precisely because no one questions them, pervade the thinking of any playwright and his audience in a given historic period; and again, the word theme is levied on to describe the dramatization of certain perennial human problems or conundrums that have puzzled us from the beginning of time.

The distinction between the first three of these meanings and the fourth one is of paramount importance to anyone seeking to understand Shakespeare's way with a play. One way of illuminating this distinction is to call attention to the very different functions of the pronoun *what* and the adverb *how*. A pronoun, we recall, may take the place of a noun. And a noun, in the familiar liturgy of our grammar schools, is the name of a person, place, or thing. It follows that if we ask the question, *What* does the play mean? We are assuming that the pronoun what stands for some discrete "meaning," some circumscribed, definable, limited "thing." The meaning of the play in this sense is static, atomistic, and detachable from other elements of the play. Moreover, it is fixed and unchanging.

Now see what happens to our thinking if we shift from pronoun to adverb and if our question, *What* does the play mean? becomes instead *How* does the play mean? To stay for another moment with our grammatical paradigm, an adverb modifies a verb. And a verb stands for an action. Then if we ask, *How* does the play mean? we are assuming that the adverb points to a process. The meaning of the play in this sense is dynamic, nuclear, organic, an integral part of the other elements of the play with which it is interrelated. This meaning, therefore, is not so much fixed as fluid; not unchanging but growing. It is this organic quality that distinguishes the themes in our fourth category from those in the other three and that prompts us to select this meaning of theme as the one best calculated to promote an understanding of Shakespearean drama.

This concept of the dynamic way theme operates in a Shakespearean play consorts well with our discoveries of how Shakespeare delineates a character, creates a world, and shapes a plot. With respect to *character,* we discovered that the surest insight was achieved by a careful focusing on the relationship of the character under observation to all the other characters in the play. Exploring the *world* of a play, we discovered in turn, put us in touch with all of that play's nerve ends, with every other element of that drama, so that the world was like a seamless web, its filaments extending from a center but without a break. And tracing the shape of a Shakespearean *plot* produced only the same discovery from another perspective: the variety and multiplicity of incidents, although suggesting exuberant narrative sprawl, on closer examination disclosed the same unity based on cunning patterns of relationship. In a word, there is a structure of characterization, there is a structure of world, there is a structure of plot, and all of these structures combine into a structure of structures whose interplay is the meaning of the drama.

All of the foregoing is true enough, but it may seem excessively schematic and it is certainly abstract. It is, therefore, time to turn to one of Shakespeare's masterpieces for concrete examples and clear illustrations of this process. *1 Henry IV*, universally acknowledged the best of Shakespeare's English history plays, constitutes almost a textbook of the ways in which a play can mean.

To begin with, *Henry IV* offers us four memorable characters: King Henry himself; Harry Percy, called Hotspur; the great buffoon, Falstaff; and Hal, the Prince of Wales. Let us take up each of these characters in turn, identify his essential qualities, sketch the special world in which he moves and has his being, indicate the plot line that he follows, and, by focusing on the *interrelationships* of these four particular characters and their worlds and plots, derive the theme, or pattern of related themes, that unifies these elements and, hence, the play in which they appear.

King Henry, significantly, makes all but one of his appearances in public. He presides over royal councils, receives emissaries, parleys with rebels, and leads armies. All but once he talks in a public voice. The reader, like Queen Victoria complaining about her Prime Minister, Gladstone, might feel that the king always addresses him as though he were a public meeting. And indeed he does. His utterances, therefore, are studied ones, delivered for a calculated effect. He lives in a world of power politics. This world is threatened externally by possible invasions from Scotland and Wales and internally by factions within his kingdom who want to unseat him. A third, and very disturbing, threat to his peace of mind takes the form of the wayward actions of his son and nominal heir.

The purpose that propels all of his actions is to bring order to his world—political peace to his kingdom and a private peace between himself and his scapegrace son. If we may speak of each principal character as having his own particular plot, then we may say of King Henry that all of his actions are in pursuit of order. This is not to say that all of his actions are prudent, although he finds them so. He cancels plans for a crusade; he declares his defeated general, Mortimer, a traitor; he demands that his victorious general, Hotspur, turn over his Scotch prisoners; he banishes Worcester from court and systematically alienates the Percys and declares them rebels at a moment when he feels sure he can defeat them with his superior forces. Betimes he lectures his son on his misbehavior and receives the latter's pledge of allegiance. He refuses amnesty to the rebels although pretending to extend such an offer, meets and defeats them at Shrewsbury, and shows himself a hard and unforgiving victor. Shakespeare, with his unerring eye for the appropriate image, finds one for King Henry: "The king has many marching in his coats," a reference to the device, used by kings in those days, of dressing other men like themselves so that they could not easily be discovered and killed in battle, to the subsequent dismay of their troops. The image aptly epitomizes the man: the king is a shrewd and practical politician; he will not scruple to employ disguise or practice some deceit in order to achieve his ends— ends which, in fairness, one must acknowledge are often very sensible ones.

The character of Hotspur, the leader of the rebels, affords an interesting contrast in every way to that of King Henry. If Henry can be said to exemplify the love of order that Queen Elizabeth strove so mightily to inculcate in her restless people, an ideal that we have already described as a legacy of medieval thought, Hotspur can be said to exemplify the Renaissance ideal of unfettered individualism. These ideals are in obvious conflict, and some commentators have suggested that Shakespeare had this in mind when he wrote the play. Be that as it may, Hotspur's individualism is of a very romantic cast. His actions appear to be motivated by a passionate desire for undying fame, for him indistinguishable from his own sense of honor. Two of his speeches—one early in the play and one late—give eloquent expression to this ideal. Fired by the prospect of unseating a king whom he regards as both unworthy and illegitimate, he exclaims:

> By heaven, methinks it were an easy leap
> To pluck bright honor from the pale-faced moon,
> Or dive into the bottom of the deep,
> Where fathom line could never touch the ground,
> And pluck up drownèd honor by the locks,
> So he that doth redeem her thence might wear
> Without corrival all her dignities. . . .
>
> *(I, iii, 201–207)*

Significantly, he wants no rivals to his fame. Later he says, in a more touching speech addressed to his men as they go forward to fight a battle that most of them feel, correctly, they are destined to lose:

> O gentlemen, the time of life is short!
> To spend that shortness basely were too long
> If life did ride upon a dial's point,
> Still ending at the arrival of an hour.
> An if we live, we live to tread on kings;
> If die, brave death, when princes die with us!
>
> *(V, ii, 81–86)*

Hotspur much of the time occupies the public world of the king, but he also lives in a world of his own, a world that bears on it the stamp of romance and romanticism. If we were asked to define the essence of *romanticism,* we could do worse than to say that it is that impulse in a person that compels him to seize life by the jugular to try to make it come to terms with him. We know the outcome every time: whether it be an Antigone, an Ahab, a Hotspur, or any other great romantic figure, the private world of such a person smashes itself on the adamantine public world.

Hotspur's plot is one that transpires in the world of public events. He defies the king and refuses to surrender his prisoners. He defends Mortimer's integrity. He joins the rebellion instigated by his uncle, Worcester, and quickly assumes the leadership of it. He is impetuous in his generalship, precipitating a battle at the wrong time and in the wrong place with fatal consequences. And yet how glorious it all is. Hotspur wins our hearts by his gallantry and ravishes our ears with his eloquence, but our heads tell us that he would never make a proper governor. And we are not surprised when, mortally wounded by Prince Hal, he expires exclaiming:

> O Harry, thou hast robbed me of my youth!
> I better brook the loss of brittle life
> Than those proud titles thou hast won of me.
> *(V, iv, 76–78)*

Another great dramatic success is Falstaff. His underlying impulse is impossible to reduce to a phrase. One comes to think of him finally as really more of an attitude than a man, although Shakespeare is at great pains to particularize the man. We know that he is fat; we know that he is old; we know that he is short of breath; we know that he is rum-soaked; we know that he is blear-eyed and white-haired. We are reminded of the portrait of a former vice president of the United States (many years ago!), who was described by one of his opponents as "a whiskey-drinking, poker-playing, evil old man."

But Falstaff transcends this picturesque particularity to emerge as a universal figure of mythic proportions. He is the lord of misrule. He is the spirit of comic irresponsibility. He is that part of all of us that prompts us to laugh when the pompous fat man slips on the banana peel. He is a kind of thrusting force of comic intelligence that reminds us that the differences between kings and waiters, princes and prostitutes, and generals and highwaymen are perhaps less significant than their similarities. He is preeminently the Critic.

Given such license by his creator, Falstaff moves freely in both worlds of the play. He is very much at home among the disreputables of the London stews whose king he is. And he can swagger about in the upper world of courtiers and warriors, albeit to the accompaniment of some very impolite stares. More important, while seeming very much a part of both worlds, he maintains a critical distance from both. Although, like so many of Shakespeare's greatest characters, he is histrionic—an actor bringing off any part he wishes to play—he is much more than an actor. He is a commentator as well, with this difference: he acts out his commentary. Falstaff can actually do what Bully Bottom only yearns to do: he can play all the parts himself! In the process of doing so, he acts out a searching criticism of both worlds and all their occupants.

Returning to the action of the play, we discover that Falstaff's plot is a series of clever reflectors and parodies and parallels of the plot lines of King Henry and Hotspur. Recalling what we discovered in Chapter 5 about Shakespeare's way with a plot, we immediately recognize the familiar Shakespearean technique. The highway robbery in which Falstaff engages is clearly intended to be a burlesque of the Percys' plot to steal a kingdom. His role playing with Hal when they take turns being king and Prince of Wales is an obvious parody of Henry's public tone and manner. Falstaff's catechism on honor, "Who hath it? He who died a Wednesday," is a devastating critique of Hotspur's posturing statements about honor and fame. His abuse of his military commission is a reminder of the gritty, sordid side of

war which offsets Hotspur's notion of war as a glorious enterprise. If the plot lines of King Henry and Hotspur are
carefully drawn to come together in a collision course,
Falstaff's plot line parallels them both, bisects them at a
critical moment, and even threatens to dissolve them in
laughter. Shakespeare never worked more boldly or more
skillfully to blend the serious with the comic.

Thematically, Prince Hal is the pivotal and focal character in the play. He moves steadily toward the drama's center, in every sense of the word. He is equally at home in all of
the worlds of the play—willing to take a moral holiday and
romp with Falstaff in the frivolous underworld, capable of
assuming full responsibility and graduating to the role of a
peerless leader of men in the serious upperworld, and
finally emerging as an emblematic figure whose actions
come to signify the play's wisdom with its suggestion of a
world that occupies the middle ground between the two
extremes. This movement toward the center is the appropriate consequence of Hal's underlying impulse—the drive to
achieve both the personal and the political equilibrium
necessary to a great king.

This impulse may be traced in all of his actions. True, we
first discover him in a disreputable tavern planning to join
Poins and Falstaff in a highway robbery. But we are never in
any doubt as to his real purpose in this exploit: Hal does not
intend to commit a crime that will render his kingdom less,
he intends to perpetrate a prank that will render his kingdom more. In a word, he sees the importance of leavening
the serious affairs of state with the yeast of humor. Proof of
this lies not only in his conversation with Poins prior to the
robbery but also with his restitution of the merchant's gold
afterwards. And so that even his sleepiest auditor will not
miss the point and fail to absolve his hero of moral taint,
Shakespeare provides Hal with one of those self-revelatory
monologues that we have already discussed as a convention
of the Elizabethan drama, utilized when the playwright
wished to set his audience straight on some important issue.

After the initial escapade, the rest of the play is marked
by the prince's steady progress toward respectability. He is

content for yet awhile to play games with his fat friend, but even in this holiday mood his remarks foreshadow his true intentions. At the play's midpoint, he accepts his father's rebuke with good grace, pledges his allegiance to the king's cause, and accepts major responsibility in the king's campaign. While continuing to display the tolerance of a resilient man toward Falstaff's shameful abusing of the king's commission, he rises to all the heroic virtues in actual battle, saving his father's life (and thereby, symbolically, transferring the kingship to himself); meeting and defeating the incomparable Hotspur in the play's climactic duel; and—significantly—bestowing much of his own hard-won fame on Falstaff and on his younger brother, John, and treating his defeated enemies, most notably the Scots' lord, Douglas, with magnanimity.

The metaphors implicit in our designating Hal's principal movement as toward the play's center and his underlying impulse as a drive toward equilibrium are a figurative means of pointing toward the play's theme. They invite still other figures. Hal may be viewed as the keystone in the arch that represents the perfect balance of tensions in this play. On the one hand we find the claims of sober public duty, represented by the figure of King Henry. On the other hand we witness the claims of whimsical private caprice, represented, albeit very differently, by both the reckless courage of Hotspur and the limitless laughter of Falstaff. Hal is a youthful prince whose destiny is to rule a kingdom. Even this young, he senses that the responsibilities of high public office can only be successfully discharged at the price of surrendering some of his individuality as a private man. He is reluctant to do so without at least savoring something of the Maytime of his youth. Shakespeare, displaying that love of paradox which readers of this book have discovered him addicted to, provides his hero with the spirit of youth in the person of a corpulent, belching, dissolute old knight ("thou latter spring" Hal calls him). From Falstaff, Hal learns—or, perhaps, relearns, as he seems to have been born wise—that all work and no play makes Henry a dull king and, what is worse, an unwise king. But Hal is still more sophisticated.

He is the balanced man. He knows that frivolity, too, has its limits. ("If all the year were playing holidays, / To sport would be as tedious as to work. . . ."). But unlike his father, who describes himself as wan with care, Hal knows the value of holidays ("But when they seldom come, they wished-for come, / And nothing pleaseth but rare accidents.").

Irony invests and informs every aspect of this play. Consider. We have a king who frets about the folly of a son who shows himself truly wiser than his father. We have an old, fat ruffian who can enjoy hearing himself described as "that reverend vice, that grey iniquity. . . . That vanity in years" yet who is possessed of a wit so keen and a spirit so unquenchably youthful that he can confidently expect a king's son to agree with his estimate of his own worth, "Banish plump Jack, and banish all the world!" And we have a true prince who can take the measure both of Falstaff's worth ("Poor Jack, farewell! / I could have better spared a better man.") and of his worthlessness ("Wherein is he good, but to taste sack and drink it . . . wherein worthy, but in nothing?"), leading him to reply to Falstaff's "Banish plump Jack, and banish all the world!" with the ominous forecast, "I do, I will."

To employ a different figure, we may say that Hotspur, Falstaff, and King Henry are all, in a sense, Hal's teachers and that he betters the instruction in every case. Irony, of course, is operating here: none of these teachers is consciously offering Hal lessons in conduct. Nonetheless, the Prince learns much from each of them. Hotspur serves as a model of physical courage and courtly chivalry, fine qualities in a king. But Hal correctly sees these as means, not ends, as parts—albeit valuable parts—not the whole of a man or a monarch. From Falstaff he learns the importance of not being too earnest, of maintaining the ironic attitude; but he does not permit irony to degenerate into cynicism or playfulness into irresponsibility. From his father he learns the need of curbing private whim in the interest of public good and of preserving public prudence in order to gain the common consent; but he sees that a king must not lose the common touch and that political prudence must not slide over into sly self-serving.

We have documented the presence of the pervasive irony that infuses this play. But one of the greatest ironies associated with 1 *Henry IV* was unintended. To a considerable extent this play is a study in kingship: Shakespeare exercises great care in tracing the principal events in the education of England's favorite king—the Prince of Wales of this play, the Henry V of the play to follow. But despite his care and despite his success in making Hal the thematic center of his play, he failed to make him as dramatically interesting as his two great foils—Falstaff and Hotspur. This is not a debatable opinion. Anyone who has seen a performance of the play or who has read it with understanding will immediately agree with this judgment—as have over three centuries of readers and spectators. And actors as well. Ask any competent Shakespearean actor which of the roles he would prefer to play—Hotspur or Hal—and you will receive only one answer. (If the choice were between Falstaff and Hal, the answers would be equally conclusive, save that the demands of the Falstaff role would not permit many actors to make such a choice.) The question, Is this an example of artistic failure? demands some sort of answer.

If we return to one major premise that underlies much of the argument of this book—namely, that the closest we come to grasping Shakespeare's unique artistry is when we focus on his technique of orchestrating all of the elements of drama in his plays rather than emphasizing any one of them—we are on our way to providing a satisfactory answer to the question. If one insisted that theme was the most important element in 1 *Henry IV*, and—quite correctly— that the character of Prince Hal is both pivotal and focal to an understanding of the play's theme, then one would be compelled to conclude that Shakespeare's failure to make Hal as dramatically appealing as Falstaff and Hotspur represents a serious artistic lapse. But if one starts with the premise that theme is but one of the play's elements and that it is toward the *interplay* of all of the elements— character, world, plot, theme, and language—that we should look in order to discover how the play means so as ultimately to reach a sound conclusion as to what it means, then we may not only absolve Shakespeare of an artistic failure but we may even argue that the very fact of Hal's diminished dramatic interest in comparison with Falstaff and Hotspur is completely consistent both with Shakespeare's theme in this play and with his means of giving it expression.

Specifically, if we have watched Prince Hal make the discovery that the price of public responsibility (which a good king must have) is the loss or supression of some private idiosyncrasy (in which the private citizen may indulge because the state does not feel the consequences but in which the king may not engage), and if we have watched this highly intelligent monarch in the making achieve the pragmatic wisdom that permits him to understand that all the important choices in this life are attended by loss as well as gain and the corollary insight that discovers that no human choice can be a completely satisfactory one, then must we not conclude that this balanced position will foreclose the extremist alternatives that make for exciting and colorful behavior? In a word, the wise monarch—*wisdom* being defined as the possession of the governor who rejects extremes and seeks the mean—will eschew the very qualities that make for exciting and dramatic conduct. Hal, as a man who can—and wishes to—achieve this balance, will not possess the flamboyance of a Hotspur or the irrepressible comic extravagance of a Falstaff. He will be the better king and the better person, but they will always remain the more interesting dramatic characters.

Concerning these characters and this play, one more observation may be made. Many readers—especially those who go on to read *2 Henry IV,* in which Hal assumes the kingship and repudiates Falstaff—argue that Falstaff retains our sympathies to the end and that the character of Hal emerges as a replica of the more unlovely qualities of his father, notably his coldly practical turn of mind. To these readers we must say that Shakespeare is never sentimental even when we are. So fecund is his genius that he does not need to dote on his creations the way we sometimes do. Thus he can watch the newly crowned Henry V carry out in fact what he once prophesied he would ("Banish plump Jack, and banish all the world!" "I can, I do!") and not grow indignant. Moreover, as an artist, Shakespeare never confuses dramatic characters with real persons. He can enjoy the final irony that he invites us to enjoy with him. Because we are dealing with art and not with life, we may have it both ways: we may applaud the prince for *facing* responsibility and simultaneously applaud Falstaff for *outfacing* it.

7
STYLE AND IMAGE

A. STYLE

> I am much deceived but I remember the style.
> (*Love's Labor's Lost, IV, i, 95*)

Occasionally we must be startled into a renewed awareness of the obvious. Man is preeminently the talking animal. His greatest invention is language. And language is speech before it is writing. The greatest writings in English—Shakespeare's plays—were composed to be spoken. And until we speak them—timidly and fumblingly at first, if need be, trippingly on the tongue with practice—we cannot be said to have experienced Shakespeare.

There is no argument here. Every lover of Shakespeare recognizes this. Whatever it may be that first attracts audiences to Shakespeare, it is the language that holds them fast. It was this way from the beginning. Probably more so then. In two respects Shakespeare's original audiences were distinctly different from his present ones: Many among them could not read. And all of them had been trained—more often than not unconsciously—to be good listeners. The final chapter of this book explains why this was so. For now, it is enough to say that the evidence of contemporary public speeches, sermons, plays, and other forms of oral discourse proves that Elizabethan audiences were strenuous listeners who took immense delight in the music-like patterns that exhibit the tonal magic of the spoken word.

The analogy with music is compelling. If by music we mean rhythm, measure, melody, harmony, concord, discord, euphony, cacophony, repetition and refrain, and point and counterpoint, we find all of these and more in Shakespeare's cunningly composed speeches set down to be delivered by superbly trained actors to eagerly receptive audiences. There is nothing pedantic about all this. The appeals are as primitive as the human nervous system and as universal as the human pulse beat. And it is to these visceral appeals of Shakespeare's language that we turn first.

We human beings are not only talking creatures, we are also rhythmic ones. Our heart beats, our pulse counts, our breathing out and breathing in, even our normal walk—all are reminders of the rhythmic patterns we live by. We must live and move rhythmically to be comfortable. But rhythm is more than a necessity. It is a delight. Our music, dance, poetry, sports find their deepest appeals in rhythm. And so does our speech.

> Speak the speech, I pray you, as I pronounced it to you, trippingly on the tongue. But if you mouth it, as many of our players do, I had as lief the town crier spoke my lines.   *(Hamlet, III, ii, 1–4)*

And although Hamlet is speaking prose, his cadences are nearly as measured, balanced, and recurrent as are those of ordered verse.

Measure, balance, and patterned recurrence—these qualities of rhythm suggest artifice. True, many of our rhythmic movements seem instinctive. We are not taught how our hearts should beat; and as we shall see, the greatest art approximates this seemingly unconscious movement. But artists are made, not born; art is learned, not acquired on instinct. And as anyone who has learned to swim or play tennis will recall, we learn rhythmic skills most easily using fixed measures.

So, wishing to catch and respond to Shakespearean rhythms, we will do well to begin with the *line* that lies at the core of most of his verse—the five-stress, ten-syllable line known as *iambic pentameter.* This line in its strictest form has a decided pause at the end, a secondary pause near the middle (the so-called *caesura*), and a steady progression of five unstressed syllables alternating with five stressed syllables. It may be diagramed thus, with ⌣ representing an unstressed syllable, ′ signifying a stressed syllable, / a medial pause, and // a decided pause at the end of a line:

$$ ⌣ ′ ⌣ ′ / ⌣ ′ ⌣ ′ ⌣ ′ // $$

Here are examples from three early plays.

> Sŏ Í tŏ hér, / ănd só sĕ yiélds tŏ mé / /
> *(The Taming of the Shrew, II, i, 136)*

> Shăll Í bĕ pláin? / Ĭ wish thĕ bastărds déad . . . / /
> *(Richard III, IV, ii, 18)*

> Ĭt is thĕ Eást, / anĕ Júliĕt is thĕ sún! / /
> *(Romeo and Juliet, II, ii, 3)*

Concerning *scansion*—the distribution of principal and secondary stresses or accents in successive lines of poetry or verse—let us say at once that there are no absolutes. At best, the notations of a reader with a good ear will be understandable to another reader with a good ear. But there will never be absolute agreement on the disposition of every stress. Nor need there be. So long as the person making the notations is correct about the principal pattern of stresses and sufficiently sensitive to deliberate variations from that pattern, he will command the confidence of his reader and their mutual agreements will be functional, if not absolute. Thus, for example, each first foot of the second and third illustrations reproduced above might well be read as a *trochee:* "Shăll Í" and "Ít ĭs." Even so, the essential characteristics of this strict form of the model iambic pentameter line remain unchanged.

Shakespeare made this iambic pentameter line the foundation of nearly three-fourths of the 104,000 lines he wrote in 37 plays spanning his entire career of over twenty years. But even from the beginning, he played with this line, testing its resiliency, its capacity for countermotion within the frame of its expected motion. The model just illustrated is a kind of theoretical norm that serves as a point of departure for the many variations—in meter, in pauses, in cadence, in tempo—which give the qualities of living speech to what would otherwise be a monotonous metronomic measure. As a matter of fact, actual model lines are hard to find, so common are the variations from the norm. Evidence for this may be found in the three examples just cited: even these regular measures, as we discovered, are susceptible of more than one pattern of scansion. These variations may be compared to the countless little improvisations with which a skillful dancer improves on a basic dance step. It would be impossible to illustrate all conceivable variations, but here are a few representative examples.

A single variation in the *metrical pattern* by inverting the order of the accents, substituting a *trochee* for an *iamb:*

> Fŏr Í ăm roúgh ănd wóo nŏt líke ă bábe.
> *(Shrew, II, i, 137)*

A double variation in the *metrical pattern,* not only substituting a *trochee* for an initial *iamb,* but also adding a syllable within the line, substituting an *anapest* for an *iamb* so as to speed up the tempo:

> Í ăm ă géntlĕmăn óf Vĕrónă, sír
> *(Shrew, II, i, 47)*

A triple variation in the *metrical pattern* by adding to the *trochee* and the *anapest* an unstressed syllable at the end of the line— a very common practice:

> Ănd kiss me, Káte, 'Wé wíll be márrĭed ă Súndăy.'
> *(Shrew, II, i, 326)*

A variation in the *pause pattern* that makes the line "run on" or overflow into the succeeding line:

I tell you, / 'tis incredible to believe
How much she loves me. / / O the kindest Kate! / /
(*Shrew, II, i, 308–309*)

A variation in the *pause pattern* that moves the *caesura* forward in the line and substitutes a *spondee* for the initial *iamb* with a subsequent gain in "naturalism" akin to actual speech:

Soft you! / a word or two before you go. / /
(*Othello, V, ii, 338*)

A variation in the *pause pattern* that introduces a "double caesura," to achieve a rhythm and a tempo suggesting inexpressible weariness:

To-morrow, / and to-morrow, / and to-morrow / /
(*Macbeth, V, v, 19*)

A radical variation in both the metrical and pause patterns which creates in context (Lear holding the dead Cordelia in his arms, asking when she'll breathe again) what may well be the most heartbreaking line in English dramatic poetry:

Never, / never, / never, / never, / never. / /
(*King Lear, V, iii, 309*)

These details of Shakespearean prosody affect the *sounds* as well as the *rhythms* of his language in various subtle ways. But we will reserve a more complete discussion of such details for the next chapter, in which we will look at the distinguishing characteristics of Shakespeare's rimed verse, his blank verse, and his prose.

Meanwhile, let us direct our attention to some tonal patterns that appear with such frequency in Shakespeare's plays that we will wish to acquire an easy familiarity with them. If we aquire this familiarity, it will help us to adjust our ear more quickly than we otherwise could to the rhythms of the spoken word when we listen to Shakespeare on the stage or the screen. And we will greatly improve our reading comprehension as well, since we will learn to read for the music as well as the meaning of the lines that might otherwise lie mute upon the printed page.

To two of these tonal patterns we may assign the term *styles,* which is to say that they embrace characteristic ways of selecting certain kinds of words and stitching these together into sentences in distinctive fashion. Unlike such writers as Poe, Dickens, Wilde, Shaw, and Hemingway, whose ways with words are so idiosyncratic as to stamp almost every sentence they write with their own name brand, Shakespeare has no single style—unless, to echo the graceful compliment of Mark Van Doren, we discover it in his way of writing well, so that he cannot be imitated except by someone who says things both as clearly and as interestingly as he did.[1] But if Shakespeare has no single style, if to him we cannot apply the famous aphorism of Buffon, "The style, it is the man himself," he nevertheless does employ some ways of writing dialogue with sufficient frequency so that we can apply the word style to them. We may call two of these the *rhetorical style* and the *colloquial style.* And we shall define these terms by systematically listing the differences between them.

The rhetorical style, first of all, is addicted to symmetry, whereas the colloquial style appears to be asymmetrical. The rhetorical style puts great emphasis on regular forms and patterns, whereas the colloquial style would appear to be without any fixed form or systematic pattern. The rhetorical style makes very conscious and deliberate use of artifice, whereas the colloquial style, like the protesting Polonius, seems to "use no art at all." Characteristically, the rhetorical style builds constantly to a climax, whereas the colloquial style may appear relatively shapeless, directionless, and even anticlimactic.

The rhetorical style is admirably suited to public address and is often found in that form, whereas the colloquial style is the natural vehicle for private conversation. The purposes of the rhetorical style may fairly be summed up as the desire for clarity, for emphasis, and for forceful conviction; the purposes of the colloquial style, by contrast, are achieved by discovering the unique means of conveying the sounds of a unique voice. The former style satifies our love for unity; the latter style, our complementary love for variety. The rhetorical style may, and does, emerge from the mouth of almost any Shakespearean character; the colloquial style is confined to those characters who are permitted by their author to speak in a naturalistic manner. The rhetorical style thus looks backwards in the direction of convention, whereas the colloquial style looks forward in the direction of naturalism. The rhetorical style can be, and is, used by Shakespeare in all three of the media of language in which he worked—rimed verse, blank verse, and prose; but the colloquial style, because of its informal nature, resists the strait-jacket of rimed verse and is found only in blank verse and prose—as one might suspect, more often in prose.

Shakespeare appears to have made use of both of these styles almost from the beginning of his career as a playwright, although his earlier plays—especially the early histories—are largely composed in the rhetorical style, and his later plays are distinguished, in part, from his earlier work by a heavier representation in them of the colloquial style. Still, it is important to note once more that Shakespeare seems to have discovered almost from the outset all of the techniques he was to employ, and, conversely, that he never abandoned, even in his last work, most of the techniques he used at the beginning. Thus we can hear the colloquial style issuing from the mob led by the rebel, Jack Cade, as early as *2 Henry VI*. And we can discover the rhetorical style plentifully sprinkled through the speeches of many characters in a play written as late as *Coriolanus*.

Illustrations of both styles are, therefore, not difficult to find in most of the plays. But before we examine some characteristic examples of each, we need first to identify three patterns that may be discovered in the rhetorical style— patterns that represent, in somewhat simplified fashion, the devices that lie at the center of the rather complex system of rhetoric with which the Elizabethans delighted themselves.

The rhetorical style is strongly marked by *repetition*— repeated words, repeated phrases, repeated sounds, and, most subtly, repeated rhythms. (Rime is the most noticeable form of repeated sound, but repetition of vowels, called *assonance,* and repetition of initial consonants, called *alliteration,* appear even more frequently.) The logical effect of repetition is emphasis; the physiological effect is hypnosis. (It is no accident that spells, charms, and incantations depend heavily on repetition.)

The rhetorical style is also distinguished by *parallelism.* Usually, parallelism finds its expression in balanced grammatical units, and we think of it as a device involving sentence structure; but sometimes it goes to meaning as well, and then the parallelism may be semantical as well as structural. A third characteristic of the rhetorical style, *balanced antithesis,* is a corollary of the second: the balance is in the rhythm and the structure (which is to say, in the grammar); the antithesis is in the meaning. The result is a singularly pleasing pattern: parallel structures encasing contrasting meanings.

These highly formal qualities suggest that the rhetorical style is rather easily identified. Often it is. But Shakespeare works cunningly and sometimes masks these very formal qualities in a passage of great pith and moment whose emotional content conceals both its structural and its intellectual frameworks. We might say that with Shakespeare the rhetorical style assumes both normal guises and artful disguises. Examples serve best to clarify principles. We begin with an extreme example which, like the artist's caricature, is easily seen, with its big nose, warts, and all showing conspicuously.

Early in *Richard III,* Richard Crookback bursts in on the lonely funeral procession of Henry VI, that sainted but inept king whom he and his brothers have first overthrown and then murdered, Richard himself having played the executioner. The sole mourner is Henry's lovely daughter-in-law, Lady Anne, whose young husband Richard has also slain. Richard peremptorily disperses the pallbearers and confronts Anne with the preposterously bold suggestion that she marry him. At first she showers him with curses and vituperation, but he is undaunted. He assaults her with words, and she defends herself briskly with the same weapons. Their skirmish provides us with an admirable example of the rhetorical style. (The line numberings and various markings are to facilitate the discussion of this passage that follows.)

Richard
1   Lady, you know no rules of charity,
2   Which renders good for bad, blessings for curses.

Anne
3   Villain, thou knows't nor law of God nor man:
4   No beast so fierce but knows some touch of pity.

Richard
5   But I know none, and therefore am no beast.

Anne
6   O wonderful, when devils tell the truth!

Richard
7   More wonderful, when angels are so angry.
8   Vouchsafe, divine perfection of a woman,
9   Of these supposèd crimes to give me leave
10 By circumstance but to acquit myself.

Anne
11 Vouchsafe, diffused infection of a man,
12 Of these known evils, but to give me leave
13 By circumstance t'accuse thy cursèd self.

Richard
14 Fairer than tongue can name thee, let me have
15 Some patient leisure to excuse myself.

Anne
16 Fouler than heart can think thee, thou canst make
17 No excuse current but to hang thyself.   (*I, ii*, 68–84)

Reading this passage aloud, we can *hear* the workings of the rhetorical patterns we have been discussing. Looking closely at the passage, we *see* the patterns we have been hearing. Repeated words and phrases are encircled. Alliteration may be heard in the pairing of *d*ivine and *d*iffused in lines 8 and 11, a sound pattern rendered even more emphatic by the accompanying double rime of per*fection* and in*fection*. The repeated words and phrases are reinforced by the parallel grammatical structures that encase them. All the way through this dialogue you can both see and hear the grammatical parallels ("Lady, you know / Villain, thou know'st"; "O wonderful, when devils . . . / More wonderful when angels. . . ."). Examples of balanced antitheses are underscored with wavy lines.

When analyzed and stripped in this fashion, the style appears wonderfully artificial. And, surely, it is. But to say so is not an act of denigration. In this play, particularly, the style is functional—which is to say that its artificiality perfectly fits both the play and its principal character. Richard III is a roaring stage villain in whom we delight but do not believe. That is why we can enjoy, even admire, a witty, eloquent amoral monster like Richard without either identifying or empathizing with him. Because we do not really believe in him, we can have it both ways: we can thoroughly enjoy his histrionic brand of Machiavellianism without suffering any moral contamination ourselves. The artifice triumphs over ugly reality.

A style called rhetorical might be supposed to find its fullest expression in public address. Nowhere is public address used more often than in Shakespeare's Roman plays and nowhere in these more often than in *Julius Caesar*. Indeed, critics have discovered that the rhetorical style in that play is not only functional but also *structural:* the play may be viewed, from this perspective, as a series of efforts to capture the emotions and influence the conduct of the Roman populace by means of artful rhetoric. The most famous instance of this public persuasion is the turning point of the play: The mob is first persuaded by Brutus that the assassination of

Caesar was both necessary and right. Then Antony turns both their hearts and heads around, and they "Cry havoc and let slip the dogs of war." But this example is both too familiar and too long to reproduce here.

A briefer example may be found at the play's beginning, where we discover two Roman tribunes alternately scolding and pleading with the mob. Here is Marullus, one of the tribunes, upbraiding them for their fickleness:

Wherefore rejoice? What conquest brings he home?
What tributaries follow him to Rome
To grace in captive bonds his chariot wheels?
You blocks, you stones, you worse than senseless things!
O you hard hearts, you cruel men of Rome.
Knew you not Pompey?

. . . .

And do you now put on your best attire?
And do you now cull out a holiday?
And do you now strew flowers in his way
That comes in triumph over Pompey's blood?
Be gone!
Run to your houses, fall upon your knees,
Pray to the god to intermit the plague
That needs must light on this ingratitude.
                              (I, i, 32–37, 48–55)

We need no diagrams or special markings to see and hear the devices that make up the rhetorical style here: the *repetition* of words ("you . . . you . . . you . . . you . . . you"), clauses ("And do you now . . .?"), and questions ("What conquest . . .? What tributaries . . .?"; the *structural parallelism* of not only questions, but also epithets ("blocks . . . stones . . . hard hearts . . . cruel men") and imperatives ("Run to your houses, fall upon your knees, / Pray to the gods"); and the *balanced antitheses* that are partly masked because half of them are contained in rhetorical questions and the other half in imperative sentences ("put on your best attire?" versus "run to your houses"; "cull out a holiday?" versus "fall upon your knees"; "strew flowers in his way?" versus "pray to the gods").

Confronted with this conspicuous display of linguistic artifice, one might be tempted to assume that this is the mannerism of a youthful playwright, more interested in how he is saying something than in what he is saying. But Shakespeare does not work this way: he rarely rejects in his late plays a device he learned to handle in the early ones. Rather, he continues it—but he refines it. Evidence of the persistence of the rhetorical style, but a rhetorical style somewhat refined, which is to say, somewhat less obvious, may be found in the utterances of his two most eloquent speakers, Falstaff and Hamlet.

We turn first to Falstaff. Early in *2 Henry IV,* Falstaff is accosted in the streets by the Lord Chief Justice, who accuses him not only of himself having a bad character but also of leading astray the young Prince. Falstaff replies to his accuser, and in the ensuing conversation between the two old men we find some of the same thrust and parry that we discovered in the Richard-Anne dialogue. But this time it seems more fluid, more spontaneous; one wants to say more naturalistic. Nevertheless, all of the rhetorical devices we have been glancing at are present here; they are simply better concealed. Here is a sample—brief but long enough to illustrate the patterns:

Chief Justice   Well, the truth is, Sir John, you live in great infamy.

Falstaff   He that buckles himself in my belt cannot live in less.

Chief Justice   Your means are very slender and your waste is great.

Falstaff   I would it were otherwise. I would my means were greater and my waist slenderer.   *(I, ii, 129–135)*

If after even this brief exposure our ear has caught the rhythms of the rhetorical style, we may be surprised to discover that the preceding passage is written in prose. It is, to be sure; but the rhetorical style that encompasses it is nearly as firm as that we have been seeing and hearing in blank verse. Starting with the smallest and simplest pattern and working toward the largest and most complex, we may tick off the evidence. We find alliteration in line 2: "*b*uckles ... *b*elt" and "*l*ive ... *l*ess." We find word repetition: "I would ... I would," "means ... means," and, aurally, because this is a pun, "waste ... waist." We find structural parallelism: "means are slender" and "waste is great." And, triumphantly, because we are listening to the words of an artful dodger, we find everywhere balanced antitheses: "live in great ... live in less," "means are very slender ... means are greater," "waste is great ... waist slenderer."

Hamlet often speaks just as artfully and also in prose. Here are two familiar passages from Hamlet's advice to the players, removed from their larger context so as to expose their rhetorical patterns. But this removal should not obscure the fact that these rhetorical patterns are firmly woven into the fabric of the longer speech from which these excerpts are taken, so engrafted into Shakespeare's mode of expression is this way of writing. When Hamlet says,

> Suit the action to the word, the word to the action ...
> *(III, ii, 16)*

we have a neat display of repeated words ("word ... word," "action ... action"), of grammatical and rhythmic parallelism ("to the word ... to the action"), and of balanced antithesis by means of word inversion ("the action to the word, the word to the action"). And when, a few lines later, he says:

> Now this overdone, or come tardy off, though it make the unskillful laugh, cannot but make the judicious grieve ...   *(III, ii, 23–25)*

we discover literal repetition in "make the" and a combination of grammatical parallelism and semantic antithesis in the matching clauses "make the unskillful laugh" and "make the judicious grieve."

A final and notable instance of how these patterns may appear anywhere is discovered in the cryptic and paradoxical utterance Hamlet makes to Horatio about destiny just before he consents to the fencing match in which he will be slain. Notice how far Shakespeare has gone in making a mannered style serve a functional purpose. The rhetoric seems now to be growing out of the meaning: the means have become successfully absorbed by the ends.

> If it be now, 'tis not to come; if it be not to come, it
> will be now; if it be not now, yet it will come. The
> readiness is all. *(V, ii, 209–211)*

Words and phrases are repeated throughout these two sentences. All three clauses in the first, long sentence are parallel in structure: a dependent clause in each instance is followed by the main clause. And the first of these two complex clauses offers a clear example of balanced opposites, in the form of a paradox. But, *mirabile dictu,* we have forgotten all about the architecture, caught up as we have been by the power of the emotion and the pregnancy of the meaning. We have moved from a rhetoric that is self-conscious and mannered to a rhetoric that is organic, from the "outward flourishes" to the "heart's core."

More than once in this book we have found occasion to point out the significance of Shakespeare as a transitional writer in the unfolding history of English literature. We have employed the metaphor of Janus, the Roman god who looks two ways—forward to the future, backward to the past. This figure asserts itself once more when we consider a second style that Shakespeare favors, the style to which we have assigned the name *colloquial.* The detailed comparison we drew earlier between the colloquial and the rhetorical styles will explain our invoking the Janus metaphor: the rhetorical style looks backward to an older tradition and a set of recognizable conventions; the colloquial style looks forward to the conversational rhythms and idioms that will flower in the English novel and, still later, become the accepted language of modern naturalistic drama.

One possible ambiguity must be removed before we proceed to look at some specimens of this style. By colloquial, we shall not mean simply rustic dialect or so-called substandard speech (although such speed is embraced by this term). We shall mean, rather, *informal* speech of the kind we are designating when we speak of everyday conversation. The *vocabulary* will be familiar, simple, homely, often earthy; the *sentence structure* will be irregular, following the fits and starts of informal, unselfconscious conversation; and the *idiom* will be private and personal, not the words people reach for when they are aware of an audience. As our detailed comparison with the rhetorical style suggested, the colloquial style will *appear* to be artless. But, of course, it will not be. The artfulness will, if anything, be greater because it is nearly completely concealed. Nonetheless, we will be able to recognize the presence of some of these formal elements. But they will appear with a difference: either they will come on in disguise or the patterns will operate to illuminate the character and situation.

First, an example in prose. Falstaff, in his role as a recruiting officer for the king's army, has swaggered into Gloucestershire, there to impress into the army some hapless farm fellows as "food for powder." The local justice of the peace who is serving up the victims turns out to be one Robert Shallow, fifty years ago Falstaff's boon companion in youthful escapades, now shrunk "into the lean and slippered pantaloon," with "his manly voice / Turning again toward childish treble," but not, it seems, turned off, as will appear by the following:

Falstaff   I am glad to see you, by my troth, Master Shallow.

Shallow   O, Sir John, do you remember since we lay all night in the Windmill in Saint George's Field?

Falstaff   No more of that, good Master Shallow, no more of that.

Shallow   Ha! 'Twas a merry night. And is Jane Nightwork alive?

Falstaff   She lives, Master Shallow.

Shallow   She never could away with me.

Falstaff   Never, never, she would always say she could not abide, Master Shallow.

Shallow   By the mass, I could anger her to the heart. She was than a bona-roba. Doth she hold her own well?

Falstaff   Old, old, Master Shallow.

Shallow   Nay, she must be old. She cannot choose but be old. Certain she's old, and had Robin Nightwork by old Nightwork before I came to Clement's Inn.

Silence   That's fifty-five years ago.

Shallow   Ha, cousin Silence, that thou hadst seen that that this knight and I have seen! Ha, Sir John, said I well?

Falstaff   We have heard the chimes at midnight, Master Shallow.

Shallow   That we have, that we have, that we have, in faith, Sir John, we have.

(*2 Henry IV, III, ii, 182–205*)

Here, to be sure, we have repetition aplenty. But see how it is cut to the cloth of character and situation. Justice Shallow's repeated words are like the dribblings from a leaky tap, and Falstaff's repeated "Master Shallow" is intoned like the reiterations of a schoolmaster speaking to an inattentive and not too bright pupil.

Another, and famous, example of this boneless garrulity appears in a monologue, in blank verse, and—interestingly—in an earlier play, *Romeo and Juliet*. We hear Juliet's Nurse fix with fussy precision the day of Juliet's birth in a reminiscence that is at once sentimental and sniggering.

Even or odd, of all days in the year,
Come Lammas Eve at night shall she be fourteen.
Susan and she (God rest all Christian souls!)
Were of an age. Well, Susan is with God;
She was too good for me. But, as I said,
On Lammas Eve at night shall she be fourteen;
That shall she marry; I remember it well.
'Tis since the earthquake now eleven years;
And she was weaned (I never shall forget it),
Of all the days of the year, upon that day;
For I had then laid wormwood to my dug,
Sitting in the sun under the dovehouse wall.
My lord and you were then at Mantua.
Nay, I do bear a brain. But, as I said,
When it did taste the wormwood on the nipple
Of my dug and felt it bitter, pretty fool,
To see it tetchy and fall out with the dug!
Shake, quoth the dovehouse! 'Twas no need, I trow
To bid me trudge.
And since that time it is eleven years,
For then she could stand high-lone; nay, by th' rood,
She could have run and waddled all about;
For even the day before, she broke her brow;
And then my husband (God be with his soul!
'A was a merry man) took up the child.
'Yea,' quoth he, 'dost thou fall upon thy face?
Thou wilt fall backward when thou hast more wit;
Wilt thou not, Jule?' and, by my holidam,
The pretty wretch left crying and said, 'Ay.'
To see now how a jest shall come about!
I warrant, an I should live a thousand years,
I never should forget it. 'Wilt thou not, Jule?' quoth he,
And, pretty fool, it stinted and said 'Ay.'

(I, iii, 16–48)

It is a tribute to the naturalism of the colloquial style that,
hearing Lady Capulet break in with

> Enough of this. I pray thee hold thy peace.

most of us would dissent, satisfied to trace for a little while
longer the meandering stream of the Nurse's discourse. In
any event, it is not difficult to discern the presence of the by
now familiar patterns of rhetoric—to hear the pattern of
assonance in the long *e* of the first two lines, to hear the
pattern of alliteration in the *sh* of *shall* and *she* and the *s* of
Susan and *souls* of lines 2 and 3, to hear the repetitions of
"Lammas Eve at night shall she be fourteen" and the paral-
lelisms of "The pretty wretch left crying and said, 'Ay' "
with the "pretty fool, it stinted and said, 'Ay.' " Yet even
with this clear-cut demonstration of an undergirding for-
malism, so fluid is movement of this passage and so perfect is
the fit of word to character and situation that we are right in
concluding that we are listening to a different style.

We have been trying to familiarize ourselves with two of
the most important and interesting tonal patterns in Shakespeare's plays. We have assigned these the names rhetorical
style and colloquial style, and we have sharply distinguished
between the two. Yet we are compelled to recognize that
elements of what we have called the rhetorical style are
found also in the colloquial style. Still, this seeming paradox
can be resolved. If we think of these two styles as two bands,
albeit somewhat far apart, on the same spectrum, we will
guard against the false notion that they are contraries. We
may say that they are not different in kind but different in
degree. Both styles have patterns, but the one is characterized by qualities we call *formal,* and the other by qualities
we term *informal.*

There remains another difficulty. A fairly sustained focus
on one of the elements of drama—here on language—runs a
very real risk: we may begin to see that element atomistical-
ly, as a thing apart, instead of molecularly, as a part of the
larger whole. This is a danger we should avoid. We may
rescue ourselves if we return to the process subsumed in the
word *orchestration:*language (no matter what stylistic pattern
it assumes) is at work in a larger context that includes the

character of the speakers, the movement of the *plot* that charts their struggles, the *world* that both envelopes and informs the conflict that is integral to all drama, and the *theme,* or significant comment on human behavior, that emerges from and at the same time unifies this combination of elements. At this point we need a small example of this orchestration—an example of the way a style issues from a larger context and at the same time realigns the several elements of the drama to create a scene that possesses its own right harmonies.

We discover such an example in a scene toward the end of *King Lear.* Following a period of systematic abuse at the hands of those to whom he thought he had given all—abuse that had driven him to madness—Lear, ministered to by his loving daughter, Cordelia, and her doctor, emerges from a long but restorative sleep to find himself before this very daughter he had once spurned. There follows a dialogue that fuses all the elements of drama into one current of passion and poetry that produces an electrifying effect.

Cordelia	How does my royal lord? How fares your Majesty?
Lear	You do me wrong to take me out o' th' grave.
	Thou art a soul in bliss; but I am bound
	Upon a wheel of fire, that mine own tears
	Do scald like molten lead.
Cordelia	Sir, do you know me?
Lear	You are a spirit, I know. Where did you die?
Cordelia	Still, still, far wide!
Doctor	He's scarce awake. Let him alone while.
Lear	Where have I been? Where am I? Fair daylight?
	I am mightily abused. I should e'en die with pity
	To see another thus. I know not what to say.
	I will not swear these are my hands. Let's see—
	I feel this pin prick. Would I were assured
	Of my condition.
Cordelia	O look upon me, sir,
	And hold your hand in benediction o'er me.
	You must not kneel.

Lear   Pray, do not mock me.
        I am a very foolish fond old man,
        Fourscore and upward, not an hour more nor less;
        And, to deal plainly,
        I fear I am not in my perfect mind.
        Methinks I should know you, and know this man;
        Yet I am doubtful, for I am mainly ignorant
        What place this is; and all the skill I have
        Remembers not these garments; nor I know not
        Where I did lodge last night. Do not laugh at me;
        For, as I am a man, I think this lady
        To be my child Cordelia.
Cordelia   And so I am! I am!
Lear   Be your tears wet? Yes, faith. I pray weep not.
        If you have poison for me, I will drink it.
        I know you do not love me; for your sisters
        Have (as I do remember) done me wrong.
        You have some cause, they have not.
Cordelia   No cause, no cause.
                                (IV, vii, 44–75)

Read slowly and carefully, this passage—even when, as here, it is taken out of the larger context of the play—discloses how the elements of drama that we have been considering can be woven by language into a stunning pattern of music and meaning.

B. Image

> . . . the true and perfect image of life indeed.
> *(1 Henry IV, V, iv, 117)*

> `And let us, ciphers to this great accompt,
> On your imaginary forces work.
> *(Henry V, Prologue, 17–18)*

It was Alexander Pope who established one infallible criterion of artful writing: "The sound must seem an echo to the sense." Our tribute to this truism is reflected in this chapter's opening reminder that Shakespeare's plays were composed to be spoken. But if these dramatic poems had their origins on the stage in words to be heard, they came to their fullest flowering on the printed page in words to be read. And for most of the nearly 400 years that have passed since the plays were printed, the number of their readers has exceeded the number of their auditors. This is partly accounted for by the fact that their appeal to the eye and mind is as immediate and strong as is their appeal to the ear. To play a variation on Pope's theme, then, we may say that the sense must be the mentor to the sound.

With this distinction between sound and sense, we discover an important distinction between two other terms— *verse* and *poetry*. The differences between verse and poetry are many and elusive. This is not the place to suggest them all. But one that is significant serves our present purpose. The sine qua non of good verse is polish. The sine qua non of true poetry is power. The effect of polish cannot be achieved without the most careful attention to matters of form. The effect of power cannot be achieved without a pregnant thought. Good verse may be nearly devoid of sense if it is sufficiently appealing in sound. Good poetry must represent a wedding of sound and sense. Its appeal to the ear must be matched by its appeal to the mind. Shakespearean poetry achieves this added dimension in part by means of imagery.

This statement requires a little explanation. An *image*

suggests most immediately a visual sense experience represented in words, a kind of picture. But when we introduce the phrase *represented in words,* we introduce the imagination. (It is no accident that the words *image, imagery, imaginary,* and *imagination* are closely related.) The imagination, in turn, suggests two mental functions: we first see in our mind's eye the object represented by the verbal image; and then we determine the *significance* of what we see (or hear, smell, taste, or feel, if other sense experiences are being invoked). It is this process of conveying sense experience and at the same time transmuting it to something significant in which Shakespeare surpasses all the writers of his own age and most writers before and since by common agreement among the critics.

As so often happens, we find Shakespeare giving clearer expression to these thoughts in poetry than we can possibly do in prose. With a gentle irony that is so often his trademark, he puts what is perhaps the most memorable statements ever made about the poetic imagination in the mouth of a man whose bent of mind is more rational than imaginative. In *A Midsummer Night's Dream,* Duke Theseus, commenting to his bride, Hippolyta, on the antics of lovers, likens them to both lunatics and poets: "The lunatic, the lover, and the poet / are of imagination all compact. . . . " Expanding on the poet's exercise of his imagination, Theseus says:

> The poet's eye, in a fine frenzy rolling,
> Doth glance from heaven to earth, from earth to heaven;
> And as imagination bodies forth
> The forms of things unknown, the poet's pen
> Turns them to shapes, and gives to airy nothing
> A local habitation and a name.   *(V, i, 12–17)*

By exercising his imagination, Shakespeare is saying, the poet creates a set of images (representations of experiences that come to us through any or all of our senses), and then by his artistry transfers these to *our* minds so that we see and think what he sees and thinks.

See and think—two processes. Let us begin with the process of seeing. Thomas Gray, the author of "Elegy Written in a Country Churchyard," once said in a burst of enthusiasm, "Every word in Shakespeare is a picture!" While literally false, of course, this is the kind of falsehood that conveys truth. Nor is it necessary to quibble over the fact that imagery appeals to all of the senses. In the world of drama, sight images outnumber all the others combined, since a dramatic world, like the real world it mirrors, is largely a world of seen things.

Sometimes, especially when his sole purpose is to get us to see, Shakespeare is content to paint a scene with literal images that have no secondary, or figurative, meaning. Oberon, the king of the fairies in *A Midsummer Night's Dream,* describes to Puck, his mischievous messenger, a place where the sleeping Titania may be found.

> I know a bank where the wild thyme blows,
> Where oxlips and the nodding violet grows,
> Quite over-canopied with luscious woodbine,
> With sweet musk-roses, and with eglantine.
>
> (*II, i, 249–252*)

The rime renders this as pretty to the ear as does the imagery to the eye. But prettiness is no criterion to Shakespearean scene painting. Here is the subhuman, Caliban, describing a place on his island to the drunken butler, Stephano:

> I prithee let me bring thee where crabs grow;
> And I with my long nails will dig thee pignuts,
> Show thee a jay's nest, and instruct thee how
> To snare the nimble marmoset; I'll bring thee
> To clust'ring filberts, and sometimes I'll get thee
> Young scammels from the rock. Wilt thou go with me?
>
> (*The Tempest, II, ii, 163–168*)

Both the "pretty" scene described by Oberon and the homely scene described by Caliban are vividly realized by the reader or listener.

With none of the stage scenery or spotlights of the contemporary stage to work with, Shakespeare provides his audience with literal verbal images that take their place. So, in *The Merchant of Venice,* we hear Lorenzo saying to Jessica,

> How sweet the moonlight sleeps upon this bank!
>
> *(V, i, 54)*

and we see this scene without the aid of stage flats or lights. Again, in vivid contrast, we can listen to Lear rage against the wind and rain:

> Blow, winds, and crack your cheeks. Rage, blow.
> You cataracts and hurricanoes, spout
> Till you have drenched our steeples . . .
>
> *(III, ii, 1–3)*

and we need no fire hose or wind machines to produce the terror of this storm.

Once, to be sure, even Shakespeare thought verbal images were not enough. In the Prologue to *Henry V,* we repeatedly hear him speaking directly to us, as if despairing that words can take the place of things.

> Suppose within the girdle of these walls
> Are now confined two mighty monarchies
>
> . . . .
>
> Piece out our imperfections with your thoughts
>
> . . . .
>
> Think, when we talk of horses, that you see them
> Printing their proud hoofs i' th' receiving earth. . . .
>
> *(Prologue, 19–20, 23, 26–27)*

But this is not his ordinary way. Nor should we take this one despairing request too seriously. When Shakespeare chooses to be descriptive, he is normally describing scenes and events off stage: recall the description by Enobarbus of

Antony's first meeting with Cleopatra, Hotspur's report of how he came to deny his prisoners to Henry IV, the bloody Captain's account of Macbeth's great victory over the rebels and invaders, and many more such scenes. By this means, he works on our "imaginary forces" much like the modern novelist and to the same effect. Neither he nor we are pinned to "this unworthy scaffold" nor confined "within this wooden O," as Shakespeare once referred to his stage and his theater. Instead, moving expansively like Keats' explorer, we stare with a wild surmise at English palaces and Viennese prisons, Roman forums and Venetian courtrooms, Forests of Arden and blasted Scottish heaths—all with our mind's eye.

To the literal-minded this can be pretty heady stuff. The rationalistic Theseuses of this world are apt to think this is a sort of trick, and protest.

> Such tricks hath strong imagination
> That, it if would but apprehend some joy,
> It comprehends some bringer of that joy;
> Or in the night, imagining some fear,
> How easy is a bush supposed a bear!
> *(A Midsummer Night's Dream, V, i, 18–22)*

But the skepticism of a Theseus is superficial. If Shakespeare works on our imaginary forces in order to get us to *see* things, he is seldom content with just that. More importantly, he wants us to *interpret* what we see, to grasp its significance. And so he gives the final word to the wise bride, Hippolyta, who shows a truer understanding than her skeptical husband of the purpose of artistic imagination. Commenting on the midsummer night's dream that has enthralled at once four Athenian lovers, the fairy queen, Titania, and Bully Bottom, the leader of the "hempen homespuns," she concludes:

> But all the story of the night told over,
> And all their minds transfigured so together,
> More witnesseth than fancy's images
> And grows to something of great constancy;
> But howsoever, strange and admirable.
> *(V, i, 23–27)*

How Shakespeare achieves by imagery these somethings "of great constancy" that are both "strange and admirable" we will now undertake to discover. We shall trace the development of verbal imagery from its most limited possibilities—that is, as pure description and sense impression—to its nearly limitless possibilities as that kind of figurative language that we may call *symbolic.* Although neither very long nor very difficult, this intellectual journey will nonetheless take us through five stages. We shall start with an example of what we will call *pure image,* move from there to the most obvious of comparisons called a *simile,* go from there to the less obvious *descriptive metaphor,* move from there to what we shall call the *dramatic metaphor,* and, finally, arrive at the most complex form of figurative language, the *symbol.* To ensure both brevity and clarity, we shall focus on one nuclear image throughout, and that image, appropriately enough, will be the stage. As always, we shall depend as heavily as possible on Shakespeare's own words.

We turn once more to *A Midsummer Night's Dream* to discover our example of a pure image. Bottom, the weaver, and his little company of "rude mechanicals," Peter Quince, a carpenter; Francis Flute, a bellows mender; Tom Snout, a tinker; Snug, a joiner; and Robin Starveling, a tailor, are gathered in a woods outside Athens to rehearse a version of *Pyramus and Thisbe* which they hope to present to Duke Theseus on the occasion of his nuptials. Bottom says brightly, "Are we all met?" Peter Quince, the play's director, replies:

> Pat, pat; and here's a marvellous convenient place
> for our rehearsal. This green plot shall be our stage,
> this hawthorn brake our tiring house, and we will do
> it in action as we will do it before the Duke.
>
> *(III, i, 2–5)*

There you have a simple image, simply set forth by a simple man, of a patch of green grass to serve as a stage and an adjacent hawthorn thicket to serve as a dressing room. This is Shakespearean scene painting with all its emphasis on *thingness,* converting by words a section of the bare platform stage of the Globe Theater into a specific place in the woods. It serves no other purpose.

When we leave literal language for figurative language we take an enormous step. With figurative language, the writer is always engaged in making a comparison, and one of the things he is comparing (the *figurative* thing) is not present in the setting. The most obvious such comparison is one that names both the literal thing and its figurative counterpart and then joins them with a verbal equal sign usually in the form of the words *like* or *as*. This kind of comparison is called a *simile*. Its function is simple. It either clarifies or makes vivid or both.

Toward the end of *Richard II,* the old Duke of York describes to his wife the progress into London of Henry Bolingbroke, who has just usurped the kingship of the hapless Richard. Having listened to her husband's account of Bolingbroke's triumphant entry, the Duchess asks: "Alack, poor Richard! Where rode he the whilst?" To which York replies:

> As in a theatre the eyes of men,
> After a well-graced actor leaves the stage,
> Are idly bent on him that enters next,
> Thinking his prattle to be tedious,
> Even so, or with much more contempt, men's eyes
> Did scowl on gentle Richard.   *(V, ii, 23–28)*

Let us summarize what we have here. Two images—that of a deposed king coming to London, and that of a minor actor coming on stage—dissimilar in most respects, suggest a striking similarity to the mind of a dramatic poet. He joins these two images in a kind of equation, with two form words, *as* and *even so,* serving as his equal signs. The poet invites us to savor the comparison, but he does most of the work for us, guiding us gradually and patiently through the process of meaning expanded by an interesting comparison.

We come now to metaphor, and when we do we are dealing with an instrument of thought and expression so powerful that it moved the first and perhaps the most influential of the critics of Western culture, Aristotle, to say:

> The greatest thing of all by far is to be master of metaphor. It is the one thing that cannot be learned from others: and it is also a sign of original genius, since a good metaphor *implies* the *intuitive perception* of the similarity in dissimilars.[2]

The operative terms here, which I have italicized, are *implies* and *intuitive perception.* Unlike the comparison found in a simile, the comparison discovered in a metaphor is not stated but implied. Instead of an equation, we have a substitution. In the mind of the writer, and therefore of the understanding reader, the image and the thing to which it is being compared become fused. The comparative process is thus immensely speeded up: the reader must make the imaginative leap with the writer, without such verbal handholds as *like* or *as.* Moreover, metaphor is almost infinitely complex in the ways in which it creates new ranges of meaning through inference, association, or suggestion.

Shakespeare's most famous metaphor involving the image of the stage is known to you all.

> All the world's a stage,
> And all the men and women merely players. . . .
> *(II, vii, 139–40)*

But before continuing with this familiar speech of Jaques from *As You Like It,* we shall direct our attention for a moment to the passage that immediately precedes it and thus establish a context for these lines which, with the exception of Hamlet's "To be, or not to be" are probably those most frequently quoted from Shakespeare.

Orlando, the romantic hero of *As You Like It,* has been exiled and is traveling in the Forest of Arden without food or shelter, somewhat handicapped by the company of his aged and ill retainer, Adam. Leaving the latter exhausted in a sheltered place, he comes upon Duke Senior and some of his men, who are living a kind of Robin Hood existence in the forest, and breaks in on them with a drawn sword, threatening them and demanding food. To his surprise, he receives a very civil welcome. Shamefaced, he explains his desperate circumstances and is told to return with Adam to be the Duke's welcome guests at dinner. As Orlando departs, Duke Senior turns to his men and moralizes in this metaphor:

> Thou seest we are not all alone unhappy:
> This wide and universal theatre
> Presents more woeful pageants than the scene
> Wherein we play in.   (*II, vii, 136–139*)

This gives the melancholy Jaques his cue, and, seizing it, he enlarges on the Duke's metaphor in the passage you know so well.

> All the world's a stage,
> And all the men and women merely players;
> They have their exits and their entrances,
> And one man in his time plays many parts,
> His acts being seven ages.   (*II, vii, 139–143*)

Jaques proceeds to outline these seven ages in a series of memorable images (not metaphors!), ending lugubriously with man in his second childishness, "Sans teeth, sans eyes, sans taste, sans everything." In doing so, he converts his succession of images into symbols of everyman; but his sour view of humanity is not Shakespeare's. The playwright, with cunning irony, sandwiches this piece of eloquent misanthropy between two actions that give it the lie: Duke Senior's generous treatment of Orlando *before* and Orlando's loving care of old Adam, whom he carries in on his back, *after*. We will, however, postpone for a little while the discussion of how an image becomes elevated to the status of a symbol.

For a moment or two, let us direct our attention to some similarities between these two metaphors of the world as a theater and a stage and the simile involving Richard II. Different as they are in their particulars, they have several things in common: they are both quite formally stated, they are both fully developed, and they both move at a rather leisurely pace. We have ample time to digest the imagery and translate the images and the comparisons into an idea. They have, in short, the qualities of "set pieces," and we are not surprised to learn that they are often removed from their contexts in order to serve as the subject for oral recitations, both in the classroom and on the public platform. Shakespeare never entirely gives over writing these purple passages with their formal and ornamental qualities. But as he develops his powers as a dramatic poet, his use of metaphor undergoes some changes. Two of these changes are worth illustrating.

Still using the metaphor of the world as a stage, Shakespeare now accelerates his pace and compresses his figure. Here are three such examples taken from as many plays that span a period of nearly ten years. At the beginning of *The Merchant of Venice,* Antonio, responding to Gratiano's persistent questions concerning his melancholy manner, declares:

> I hold the world but as the world, Gratiano—
> A stage where every man must play a part,
> And mine a sad one.   *(I, i, 77–79)*

Equally quick but more cryptic is the statement of the Duke, early in *Measure for Measure,* as he explains to his deputy, Angelo, his intention to take a kind of moral holiday from being a governor.

>   I love the people,
> But do not like to stage me to their eyes. . . .
>   *(I, i, 67–68)*

Note how he converts the word *stage* into a verb (which prompts the observation that metaphor may appear in a variety of grammatical forms). Much more poignant and more powerful, than these two examples, is an example from *King Lear.* Rather late in that play, maddened Lear and blinded Gloucester meet. Characteristically, the marvelously eloquent old king pours out a flood of images and epithets that give expression to his total disillusionment with life. In the process, he catches up the stage metaphor and hurls it at us and then goes right on ranting by means of an almost surrealistic chain of imagistic associations that reminds us of the poetry of T. S. Eliot.

> When we are born, we cry that we are come
> To this great stage of fools.—This' a good block.*
> It were a delicate stratagem to shoe
> A troop of horse with felt. I'll put't in proof,
> And when I have stol'n upon these son-in-laws,
> Then kill, kill, kill, kill, kill, kill!
>
> *(IV, vi, 179–184)*

Those readers or spectators who have borne witness to the fearful cruelty of Lear's elder daughters and of the husband of one of them will feel the force of this picture of an old king in a murderous rage stealing upon his oppressors at the head of a troop of cavalry whose horses' hooves have been muffled in felt.

These last three examples illustrate Shakespeare's way of using metaphor (including his favorite metaphor of the stage) swiftly, casually, at times almost parenthetically. Here the metaphor seems more functional than ornamental, more spontaneous than self-conscious. This is what critics mean when they say that Shakespeare thinks in images. The dramatist has so fully realized his character and the situation in which that character is immediately involved that the images and metaphors seem to flow almost unconsciously from his pen.

It is only a short step to the next plane in Shakespeare's development as a user of imagery and metaphor. Now the easy flow becomes a swift torrent, and we find ourselves in the presence of what commentators usually refer to as congested metaphors, by which they mean figurative language that comes so thick and fast that the curious reader or auditor would have to stop the play and repeat the passage in slow motion in order to work out all the details of the comparisons Shakespeare lavishly flings at him. Concerning this tempo,

*felt hat?

Charles Lamb, himself using a metaphor, said, "It is as though one metaphor hardly peeks out of its shell, is hardly hatched, when another one comes and knocks it out of the nest, so to speak." This congestion bespeaks the speed of Shakespeare's thought. The process is well illustrated in a famous passage from *Macbeth*—a passage so rich in imagery and metaphor that although we immediately recall it, we may have forgotten that it contains among its many images still another from the stage.

> *Macbeth*   To-morrow, and to-morrow, and to-morrow
> Creeps in this petty pace from day to day
> To the last syllable of recorded time,
> And all our yesterdays have lighted fools
> The way to dusty death. Out, out, brief candle!
> Life's but a walking shadow, a poor player
> That struts and frets his hour upon the stage
> And then is heard no more. It is a tale
> Told by an idiot, full of sound and fury,
> Signifying nothing.
>
> *(V, v, 19–28)*

This metaphoric congestion to which critics so often allude may more aptly be termed "associative richness" or "the cumulative homogeneity of figurative language," as it is by Alfred Longueil,[3] who uses this very passage to illustrate Shakespeare's unique way of building to an emotional climax by means of closely associated imagery. He points out, for example, the way the impeded rhythm of the first line suggests the "Creeps" that begins the second; "Creeps" in turn pictures the "petty pace" of line 2; and the association of smallness with "petty" prepares us for "syllable" in line 3. The later words, "brief" and "hour," reinforce these images of meagerness. Additionally, "tomorrow" anticipates "yesterdays," and "yesterdays" is easily associated with "dusty death." "Candle" invites the suggestion of "a walking shadow," which permits the inference that the actor ("poor player") is but another kind of shadow. Finally, a whole string of words and phrases—"creeps" and "petty" and "death" and "brief candle" and "frets his hour" and "no more"—all cohere and lead up to the climactic "nothing." Shakespeare, it may fairly be claimed, surpasses all other poets in his ability to forge so continuous a chain of closely associated images.

If Shakespeare's Macbeth was so sunk in despair that he could find nothing significant in life, his creator permitted him to express his feeling in images that signified— *symbolized*—a soul in damnation. Starting as a warrior-hero, "Bellona's bridegroom," Macbeth knowingly murders his king for gain and thereafter walks the way to dusty death— the death of the heart, of the mind, of the soul—suffering the scorpion stings of conscience until he is almost past feeling anything. His utterance here is a succession of figures of speech that so exactly reflect his mood that we correctly regard these images and metaphors as organic, not artificial; as functional, not decorative. What emerges here is the portrait of a suffering man who comes to symbolize all murderous guilt.

So rich in suggestiveness is the passage in which this symbol of all conscious sin is made articulate that later writers have seized on some of its images to use as titles that epitomize (and therefore symbolize) an imaginative creation of their own. Thus, Robert Frost, writing a narrative poem about the snuffing out of a boy's life in a cruel encounter with a hungry saw, entitled it "Out, Out—," and William Faulkner called the novel that most readers consider his supreme achievement *The Sound and the Fury,* a tragic tale told, at least in part, by an idiot, Benjy.

With this passage, then, we have reached the complexity of Shakespeare's mature style. The poet does not take us by the hand and lead us through the figures. Metaphor has ceased to be an ornament, a decorative literary device, and has become instead the stuff of drama. This is what is meant by dramatic poetry: the feelings reflected, the reactions invoked, the ideas expressed are not ours or even the poet's; they are Macbeth's! We are listening to the unique voice of a unique sufferer. And yet, without ceasing for a moment to be a particular man, Macbeth has also become a symbol of all those men who carry their own hell with them as the terrifying consequence of engaging in conscious evil.

As great as this accomplishment is, there is still a greater—or, at least, a larger—one. Not only does Shakespeare elevate the image of one of his great characters to the level of a universal symbol; he also—and this seems inevitable as we observe his progress as a dramatic poet—comes to see all that he is doing as a playwright in terms of image and metaphor and symbol. At the end of his career, indeed, he not only sees all of his plays as one succession of images of the human condition, but he also seems to see life itself as a kaleidoscope of theatrical images. Or, at least, he gives his great magician, Prospero, this perspective. The following lines from *The Tempest* are deservedly famous. Besides the pleasure they confer, they serve admirably to conclude our little survey of Shakespeare's progress from pure image to complex symbol.

Prospero has conjured up for the edification of Ferdinand and Miranda a vision, in the form of a wedding masque featuring goddesses, nymphs, and reapers who sing and dance and offer life's blessing to the young lovers. Suddenly, disturbed by the recollection of Caliban's plot against his life, he causes the conjured spirits to vanish. Then, wishing to allay the alarm expressed by his prospective son-in-law at the swift change in his demeanor, Prospero offers this interpretation of his creation, an interpretation that many readers and auditors believe reflects Shakespeare's view of his own art.

> You do look, my son, in a moved sort,
> As if you were dismayed: be cheerful, sir.
> Our revels now are ended. These our actors,
> As I foretold you, were all spirits and
> Are melted into air, into thin air;
> And, like the baseless fabric of this vision,
> The cloud-capped tow'rs, the gorgeous palaces,
> The solemn temples, the great globe itself,
> Yea, all which it inherit, shall dissolve,
> And, like this insubstantial pageant faded,
> Leave not a rack behind. We are such stuff
> As dreams are made on, and our little life
> Is rounded with a sleep.   *(IV, i, 146–158)*

These last examples illustrate one of the principal functions of imagery—to prompt the imagination of the reader
(and listener) to translate concrete symbols into abstract
ideas. Thus the reader and playgoer, like the poetic
dramatist, are led to think in images. To hear Richard II
exclaim "Is not the king's name twenty thousand names? /
Arm, arm, my name!" is to be made vividly aware that the
speaker is a poet who believes in word magic but no politician
who must deal with realities. To hear Macbeth assert "My
way of life / Is fall'n into the sear, the yellow leaf" is to
recognize that spiritual sterility and moral decay, not just old
age, are taking their toll of this criminal king. To hear
Cleopatra declare, as she resolves to die, "I am marble-
constant: now the fleeting moon / No planet is of mine" is to
become aware that this most fickle, changing, and
chameleon-like of women is capable of the kind of resolution
we associate with saints and martyrs: she is capable of a
transcendental, as well as a physical, passion.

Issuing from this general function of imagery—this trans-
mutation of the concrete particular into the abstract
generalization—are several specific functions that may be
named and briefly illustrated. Imagery may be used to
foreshadow coming events, as when the first character to-
wards whom our attention is directed in *Macbeth* is the
bloody sergeant ("What bloody man is that?"); when Friar
Laurence warns the impetuous Romeo, "These violent de-
lights have violent ends / And in their triumph die, like fire
and powder, / Which, as they kiss, consume"; or when Antony is described by a worried friend as one whose "captain's
heart" has "become the bellows and the fan / To cool a gipsy's
lust."

Images may be repeated at intervals throughout a play so as
to form a pattern. Often these patterns will suggest one of the
play's principal meanings or will form an illuminating parallel with other elements in the drama so as to reinforce the
meanings that these elements yield. Thus in *Hamlet* we are
presented with a succession of images of infection and dis-
ease ("this too too sullied flesh"; "some vicious mole of nature"; "something is rotten in the state of Denmark"; a most

instant tetter barked about / Most lazarlike with vile and loathsome crust / All my smooth body"; "my wit's diseased"; ". . . your trespass . . . will but skin and film the ulcerous place / Whiles rank corruption, mining all within, / Infects unseen"; "Diseases desperate grown / By desperate appliance are relieved"; "This is th' imposthume [abscess] of much wealth and peace, / That inward breaks and shows no cause without / Why the man dies"; "But to the quick o' th' ulcer—") whose cumulative effect is to reinforce what the unfolding story reveals—that the sick state of Denmark can be saved only by the removal of the cancer at its center and that the price of this salvation will be nothing less than the life of its savior. Similarly, in *Antony and Cleopatra,* Shakespeare's clear intention of displaying an outsized hero throwing away a world to gratify a passion which, in scope and intensity, far exceeds that of mere physical appetite for a woman is everywhere achieved by a succession of cosmic images ("our general's . . . goodly eyes . . . have glowed like plated Mars"; "Let Rome in Tiber melt and the wide arch / Of the ranged empire fall! here is my space . . ."; "the universal landlord"; "Your emperor / Continues still a Jove"; "I, that with my sword / Quartered the world and o'er green Neptune's back / With ships made cities"; "His face was as the heavens, and therein stuck / A sun and moon, which kept their course and lighted / The little O, th'earth"; "His legs bestrid the ocean: his reared arm / Crested the world"; ". . . in his livery / Walked crowns and crownets: realms and islands were / As plates dropped from his pocket"; "I am fire, and air; my other elements / I give to baser life") the impact of which supports the sentiment that Dryden expressed when retelling this story: "The World Well Lost."

Twentieth-century criticism, with its special affinity for the elements of poetry, has made much of imagery generally and image patterns particularly. Beginning with Caroline Spurgeon's compendium of Shakespeare's favorite images[4] and continuing through the writings of many contemporary critics, notably W. H. Clemen,[5] one may read many ingenious and illuminating interpretations of Shakespearean passages, scenes, and sometimes entire plays—interpretations that might be likened to the discovery of Henry James's famous "figure in the carpet,"⁶ the unifying design that holds the entire fabric together. But admitting that these interpretations sometimes are impressive and recognizing that patterns of imagery do function as a unifying agency, we must not succumb to the notion that such patterns constitute "the key" to a play's meaning. Images and image patterns are, at most, parts of the whole. As we have repeatedly discovered in our examination of the other elements of drama, it is in the interrelatedness of these elements—the structure of structures—that we discover a play's artistic significance. Keeping this in mind, we will not try to find the significance of a play solely by means of its image patterns but will rather find the significance of the image patterns just so far as these can be demonstrated to be integrated into the whole play. Common sense tells us why this must be so. The recognition and tracing of verbal image patterns are the occupation of the close reader in his study. Audiences in a crowded theater must be provided with much larger and more obvious clues, primary images of a different kind, like the actors and their actions. If you wish to prepare yourself beforehand for a rare form of pleasure, you may read the playscript and alert yourself to the presence of these smaller textural clues. You will then achieve a more refined understanding of the play than your less sophisticated neighbor, but you will not necessarily achieve a truer one.

Another important function of imagery is the way it can be used to define and differentiate characters. Here we may begin with a form of self-awareness: the recognition of how all of us tend to see only what we want to see. If, then, we ask why a particular person happens to see and comment on only certain details or images from among the thousands of sensations that constantly bombard him, our answer will provide us with an acute insight into his character. It is no accident that on the subject of love, Mercutio's images are pornographic ("For this drivelling love is like a great natural that runs lolling up and down to hide his bauble in a hole"), and the Nurse's are coarsely pragmatic ("I think it best you married with the County / O, he's a lovely gentleman! / Romeo's a dishclout to him"), whereas those of Romeo and Juliet run to heavenly things ("What light through yonder window breaks? / It is the East, and Juliet is the sun"; "Give me my Romeo; and, when he shall die, / Take him and cut him out in little stars, / That he will make the face of heaven so fine / That all the world will be in love with night"). Nor are we surprised that the words of the determined politician, Bolingbroke, are full of images of lands, titles, and gages [challenges], whereas the king he will depose, Richard II, conjures up images of the sun, when thinking of himself as ruler; of Christ, when thinking of himself as a king betrayed; and of buckets full of tears and of obscure and little graves when his self-pity threatens to overwhelm him. More subtly, and more strikingly, we may trace the transfer of imagery from a villain to a hero, as we witness the cynically foul-mouthed Iago (". . . you'll have your daughter covered with a Barbary horse"; "your daughter and the Moor are making the beast with two backs") corrupt the noble Othello until the latter is reduced by his poisonous jealousy to echoing his tormentor ("Goats and monkeys!"—a cryptic and agonized reflection of Iago's earlier slander of the relationship of Cassio and Desdemona, "as prime as goats, as hot as monkeys").

Still another function of imagery—to create the appropriate atmosphere in which to envelop a particular action—scarcely needs illustration. Readers already familiar with some Shakespearean plays can provide dozens of their own examples, and novice readers will encounter them on nearly any page. Perhaps, however, it is well to remind both sets of readers that such imagery is often employed for ironic effect. Thus, the trusting King Duncan and his loyal general, Banquo, approach the deathtrap that is Macbeth's castle at Inverness exchanging these remarks that reveal Shakespeare's desire to have his listeners fully savor the irony:

King   This castle hath a pleasant seat. The air
         Nimbly and sweetly recommends itself
         Unto our gentle senses.

Banquo   This guest of summer,
          The temple-haunting martlet, does approve
          By his loved mansionry that the heaven's breath
          Smells wooingly here.   *(I, vi, 1–6)*

This final example happily illustrates our final word on
Shakespearean imagery. Although, contrary to the Baconian
heresy, Shakespeare was a widely read man, and although he
displays here and there in his plays—and richly in his nondramatic long poems—an easy familiarity with traditional
rhetoric and classical imagery, he seems instinctively to have
turned for most of his images precisely where a popular
writer writing for a popular audience ought to turn—to nature itself. Thus, Shakespeare's images are inclusive, not
exclusive. General readers will find themselves invited to
recognize the familiar—the earth, the sea, and the sky, and
the things that inhabit them: flowers, plants, animals, and all
growing things; our human concerns with food, clothing,
shelter, our health and illness, our occupations and diversions. This source of imagery is still another of the many
means by which Shakespeare, all unwittingly, bridged the
gap that would otherwise have hopelessly divided him from
the twentieth-century reader and playgoer. He is the greatest
culture hero of the English-speaking people because his plays
are truly rooted in that culture. The New York City productions of Joseph Papp, "Shakespeare in the Park," have demonstrated once more that Shakespeare is accessible to almost any English-speaking person who will pause to listen.
Books like this one are written to clarify—and, with luck,
to accelerate—the process.

8
VERSE AND PROSE

A. VERSE

> O, that's a brave man; he writes brave verses,
> speaks brave words. . . .
> *(As You Like It, III, iv, 36–37)*

Told that the word *brave* meant *splendid* to Shakespeare, we might conclude that this epigraph represents the speaker's praise of poetic talent in another. Might, that is, if we ignored the satiric tone. But brave or splendid, the bite comes through. As a matter of fact, in these remarks from *As You Like It* delivered by Rosalind's cousin, Celia, Shakespeare is having a little fun at the expense of his hero, Orlando, who writes *bad* verse; and, characteristically, he is also laughing at the whole business of verse making. This is very like Shakespeare. Under the headings *verse, poetry, poet,* and *poetical,* you will find in Bartlett's *Concordance to Shakespeare* some sixty-one comments on verse and verse making. A great many of these comments are derisive in substance or tone, albeit gently so. Most of us would not want it otherwise. When an accomplished artist speaks of his craft, a bantering tone gives us confidence in his humanity.

What, then, may we discover about Shakespeare's ways of working with verse when we turn away from this mocking commentary to the body of the work itself? We may begin by citing a few statistics. The 37 plays commonly attributed to Shakespeare contain approximately 104,000 lines. Examining the individual plays, we discover that they range (in round numbers) from a high of 3,700 lines (*Hamlet*) to a low of 1,750 lines (*The Comedy of Errors*), with an average length of 2,700 lines (*The Merchant of Venice* will serve as a representative example). About 28 percent of these lines are in prose, 7 percent are in rimed verse, and 65 percent are in blank verse—proportions, interestingly, that coincide nearly exactly with those we find in *Hamlet*. Although the proportions among the three media vary from play to play—the extremes are represented by *Richard II*, composed entirely in verse (20 percent rimed verse, 80 percent blank verse); by *Richard III*, composed almost entirely in blank verse; and by *The Merry Wives of Windsor*, composed almost entirely in prose—the averages are eloquent: verse is Shakespeare's favorite medium.

Why should this be so? There are several reasons. First, there is the influence of tradition. Until a few years before Shakespeare began to write, all popular drama in England was composed in verse—and in rimed verse at that. This tradition, moreover, stemmed from a notion of art generally and of drama particularly quite different from our modern notion. Elizabethans viewed drama, as they viewed epics and other forms of literary art, as well-wrought idealizations, not photographically faithful reproductions, of life. Art, to them, represented experience distilled and symbolized and elevated. To echo a phrase we used earlier, dramatic art presented them with images that were true *about* life but not necessarily true *to* life. Such an art form, it follows, requires an artful language. Thus verse—more measured as well as more memorable than prose—seemed the appropriate medium to achieve the patterned effects of art.

It can be persuasively argued that this Elizabethan attitude toward the language of drama is not peculiar to that time. As Eric Bentley has observed, there is something about all drama that inclines toward verse as its natural medium.[1] This inclination is not really contradicted even by today's naturalistic drama. The speech of any drama must be artfully contrived if for no other reason than that dramatic dialogue, as opposed to the meandering garrulity of everyday talk, must be made "dramatic." At a minimum, the language of drama must suggest the spontaneous give and take of genuine communication between persons and must never be permitted to sound like an author's monologue sliced up into segments that merely appear in print as dialogue. This effect of communication cannot be achieved by artlessness. Modern plays may declare themselves lifelike. But the speeches of even the most fiercely naturalistic of them can be demonstrated to reveal the operation of the time-honored principles of rhetoric. And it is only a step from the rhetorical principles imposed by dramatists on their prose to the measured cadences that characterize verse. The differences are those of degree, not of kind. Arguably, *Waiting for Godot* is closer to the language of Shakespeare than it is to the tape recordings of any actual conversations.

We have been trying to preserve the distinction between verse and poetry. Our references to verse have employed words like *measure* and *pattern,* words that emphasize sound more than sense, form more than content. And this has been deliberate. When we come, in good time, to discuss some of the qualities of Shakespearean blank verse that have made it the most notable poetic stage line in English, we shall define and illustrate the poetry of those lines. Still, at the moment we do need to draw on this honorific word to round off our explanation of why verse is by so much the dominant medium of expression in Shakespeare's plays. Poetry, it has been discovered by all writers, is the best vehicle for expressing human experience at its moments of greatest tension. Increasingly in his development as a dramatist, Shakespeare found himself focusing on such moments. Since verse is the normal vehicle for poetry, he found verse more and more nearly indispensable to the achievement of his purposes.

But as our statistics revealed, Shakespeare wrote this

dramatic verse in more than one form. The differences between rimed and blank verse account for his sparing use of
the former and lavish use of the latter. A discussion of these
differences and the ways in which he exploited both forms
for different purposes will disclose much that is important
about Shakespeare's practices as a playwright and much
that is revealing about the special nature of his plays.

RIMED VERSE

> I'll rhyme you so eight years together, dinners
> and suppers and sleeping hours excepted.
> (As You Like It, III, ii, 91–92)

Of the three media of expression available to Shakespeare
when he began to write his plays—rimed verse, blank verse,
and prose—he made, paradoxically, the smallest use of the
form with which he was presumably the most familiar. Not
only was rimed verse the common medium of the drama
immediately preceding his time, but, as we know, Shakespeare used rime in all of his nondramatic poems, fashioning
a six-line riming stanza for his *Venus and Adonis* and a
slightly more intricate seven-line riming stanza for *The
Rape of Lucrece* as well as popularizing the riming couplet at
the ends of his sonnets, a distinguishing feature of this sonnet form to which the name *Shakespearean* has since been
attached to differentiate it from the older *Petrarchan* form,
whose riming pattern is distinctly different from that favored by Shakespeare.

And yet despite this familiarity with—this delight in—
rime, Shakespeare discovered that it imposed limitations
too restricting to permit the full development of his evolving dramatic powers. One such limitation is endemic in the
language itself: English is, by comparison with French, for
instance, accounted rime poor. While this deficiency may
prove no handicap in a short lyric, it may prove disadvan-
tageous in a long poem, disabling in a full play. The writer,
straining to meet the requirements of a rime form, may be

compelled to sacrifice the precision or power of his utterance: the sound may become a substitute for, rather than an echo of, the sense.

Characteristically, Shakespeare employs comic means to show himself aware of this danger. There is a scene in *As You Like It* in which Rosalind reads aloud some of the bad verses Orlando has been hanging on the trees in the Forest of Arden, and her companion, the witty clown Touchstone, after scornfully exclaiming in prose "I'll rhyme you so eight years together, dinners and suppers and sleeping hours excepted," then parodies Orlando's feeble efforts in verse.

Orlando's earnest

'From the east to western Inde,
No jewel is like Rosalinde.
Her worth, being mounted on the wind,
Through all the world bears Rosalinde.
All the pictures fairest lined
Are but black to Rosalinde.
Let no face be kept in mind
But the fair of Rosalinde.' *(III, ii, 83–90)*

is countered by Touchstone's saucy

If a hart do lack a hind,
Let him seek out Rosalinde.
If the cat will after kind,
So be sure will Rosalinde.
Wintred garments must be lined,
So must slender Rosalinde.
They that reap must sheaf and bind,
Then to cart with Rosalinde.
Sweetest nut hath sourest rind,
Such a nut is Rosalinde.
He that sweetest rose will find
Must find love's prick, and Rosalinde.
(III, ii, 96–107)

Parenthetically, these lines permit us to observe that certain words—"wind / lined"—that no longer rime—once did. This presents no real problem. Modern readers accustomed to the "once again / down memory lane" rimes of popular songs will have no difficulty recognizing these archaic rimes in Shakespearean playscripts or adjusting to their pronunciation in the theater.

It might be argued that a writer as fecund as Shakespeare could never really suffer from poverty of invention and hence would find no handicap in seeking English rimes. But there are more subtle limitations that attach themselves to rimed verse, limitations that, ironically, are closely related to its strengths. Everyone who has ever attempted to memorize a poem knows that the rime scheme (if the poem has one) is his greatest aid and comfort. The principle of repetition undergirds most memorable expression, and rime is the most conspicuous of all forms of repetition. The riming words sound and resound in the ear and thus fix themselves in the mind. Aye, there's the rub. Although rime may serve the memorizer, it may betray the dramatist. The very memorability of such well-known lines as Hamlet's "The play's the thing / Wherein I'll catch the conscience of the king" carry with them a triple danger: they so stick in the ear and the mind that they efface the remainder of the passage of which they are a part; they invite both the injudicious actor and the too-expectant listener to neglect some necessary question of the play while each waits to pounce on this punchline; and they present a temptation to the playwright—to try to outcap his own brilliant effort with a yet more brilliant one until what seemed a happy hit becomes a mannerism, and novelty turns into staleness.

This particular limitation of rime leads us logically enough to notice other qualities of riming verse that likewise ease the memorizer's task while stifling the dramatist's need for scope and variety. I refer to the marked pauses at the ends and often near the middle of riming lines. The final words of Brutus, spoken as he prepares to die a Roman death by running on his own sword held by his slave, Strato, illustrate these pauses.

> Farewell, good Strato. Caesar, now be still.
> I killed not thee with half so good a will.
> > (*Julius Caesar*, V, v, 50–51)

It will be seen, too, that this pair of lines constitutes a distinct unit of thought and that the last syllable of each line receives a strong stress. This rather rigid pattern—of rime, pause, stress, and meaning—so regularizes the reading of these lines as to invite, in passages made up of many lines like them, a dangerous monotony in both their composition and their delivery.

Nor is our quoted example an isolated instance. Specimens of riming couplets selected at random exhibit the persistence of these qualities and this whether the couplet appears alone or as part of a longer passage of consecutive rimed couplets. Moreover—and this is by all odds the most persuasive evidence—lines having these qualities appear in plays written late as well as early in Shakespeare's career. Shakespeare's rime patterns appear to be fixed; they do not improve with age. This evidence compels the conclusion that the medium itself is a restrictive one that does not admit of the development and the variety that Shakespeare's blank verse so conspicuously demonstrates.

We have several times discovered that Shakespeare seems never to have entirely abandoned techniques he acquired during his apprenticeship as a playwright. So here. A recognition of the restrictive qualities of rimed verse did not lead Shakespeare to drop this form entirely. Instead he came to use it selectively for special purposes where the very qualities that prevented it from being a universal vehicle for discourse cause it to shine at times with a particular glitter.

Preeminent among these special uses are the songs, a delightful addition to the plays, whose popularity with both Shakespeare and his audiences is evidenced by their appearance—either as fully developed lyrics or as fragments and snatches—in twenty-one of the thirty-seven plays, covering the entire span of his career as a playwright, and including every kind of play he came to write—

tragedies and tragicomedies as well as farces, romantic comedies, and symbolic romances.

Here is one example whose qualities of rime, meter, refrain, diction, and metaphor are all brilliantly displayed within the tiny compass of six lines. The singer is a boy who is unaware of the ironical application of the words of his song to the lady to whom he is singing them, the forlorn Mariana of *Measure for Measure,* who had been spurned by her one-time fiancé, Angelo, because the death of her brother had left her dowerless.

> Take, O take those lips away,
>   That so sweetly were forsworn;
> And those eyes, the break of day,
>   Lights that do mislead the morn;
> But my kisses bring again, bring again,
> Seals of love, but sealed in vain, sealed in vain.
>
> *(IV, i, 1–6)*

Songs, as we have said, are, in a sense, an addition to the plays that contain them, although it would be a serious error to think of them as mere embellishments without any dramatic significance. We have just seen an instance of a song's ironical glancing at the fate of the lady who is listening to it. This is Shakespeare's usual way with songs and with other matter—prologues, epilogues, choruses, masques, plays within plays—inserted into the main body of the drama. Almost nothing in Shakespeare is extraneous. Everything has its special function. But that is precisely the present point: some of these functions are *special.* Shakespeare used rime to signal this fact. These inserts he composed in verse, in order to distinguish them from the larger drama of which they, like a bit of bright tile set in a plaster wall, are a part.

This notion of using rimed verse as a means of identifying and setting off some special forms of discourse led very naturally to its use as a device for italicizing or punctuating two or more lines embedded in the blank verse of regular discourse, whenever the playwright wished to give such

lines special emphasis. The favorite rime form for this purpose was a ten-syllable, five-stress pair of iambic lines,
called the *heroic couplet* because it had been popularized by
earlier narrative poets who wrote epics of knights and
heroes. Because this couplet was made up of two iambic
pentamenter lines, it was possible for the dramatist to insert
one anywhere he desired without disturbing the metrical
pattern or prevailing rhythm of the enclosing blank verse
passage. As we might guess, the favorite place for such emphasis was at the end of a speech, which sometimes coincided with the end of a conversation or the end of a scene.
Hence the assigning to them of the term *capping couplets.*

Hamlet's riming declaration of his intention to "catch the
conscience of the king," quoted earlier, marks the end of
both an extended soliloquy and a scene. The following four
lines, spoken by Edgar, the only surviving principal from
the stricken families of Lear and Gloucester, actually mark
the end of the play!

> The weight of this sad time we must obey,
> Speak what we feel, not what we ought to say.
> The oldest hath borne most; we that are young
> Shall never see so much, nor live so long.
>> (*King Lear, V, iii,* 324–327)

Note how this specimen of riming verse, written at the
height of Shakespeare's powers, in what many competent
judges feel is his greatest play, differs from the severe and
restrictive pattern we have been outlining by only so much
as the slight tendency of the third line to run on into the
fourth. Here is further proof, if any were needed, of the
limitations of this form and of Shakespeare's wisdom in
sensing these limitations early in his career and relegating
his use of rime to the special functions we have been listing.

In retrospect, this decision of Shakespeare's seems not
only wise but also inevitable. But in matter of fact, it may
not have been so simple. There was a period in his career as
a playwright when he made very heavy use of rimed verse
and this in plays that are by no means without merit. Three

of them—*A Midsummer Night's Dream, Richard II,* and
Romeo and Juliet—are accounted masterpieces. Did he do
anything different with rime in these plays which helped
him transcend the limitations we have discovered in this
form? One might well think so. We know that these plays
were all composed during his so-called lyrical period, when
he published his two long narrative poems and probably
wrote a good share of his sonnets. And we know that in all of
these plays he hit on subjects and created characters that
admirably fit the lyrical impulse. Concerning Richard II we
have spoken at some length in Chapter 3, and everyone
knows the transcendental lovers, Romeo and Juliet, and has
spent an hour or two in the magical world of one midsummer night's dream.

But a lyric poet is not the same manner of man as the hero
of a lyric poem or a lyrical play. As every artist has learned,
sometimes to his sorrow, if he cannot distance his subject he
must forfeit control. Shakespeare kept control. Even in
these highly romantic plays which are strongly impregnated
with the lyric impulse, Shakespeare was already displaying
the artist's discriminating sense. Although the quantity of
rimed verse in these plays ranges from about 17 percent in
Romeo and Juliet to 45 percent in *A Midsummer Night's
Dream,* Shakespeare unerringly selected for rime those portions of the plays—inserted prologues and choruses, highly
stylized comic exchanges as mannered as minuets, allegorical and sententious passages in which a homily is delivered
or a lesson taught, ritualistic greetings and partings—which
would gain, not lose, by the artifice of measured riming
lines. Examples are not difficult to find.

In *A Midsummer Night's Dream,* he gives rimed verse to
the faeries and to the mortal lovers when they are under
Puck's spell, reserving blank verse for the courtiers and
prose for the rude mechanicals. In *Richard II,* he uses rimed
verse to frame and summarize the naked allegory of the
garden scenes and to embody such rituals as Richard's parting from his queen, where the formal qualities of the verse
flatten out the speakers until they seem, by design, as two-

dimensional as any figures frozen in a medieval frieze. In *Romeo and Juliet,* the lovers' impassioned exchanges on Juliet's balcony and in her bedroom are all in blank verse, save for a capping couplet or two, but their shy and formal first meeting at the Capulet ball is exquisitely handled not only in rimed verse but—and here Shakespeare displays a nice balance of taste and virtuosity—with that rime encased in the form of an English sonnet.

The passage deserves to be represented in full. The angry Tybalt, rebuked by Juliet's father, has left the stage. Doubtless standing well forward on the huge platform stage on which most of the action in any Shakespearean play took place, separated from Old Capulet and the crowd of merrymakers, dancers, musicians, and serving men gathered in the rear, these two enchanted youngsters approach each other, shyly but marvelously articulate.

Romeo   If I profane with my unworthiest hand
        This holy shrine, the gentle sin is this;
      My lips, two blushing pilgrims, ready stand
        To smooth that rough touch with a tender kiss.
Juliet   Good pilgrim, you do wrong your hand too much,
        Which mannerly devotion shows in this;
      For saints have hands that pilgrims' hand do touch,
        And palm to palm is holy palmers' kiss.
Romeo   Have not saints lips, and holy palmers too?
Juliet   Ay, pilgrim, lips that they must use in prayer.
Romeo   O, then, dear saint, let lips do what hands do!
      They pray; grant thou, lest faith turn to despair.
Juliet   Saints do not move, though grant for prayers' sake.
Romeo   Then move not while my prayer's effect I take.
                    (I, v, 93–106)

If the sonnet is the most elaborate of the riming measures Shakespeare used, there are other measures that were introduced for different effects. As a master of sound, he could achieve a remarkable incantatory effect with riming tetrameters even when, as with the spells cast by the witches in *Macbeth,* the imagery is grotesque ("Eye of newt, and toe of frog, / Wool of bat, and tongue of dog"). Very early in his career, he was not averse to using the doggerel *four-teener* ("Was there ever any man thus beaten out of season, / When in the why and wherefore is neither rime nor reason?") for comic purposes, although later he would use prose in its place. In the plays, besides the three already mentioned, where rime is used most plentifully—*The Comedy of Errors, Love's Labor's Lost,* and *Pericles*—the reader will discover quatrains interspersed with the riming couplets; and, of course, the songs called for a considerable variety of stanzaic patterns.

Just as there is considerable variety in the riming measures, so also there is considerable scope in the *functions* to which Shakespeare put his rimes. In addition to those functions already cited, rime is associated with certain manifestations of the supernatural—the apparitions who speak cryptically to Macbeth, the faeries (Puck and Ariel) who cast spells, the gods who bestow their favors on mortals (Ceres blessing Ferdinand and Miranda), and the witches who weave their dark prophecies all speak in rime. And rime is the vehicle for such inscriptions as those found in the gold, silver, and lead caskets that Portia's suitors must decide among. It is used in occasional *asides* when the playwright is particularly desirous that his character's remark draw attention to itself. Sometimes, as with Friar Laurence's disquisition on the paradoxical intimacy of virtue and vice, Shakespeare introduces rime as though to underscore with sound the sense of such a didactic utterance.

But a compounding of further instances of either measure or function adds nothing to our understanding of the role of rimed verse in Shakespearean drama. The prescription for you as reader and playgoer is clear. Whenever your ear in the theater, or your eye in the study, identifies a riming pattern, you know that you are in the presence of something a little special to which the playwright is inviting you to attend. This may be something as sizable as the whole of *The Mur-*

der of Gonzago, Hamlet's "mousetrap" play within the play, or something as small in compass as Macbeth's despairing last words ("Lay on, Macduff, / And damned be him that first cries, 'Hold, enough!'"). In either case, the rime is underscoring with its insistent sound what the action on the stage or the words on the page are seeking to convey to your eye and ear and mind.

Equally important—perhaps more so for modern playgoers—the presence of rime will serve as another reminder of the unabashedly artificial qualities of Elizabethan drama. We, as moderns shaped and conditioned by naturalism in fiction, film, and drama, cannot be reminded too often that we are witnessing a sixteenth-century art object composed in a sixteenth-century tradition and utilizing sixteenth-century conventions to project an image of life as it was viewed by a sixteenth-century mind. We can depend on the universal, the timeless qualities in Shakespeare to come through: no one needs guidance with these. It is with those aspects of the plays, like rime, which the passing of time has most affected, that help may be proffered and, with good luck, found not wanting.

BLANK VERSE

And for thy fiction,
Why, thy verse swells with stuff so fine and smooth
That thou art even natural in thine art.
(Timon of Athens, V, i, 81–83)

If the uses to which rimed verse could be put in drama proved limited, it is the glory of blank verse that its uses were to seem limitless. It was Shakespeare who made them so. Blank verse was still a relatively new medium of expression in English when Shakespeare began to write. The Earl of Surrey introduced it into English around the middle of the sixteenth century in his translation of parts of Virgil's *Aeneid,* and the authors of an early English tragedy, *Gorboduc,* applied it to drama just a few years before Shakespeare was born. It was then picked up by dramatists of the eighties, chief among them Christopher Marlowe.

The most famous lines Marlowe ever wrote:

> Was this the face that launch'd a thousand ships,
> And burnt the topless towers of Ilium?

will serve to illustrate the rather limited and fixed characteristics of the blank verse line that Shakespeare inherited and that he was to convert from regularity to plasticity. Note, as you read Marlowe's lines aloud, the metronomic beat of five unstressed syllables alternating with five stressed syllables (iambic pentameter), the very marked pause at the end of each line, the absence of any additional syllables at the ends of lines, the invitation to pause slightly after the second foot in the first line (caesura), and, of course, the absence of end rime (*blank verse*).

From this somewhat rigid pattern of regular pauses and stresses Shakespeare was to depart in a number of interesting ways so as to create for himself a poetic stage line of great flexibility and power. For purposes of clarity, we will supply brief examples of each of these major departures, since concrete illustrations often illuminate what abstract discussion may darken. Then, with each of these variations from the limited, fixed pattern clearly identified, we may turn to other, somewhat longer, examples to illustrate the remarkable dramatic effects Shakespeare could achieve when he blended any or all of these distinctive techniques of pause and stress into passages of astonishing fluidity.

Let us first direct our attention to the distribution of *pauses*. Here is Shakespeare sounding like Marlowe:

> Why, I can smile, / and murder whiles I smile, / /
> And cry 'Content!' to that which grieves my heart. . . . / /
> (*3 Henry VI, III, ii, 182–183*)

Each of these lines spoken by Richard, later Duke of Gloucester, has a strong pause at the end, and the first line has a strong medial pause after the second iambic foot.

Moreover, the units of thought coincide with the pattern of pauses. Whenever a pause dictated by meaning (and often marked by punctuation) coincides with the end of a verse line, such lines are said to be *end-stopped*. If pentameter lines in succession are end-stopped, they acquire in their regularity an affinity with the heroic couplet even though they are without rime. Indeed, the blank verse line is usually thought to have evolved from the heroic couplet.

There are several ways to modify this pattern of rigid regularity in the blank verse line. One is to propel the flow of meaning from one line to the next so that the anticipated pause at the end of the line is overcome by the rush of meaning. Such lines are called *run on*. Richard, Duke of Gloucester, later Richard III, who in the preceding quotation commented with stunning frankness on his own character, here comments with equal candor on his grotesque appearance:

> Deformed, / unfinished, / sent before my time
> Into this breathing world, / scarce half made up, / /
> And that so lamely and unfashionable
> That dogs bark at me as I pass by them— / /
> (*Richard III, I, i, 20–23*)

The variations are at once apparent. Line 1 overflows into line 2, and line 3 runs on into line 4. There are variations in medial pauses as well. Line 1 has two such pauses, one at the end of the first foot, the other splitting the third iambic foot (between the final, unstressed syllable of *unfinished* and the stressed monosyllable of *sent*). Line 2 places the medial pause after the third foot. And lines 3 and 4 have no medial pauses at all. Indeed, the marked difference between the rhythms of the first two lines and the last two contributes most of all to the naturalism of this passage—the strong impression that we are listening to a living voice.

One of the surest ways to encourage the actor or reader to follow the flow of a run-on line is to end that line with an unstressed syllable.

> I am dying, Egypt, dying; only
> I here importune death awhile. . . .
>   *(Antony and Cleopatra, IV, xv, 18–19)*

The unstressed syllable *ly* at the end of line 1 prompts the reader or speaker to move swiftly on to the second line. When that unstressed syllable is an extra or redundant syllable, making a total of eleven syllables in a line, it is called a *feminine ending* (presumably by analogy with a woman's extra rib). Shakespeare made use of such endings from the outset of his career, in a ratio of about one line in seven according to one authority. Apparently, the possibilities of this device for loosening the more rigid model line appealed to him, for in the later plays the ratio had become one in three or four. We have just heard the voice of the dying Antony. Here is Cleopatra lavishing praise on her dead lover:

> His face was as the heav'ns, / and therein stuck
> A sun and moon, / which kept their course and lighted
> The little O, / th' earth.   *(V, ii, 79–81)*

The unstressed syllable *ed* at the end of line 2 encourages the reader or speaker to run on to the third line. Moreover, this same unstressed syllable, when combined with the first syllable of line 3, also unstressed, accelerates the tempo and thus encourages the swift passage from one line to the other. Note, too, the scattered pauses, marked by commas, setting up a pause pattern that works contrapuntally against the anticipated regularity of the pauses we associate with end-stopped lines.

In addition to the unstressed final syllable, Shakespeare added another device to promote run-on lines. By employing at the ends of lines words with no semantic significance—prepositions, conjunctions, relative pronouns, auxiliary verbs, and similar *form words*—he ensured both a weaker stress on such a word and a strong movement toward the next word in the following line. This technique appears with increasing frequency in the plays he wrote toward the end of his career, when he seems to have moved even further in the direction of freedom from fixed forms. Two examples from *The Tempest* should be sufficient to fix this practice in our minds. The form word in each passage is italicized. The first example is Prospero's invocation to the elves of the island of which he is lord.

> . . . you demi-puppets *that*
> By moonshine do the green sour ringlets make. . . .
>
> *(V, i, 36–37)*

And the second is his explanation to the dumbfounded Ferdinand of why he has magically dispersed the spirits he had previously invoked to heap blessings on that young prince.

> Our revels now are ended. These our actors,
> As I foretold you, were all spirits *and*
> Are melted into air; into thin air. . . .
>
> *(IV, i, 148–150)*

Nothing more emphatically illustrates Shakespeare's increasing freedom from the straitjacket of rigidly patterned verse than his practice of ending a sentence—sometimes even a speech—in the middle of a verse line. The first lines of both of the preceding quotations illustrate the practice: new sentences begin where the previous sentences broke off, in mid line. (The uncapitalized *you* of the first quotation marks the start of a new sentence as surely as if it had been preceded by a period and was capitalized, because it follows a semicolon, which has the strength of a period.) The opening lines of *A Midsummer Night's Dream*, below, not only afford another clear illustration of this practice but also serve once more to remind us, by their appearance in a relatively early play, of Shakespeare's inveterate practice: most of the techniques—both structural and textural—that he employed in his early plays, he never forsook.

> Now, / fair Hippolyta, / our nuptial hour
> Draws on apace. / / Four happy days bring in
> Another moon; / / but O, / methinks, / how slow
> This old moon wanes! / /   *(I, i, 1–4)*

We see that three of these four lines contain sentences that end midway within those lines. (Again, the semicolon in line 3 has the weight of a period.) This passage will serve, as well, to illustrate how Shakespeare can scatter pauses anywhere—in line 1 after the first syllable ("Now") and also after the third foot and in line 3 after the second, third, and fourth feet.

The effect of all of these devices—the forward rush of meaning, the unaccented final syllable, the semantically unimportant form word at the end of a line—is to free us from the fatal singsong regularity with which some persons are disposed to read all verse. Here instead we read, almost as with prose, in units of thought, following the thread of meaning where it leads us. Indeed, so persuasive are these signals inviting us to read right on that our danger is no longer that we shall read with too much metronomic regularity but that we shall ignore the notation of the verse line altogether. Although not as offensive to the ear as childish singsong, this is nonetheless an error and one that mars the poet's music. What we have in this flexible blank verse is not an invitation toward linguistic anarchy but a contrapuntal device playing a *heard* rhythm against the *anticipated* rhythm of the theoretical fixed form. We should continue to anticipate the measures of that fixed form even when the poet departs from them. Specifically, for example, we should pause ever so slightly at the end of a blank verse line even when we are being strongly invited to ignore that pause. Thus we establish in our ear the *point* against which Shakespeare's variant notations are providing the *counterpoint,* and the total effect is one of delicious concord and enriched harmony.

We probably should pause for breath here and acknowledge the complaint of the drama critic, Dan Sullivan, who exclaimed on reading these paragraphs: "You make it sound so consciously worked out. Try writing a couple of pages of blank verse at top speed and see how the beat automatically dictates much of this." Of course Sullivan is right if he is arguing that Shakespeare, unlike the mythical centipede, did not pause to count his feet. We know from the testimony of his contemporaries that Shakespeare wrote rapidly, and we are certain that none of his most flashing passages could have been produced by slow labor. But our purpose here is not to imitate Shakespeare even if we could but to appreciate *what* he did. To do so, we must employ the slow-motion camera, in the manner of the instant replay on television which permits the spectator to savor lingeringly the performance of the skilled athlete.

What we thus discover concerning Shakespeare's ways of working with rhythms and pause patterns holds true of *meters* and *patterns of stress* as well. Once more we have a sort of platonic model or norm, and once more we discover many variations and departures from that norm. Regarding stress, our platonic model is the iambic pentameter line diagramed thus:

Ă líttle móre thăn kín, ănd léss thăn kínd!

(*Hamlet*, I, ii, 65)

However, before we set about discovering the variations on this model line that are followed in actual practice, we should raise and answer a brace of questions: Why an iambic foot? And why a pentameter line?

The answers turn on what used to be called, in a quaint phrase, the genius of the language. English is predominantly iambic in its beat. This is so for at least two closely connected reasons. The Anglo-Saxon bedrock vocabulary of English is monosyllabic. And in English we signal our grammatical relationships not by inflected word endings but by a typical order of words consisting of a whole host of monosyllabic connectives (prepositions, conjunctions, relative pronouns, conjunctive adverbs, auxiliary verbs) that often combine with monosyllabic nouns and verbs to form iambic feet.

Ăn ĭf we líve, we líve to tréad ŏn kíngs . . .

(*1 Henry IV*, V, ii, 85)

Equally significant, the very large number of two-syllable
words in English that, taken alone, display a trochaic meter
(shórtnĕss, báselў), when combined syntactically in
phrases, clauses, and sentences, fall into an iambic pattern
by joining their stressed first syllables with the unstressed
words or syllables that precede them.

> Ó gentlĕmĕn, thĕ tíme ŏf life ĭs shórt!
>
> Tŏ spénd that shórtnĕss báselў wĕre tóo lóng. . . .
>
> (*1 Henry IV, V, ii, 81–82*)

An examination of Shakespearean blank verse lines taken at
random from any of the plays will uncover countless examples of these metrical patterns.

What, then, about the line length: Why pentameter?
Again the answer turns on the nature of the English language. Actual experience with verse lines of varying length
has taught poets that the pentameter line is the best length
for the sustained utterance of serious matter. If the line gets
shorter—is reduced to three feet, or, more frequently, to
four feet—it grows songlike. Splendid for some short lyrics,
it will not do for serious discourse of any length. The following comparision makes the point and makes it very fairly:
Both passages have the same central image—daffodils—and
both are from the same play, *The Winter's Tale*. But the first
one is encased in lively and saucy tetrameters (whose tempo
is accelerated by the introduction of several *anapests*):

> When daffodils being to peer,
> > With heigh! the doxy over the dale,
> Why, then comes in the sweet o' the year,
> > For the red blood reigns in the winter's pale.
> > > (*IV, iii, 1–4*)

the second in sober and earnest pentameters:

> I would I had some flowers o' th' spring that might
> Become your time of day, and yours, and yours,
> That wear upon your virgin branches yet

Your maidenheads growing. O Proserpina,
For the flowers now that, frighted, thou let'st fall
From Dis's wagon; daffodils
That come before the swallow dares, and take
The winds of March with beauty . . . (*IV, iv, 113–120*)

The differing metrical patterns and the differing tempos befit the tones and meanings of their respective passages.

Conversely, experience has shown that if the verse line in English gets any longer than five feet—say, six, called a *hexameter,* or seven, a *heptameter*—the ear denies what the eye asserts: the listener breaks up the long line into two shorter ones. The well-known ballad stanza, with its metrical pattern of alternating four- and three-foot lines, illustrates what the English ear does to a theoretically possible heptameter.

> It is an ancient Mariner,
> And he stoppeth one of three.

And when A. E. Housman actually writes a heptameter line,

O who is that young sinner with the handcuffs on his wrist?

we probably hear it as

O who is that young sinner with
   the handcuffs on his wrist?

or, alternatively, scan it as a four-beat measure,

Ŏ whŏ ĭs thăt yoŭng sínnĕr wĭth thĕ hăndcuffs ŏn hĭs wríst?

Having established the principal reasons for the predominance of the iambic pentameter line, let us look for a moment at what Shakespeare does with it. What we discover in his actual practice is a number of artful variations on the fixed pattern, in which the *iambs* (˘ ´) become *trochees* (´ ˘) or *spondees* (´ ´) or *anapests* (˘ ˘ ´) or, more rarely, *dactyls* (´ ˘ ˘). The terms used to designate these stress patterns are not important, and if we do not already know them or do not find them easy to learn we should waste no time in the process. It is enough if we hear the basic five beats through all the variations; for if our ears can pick up the anticipated regular measure, they will usually detect the pleasing departures from that measure.

Hotspur's address to his followers just before the battle of Shrewsbury, on which we have already levied, will serve to illustrate some of these variations in stress. We will first reproduce the six-line passage. Then we will take up each successive line and supply two versions of it: the first we will lable *point*, by which we signify the model line or norm we *expect* to hear; the second we will label *counterpoint*, the line we *actually* hear if we are reading for the meaning Shakespeare invited us to find there.

> O gentlemen, the time of life is short!
> To spend that shortness basely were too long
> If life did ride upon a dial's point,
> Still ending at the arrival of an hour.
> An if we live, we live to tread on kings;
> If die, brave death, when princes die with us!
>
> *(1 Henry IV, V, ii, 81–86)*

Point Ŏ géntl̆emén, t̆he tíme ŏf lífe ĭs shórt!

Counterpoint Ó géntl̆emĕn, t̆he tíme ŏf lífe ĭs shórt!

Point T̆o spénd thăt shórtnĕss básely̆ wére tŏo lońg

Counterpoint T̆o spénd thăt shórtnĕss básely̆ wĕre tóo lońg

Point Ĭf lífe dĭd ríde ŭpón ă díal̆'s poínt,

Counterpoint Ĭf lífe dĭd ríde ŭpŏn ă díalˇs poínt,

Point Stĭll endĭng át the arríval óf ăn hóur.

Counterpoint Stíll endĭng ăt the ărríval ŏf ăn hóur.

Point Ăn íf wĕ líve, wĕ líve tŏ tréad ŏn kíngs;

Counterpoint Án ĭf wĕ líve, wĕ líve tŏ tréad ŏn kíngs;

Point Ĭf díe, brăve déath, whĕn príncĕs díe wĭth uś!

Counterpoint Ĭf díe, bráve déath, whĕn príncĕs díe wĭth uś!

  · In the preceeding paradigm, we are, of course, using a musical metaphor. The meaning of this metaphor may be extended. What we have called point may be likened to a *sense of order:* this finds its expression in the model, the norm, the metrical pattern we anticipate. What we have called counterpoint may be likened to a *kind of freedom:* this finds its expression in the actual, the departures from the norm, the metrical pattern we really hear. By keeping both in mind and both, so to say, in our ear, we have it both ways: like the poet, we keep the platonic model and the actual performance in a state of tension, thus deriving the exquisite pleasure that attends any act of reconciling seeming opposites, or, to put it another way, discovering unity in variety.

  By just such techniques of pause and stress, Shakespeare won a dramatist's freedom to achieve the effects he desired. Among all of these effects, the one acknowledged in his own day and ever since as his unique and supreme achievement is the one alluded to in the epigraph to this section: "Thou art even *natural* in thine art." All of Shakespeare's other achievements with language abide our question. This one alone cannot be fully explained—only illustrated.

Here is one of the earliest examples of "natural" speech, expressed in the colloquialisms of Old Capulet as he sternly rebukes his nephew, Tybalt:

> He shall be endured.
> What goodman boy! I say he shall. Go to!
> Am I the master here, or you? Go to!
> You'll not endure him, God shall mend my soul!
> You'll make a mutiny among my guests!
> You will set cock-a-hoop, you'll be the man!
>
> (*Romeo and Juliet, I, v, 76–81*)

And here is one from *1 Henry IV,* where Hotspur reacts to the king's peremptory demand for the surrender of his prisoners in a torrent of words the tempo of which explains his nickname:

> I'll keep them all!
> By God, he shall not have a Scot of them!
> No, if a Scot should save his soul, he shall not.
> I'll keep them, by this hand!
>
> . . . .
>
> Nay, I will! that's flat!
>
> (*I, iii, 213–216, 218*)

Playing on this great instrument, the blank verse line, he can use simple monosyllables to display Antony's guile:

> I am no orator, as Brutus is,
> But (as you know me all) a plain blunt man . . .
>
> (*Julius Caesar, III, ii, 217–218*)

and antiphonal sentences to reveal Othello's distracted mind as he speaks alternatively to the emissary from Venice and to the stunned Desdemona:

> Ay! You did wish that I would make her turn.
> Sir, she can turn, and turn, and yet go on

And turn again; and she can weep, sir, weep;
And she's obedient; as you say, obedient,
Very obedient.—Proceed you in your tears.—
Concerning this, sir—O well-painted passion!—
I am commanded home.—Get you away;
I'll send for you anon.—Sir, I obey the mandate
And will return to Venice.—Hence, avaunt!
                              (*Othello, IV, i, 245–253*)

But the results cannot be explained in technical words like
monosyllables and *antiphonal.* Here are two examples of
phrasal repetition, but they are as far apart as are the worlds
of their speakers. First we have Shylock responding to Bassanio's request for a loan:

Three thousand ducats—well.
. . . .
For the three months—well.
. . . .
Antonio shall become bound—well.
. . . .
Three thousand ducats, for three months,
and Antonio bound.
              (*The Merchant of Venice, I, iii, 1, 3, 6, 10*)

and then Hamlet quizzing the castle guard about the mysterious appearance of his father's ghost:

Indeed, indeed, sirs, but this troubles me.
. . . .
Very like, very like. Stayed it long?
                          (*Hamlet, I, ii, 224, 237*)

Nor need the speakers be major characters to be anointed
with this natural eloquence. Cleopatra's waiting-maid,
Charmian, can greet the death of her incomparable mistress
with these homely words and acts:

> Now boast thee, death, in thy possession lies
> A lass unparalleled.
> ·······································
>   Your crown's awry;
> I'll mend it. and then play—
>   (*Antony and Cleopatra, V, ii, 314–315, 317–318*)

and even the somewhat wooden, if worthy Horatio, on the ramparts of Elsinore can in response to the sentinel's challenge, "What, is Horatio there?" reply dryly,

> A piece of him.   (*Hamlet, I, i, 19*)

The foregoing examples illustrate what we may call naturalism in speech absolute. Because they possess universal qualities, one feels that they would sound natural in any century in which English is spoken. But "oft it chances in particular men" that they have a way of speaking—a *tone* that is uniquely theirs. What goes to make up this tone is what goes to make up the speaker himself and so is not subject to cataloguing. Speeches like the following, therefore, may be viewed as capsule biographies. And in each case the capsule is language. Of all the characters in Shakespeare, it seems fair to say that only Othello could have said:

> Keep up your bright swords, for the dew will rust them.
>   (*I, ii, 59*)

only Richard II:

> Let's talk of graves, of worms, and epitaphs,
> Make dust our paper, and with rainy eyes
> Write sorrow on the bosom of the earth.
>   (*III, ii, 145–147*)

only Lear:

>   Let me have surgeons;
> I am cut to th' brains.
>   (*IV, vi, 189–190*)

only Macbeth:

> I am in blood
> Stepped in so far that, should I wade no more,
> Returning were as tedious as go o'er.
>
> *(III, iv, 136–138)*

only Shylock:

> No, not take interest—not as you would say
> Directly intr'est. Mark what Jacob did . . .
>
> *(The Merchant of Venice, I, iii, 72–73)*

only Hotspur:

> . . . for I will ease my heart,
> Albeit I make a hazard of my head.
>
> *(1 Henry IV, I, iii, 127–128)*

only Hamlet:

> Mother, good night. Indeed, this counsellor
> Is now most still, most secret, and most grave,
> Who was in life a foolish prating knave.
> Come, sir, to draw toward an end with you.
> Good night, mother.
>
> *(III, iv, 214–218)*

And, although today it is considered neither fashionable nor wise to allude to the voice of any character as the voice of Shakespeare himself, it does not seem too rash to conclude that we are listening to the playwright when, speaking through his magician-impresario, Prospero, he seems to anticipate his own retirement.

> But this rough magic
> I here abjure; and when I have required
> Some heavenly music (which even now I do)
> To work mine end upon their senses that

This airy charm is for, I'll break my staff,
Bury it certain fathoms in the earth,
And deeper than did ever plummet sound
I'll drown my book.

(The Tempest, V, i, 50–57)

B. PROSE

These numbers will I tear, and write in prose.
(Love's Labor's Lost, IV, iii, 52)

Molière's newly rich M. Jourdain unconsciously perpetrated the best joke ever made about *prose* when he expressed astonishment at the revelation that he had been speaking prose all his life without knowing it. The assumption underlying this joke on an uneducated man is, of course, that all educated people *do* know the difference between prose and verse. But life's ironies have a way of chastening the pride of the informed as well as the ignorant. A very likely joke on the educated is that whereas they do know the *differences* between prose and verse, they do not recognize the *similarities!*

Recognition of these similarities is important for anyone seeking to understand Shakespeare's plays. Shakespeare's prose is a medium of expression as rich in its rhythms, its imagery, its metaphors, and its patterns of rhetoric as is his verse. One proof of this is the way in which actors move from Shakespearean blank verse to prose and back again without jarring the ears or distracting the attention of their audiences. (The same claim cannot be made for the transfer to rimed verse, for reasons made clear earlier in this chapter.)

This proof can be tested in the study as well as in the theater. Consider, for example, the matter of rhythm. It is common for persons attempting to distinguish prose from verse to state or imply that verse is "rhythmic" whereas prose is not. This is a mistake and a fairly serious one. It is a mistake based on a confusion between what is *metrical* and what is *rhythmic*.

An analogy will be useful here to clear up the confusion. The movement of prose might be likened to the complex variety of steps taken by a dancer in what is loosely called modern ballet or modern dance. None of the dancer's movements is exactly repeated; he goes from one step to another without developing the kind of pattern we associate with repetition. Yet the dance has an overall rhythmic pattern, and it has a set of distinctive particular rhythms. Verse, in contradistinction, moves like a classical ballet dancer in a set or series of formal dance steps, establishing patterns that please precisely because they are repeated and therefore are predictable. We can agree, I think, that both dancers are displaying rhythm, but only the dancer of classical ballet is displaying that form of regular and regularized rhythm we call *measured* and which in verse is called *meter*.

We can verify this for ourselves by drawing on two passages from Shakespeare, with Hamlet as the speaker in both instances.

No one can miss the rhythm—and the measure!—of these few blank verse lines in which Hamlet, holding up two locket pictures of his father and his uncle, compels his adulterous mother to confront the image of her first husband.

> Look here upon this picture, and on this,
> The counterfeit presentment of two brothers.
> See what a grace was seated on this brow:
> Hyperion's curls, the front of Jove himself,
> An eye like Mars, to threaten and command,
> A station like the herald Mercury
> New lighted on a heaven-kissing hill—
> A combination and a form indeed
> Where every god did seem to set his seal
> To give the world assurance of a man.
>
> *(III, iv, 54–63)*

Is the following prose passage, spoken to the players, any less rhythmical? (I did not say metrical.)

> O, there be players that I have seen play, and
> heard others praise, and that highly (not to speak
> it profanely), that neither having th' accent of
> Christians, nor the gait of Christian, pagan, nor
> man, have so strutted and bellowed that I have
> thought some of Nature's journeymen had made
> men, and not made them well, they imitated hu-
> manity so abominably.   *(III, ii, 27–33)*

If by rhythm we mean a discernible movement that establishes in our ear and nervous system the pleasing suggestion
of pattern—but not necessarily an exactly repeated
pattern—then Hamlet's prose is as rhythmical as his verse.

What holds true of rhythm holds equally true of imagery
and metaphor. Shakespeare seems not to have regarded
prose as inferior to verse, as the work of some of his contemporaries suggests they sometimes did. Thus, he employed
his imagination as abundantly in the one medium as the
other. Here are two passages, the first in blank verse and the
second in prose, that have a common subject—the sea and
the thought of drowning in it. The effects he achieves in
these two utterances are as different as any two things can
be, but this startling difference is achieved by *tone,* not by
either the number or the inventiveness of the images they
contain. The first speaker is the Duke of Clarence, who,
moments away from his murder at the hands of Richard
Gloucester's hired assassins, recounts a premonitory dream
of death by drowning, which includes these lines:

> O Lord! methought what pain it was to drown!
> What dreadful noise of waters in mine ears!
> What sights of ugly death within mine eyes!
> Methoughts I saw a thousand fearful wracks;
> A thousand men that fishes gnawed upon;
> Wedges of gold, great anchors, heaps of pearl,
> Inestimable stones, unvaluèd jewels,
> All scatt'red in the bottom of the sea:
> Some lay in dead men's skulls, and in the holes

> Where eyes did once inhabit, there were crept
> (As 'twere in scorn of eyes) reflecting gems,
> That wooed the slimy bottom of the deep
> And mocked the dead bones that lay scatt'red by.
>   (*Richard III, I, iv, 21–33*)

The second speaker is honest old Gonzalo, who, like Ahab's doughty second mate, Stubb, can jest in the face of death when his ship seems about to go down. Gonzalo's jest is leveled at the ship's bumptious boatswain.

> I have great comfort from this fellow: methinks
> he hath no drowning mark upon him; his com-
> plexion is perfect gallows. Stand fast, Good Fate,
> to his hanging! Make the rope of his destiny our
> cable, for our own doth little advantage. If he be
> not born to be hanged, our case is. misera-
> ble. . . . I'll warrant him for* drowning, though
> the ship were no stronger than a nutshell and as
> leaky as an unstanched wench.
>   (*The Tempest, I, i, 26–31, 43–45*)

The tone of the first passage is one of tremulous fear—we hear the quaver in the speaker's voice and feel the shrinking of his flesh. The tone of the second passage is one of jaunty fearlessness—the voice is as firm as the spine of its speaker. But would anyone deny that the witty imagery of the second is fully as inventive as the morbid, "Gothic" fantasies of the first?

As with rhythm and imagery, so with patterns of rhetoric. In the chapter just before this one, the qualities of artful repetition and symmetry that distinguish rhetorical discourse were catalogued and illustrated. For now it is sufficient to demonstrate their equally effective use in verse and prose.

No character in all of Shakespeare employs the parallels, balances, contrasts, and symmetries that characterize rhetorical speech more artfully than Richard III and

*guarantee him against

nowhere does he do so with more skill than when he woos,
and takes the distraught Lady Anne by storm. He simply
mesmerizes her with language. Here is a sample of his virtuosity:

> Teach not thy lip such scorn; for it was made
> For kissing, lady, not for such contempt.
> If thy revengeful heart cannot forgive,
> Lo, here I lend thee this sharp-pointed sword,
> Which if thou please to hide in this true breast
> And let the soul forth that adoreth thee,
> I lay it naked to the deadly stroke
> And humbly beg the death upon my knee.
> Nay, do not pause: for I did kill King Henry—
> But 'twas thy beauty that provokèd me.
> Nay, now dispatch: 'twas I that stabbed
>   young Edward—
> But 'twas thy heavenly face that set me on.
>   *(I, ii, 171–182)*

Ornately patterned verse, indeed! But is the following piece
of impudent parody by Falstaff pretending to speak to the
Prince of Wales in the sententious tones of his kingly father
any less ornately patterned?

> That thou art my son I have partly thy mother's
> word, partly my own opinion, but chiefly a vil-
> lainous trick of thine eye and a foolish hanging of
> thy nether lip that doth warrant me. If then thou
> be son to me, here lies the point: why, being son to
> me, art thou so pointed at?
>   *(1 Henry IV, II, iv, 384–389)*

If the purpose of all of these examples is to illustrate the
presence of some significant similarities between Shakespeare's prose and his verse, the differences between the two
mediums are nonetheless real and interesting. All three of
the preceding prose passages will be seen—will be heard!—
to have a lifelike quality, a certain smack of the colloquial,

an idiosyncratic flavor that supports the illusion that the words we are hearing have been uttered by a living man.

Two explanations for this lifelike quality may be advanced without recklessness. Shakespeare wrote his prose in an age that made no sharp distinction between literary dramatic prose and the prose of common speech. The speech of Elizabethan London, and, indeed, of Elizabethan rural England, like the speech of many Irishmen today, appeared capable of richer and more variegated effects than does our modern prose. No writer ever possessed a sharper ear than did Shakespeare for the uninhibited natural rhythms and the unselfconscious color tones of everyday speech, as is evidenced by the language of his comic characters, his Bottoms and his Dogberrys.

Additionally, the very act of writing prose to be spoken in dialogue might be said to invite the writer to hit on the give-and-take, cut-and-dash rhythms and the familiar and even idiosyncratic diction of living speech. But this explanation cannot stand alone without careful qualification. For it is evident that as much might be said for verse, since it, too, like all language in drama, must be pressed into service as dialogue—the playwright's sole form of expression.

Although they are, I think, suggestive, both these "explanations" are only partial and incomplete, therefore not fully satisfactory. The effort at a more complete explanation brings us naturally to consider the special uses to which Shakespeare put his prose. It is here that we will discover why so much of it has that combination of nervous rhythms, colloquial diction, and homely idiom that makes it lifelike. As is so often the case with Shakespeare, this process of discovery will find us tracing his evolutionary movement from the conventional to the unique.

We have repeatedly seen that Shakespearean plays make no effort to be naturalistic. They rely for the most part on nonillusionistic means to achieve the idealized ends that characterize the Renaissance concept of drama. Nevertheless, as we have observed from time to time, they occasionally reveal the playwright making concessions to that kind of credibility which we associate with realism. (We may mention the use of both the upper and the main platform, together with scaling ladders, to depict the siege of Harfleur in *Henry V.*)

In response to the need for a certain minimal credibility, several conventions concerning the use of prose had become established in British drama before Shakespeare began to write plays. Kyd, Marlowe, Greene, and Peele, among others, had developed these uses, and Shakespeare followed their example. Two of these conventions—the use of prose in letters and proclamations and in the speech of madmen—are by their very nature exceptional; the third— its use for comic matter—is commonplace. These three conventional uses of prose, and Shakespeare's departures from two of them, deserve a few words of explanation.

Letters and proclamations were apparently viewed by dramatists (and, it may be assumed, by their audiences) as a kind of intrusion into the play of something from the world without. Since no one in real life (the world without) wrote either of these forms in verse, it was thought too great a departure from reality to translate them into verse in a play. At the same time, then as now, madmen were viewed as abnormal. Since verse was the normal form of discourse in the earlier drama, any departure from the normal, as in the deranged speech of one who is mad, would be best signaled and expressed in prose. Finally, because comic matter was viewed by these forerunners of Shakespeare as a kind of decline into absurdity from the loftier levels achieved by serious verse, the doggerel originally spoken by comic characters, with its looping rhythms and ragged meters, was easily converted into prose.

Shakespeare adopted these conventions. *Macbeth* conveniently provides vividly clear examples of all three. The first may be found in the letter from Macbeth to his wife telling her of his singular meeting with the three witches ("They met me in the day of success, and I have learn'd by the perfect'st report they have more in them than mortal knowledge."); the second, in Lady Macbeth's sleepwalking scene wherein we witness the actions and hear the words of a mind deranged by guilt ("Out, damned spot! Out, I say! One—two—why then 'tis time to do't. Hell is murky. Fie, my lord, fie! a soldier and afeared?"); the third, in the scene in which the drunken porter acts out a grim little comedy of his own devising as he sleepily attends to the knocking at the gate of Macbeth's castle soon after the dreadful murder of King Duncan ("Here's a knocking indeed! If a man were porter of hell gate, he should have old turning the key.")

Apparently, neither letters nor proclamations presented Shakespeare with the need or the incentive to depart from the prose style convention. But scenes of madness and, more especially, comic scenes inspired more varied responses.

It is true that most of Shakespeare's madmen—real or simulated—speak in prose. Thus we observe his maintaining the convention when he permits Hamlet to assume "an antic disposition" ("I am but mad north-northwest. When the wind is southerly I know a hawk from a handsaw.") But in the same play, when it suits his purposes to do so, he gives the truly mad Ophelia a kind of broken music to speak—one moment prose ("Well, God dild you. They say the owl was a baker's daughter."), the next moment a kind of bawdy verse in which he appears to have anticipated much that Freud would later strive to teach us about the workings of the psyche ("Then up he rose and donned his clo'es / And dupped the chamber door / Let in the maid, that out a maid / Never departed more"). And he mixes forms of discourse even more astonishingly in those scenes midway through *King Lear* in which he brings together a most curious trio—the maddened king; a disinherited son, Edgar, who is simulating madness to avoid detection; and what the Elizabethans called a natural fool, Lear's court jester—and then permits these three to deliver up a mélange of prose, riming verse, blank verse, and snatches of song and doggerel which yield a language of pain and poignancy that is without antecedent or parallel.

Concerning comic matter, Shakespeare did not so much violate the convention as expand it. Low-comedy scenes (scenes involving the hostlers in *1 Henry IV,* the Montague and Capulet servants in *Romeo and Juliet,* the "watch" in *Much Ado About Nothing,* the rude mechanicals in *A Midsummer Night's Dream*) are in prose. So are realistic scenes of everyday life (almost all of the scenes in *The Merry Wives of Windsor,* the king's conversation with his soldiers on the eve of the battle of Agincourt in *Henry V,* Hamlet's talking with the players, Malvolio's receiving and issuing of household orders in *Twelfth Night).* And scenes of bantering give-and-take, even when the speakers are of the upper classes, are often in prose (Beatrice and Benedick's word duels in *Much Ado About Nothing,* Rosalind's teasing of Orlando in *As You Like It).*

But Shakespeare expanded the functions of prose. An offshoot of comic prose is the language of his satirists. Probably the most foulmouthed satirist in all of Shakespeare is Thersites in *Troilus and Cressida:* he rails, in prose, against the very unheroic heroes in the Greek army, in a play whose author is almost as unsparing of these worthies as is his scabrous spokesman. But not all of Shakespeare's satirists engage in vituperation. Indeed, some of the best satiric passages emerge from such gently witty critics of folly as Rosalind. And Falstaff's sallies are never bitter. Still, the art of denigration is one form of eloquence, and Shakespeare discovers in prose the proper vehicle for its expression. Casca's contemptuous description of the Roman mob (" . . . clapped their chopt hands, and threw up their sweaty nightcaps, and uttered such a deal of stinking breath. . . . "), Iago's obscene goading of Brabantio (". . . you'll have your daughter covered with a Barbary horse; you'll have your nephews neigh to you. . . . "), and Edmund's cynical characterization of his father's pious concern over heaven's displeasure with human wickedness ("An admirable evasion of whoremaster man, to lay his goatish disposition on the charge of a star") come to mind.

It is only a step from satire and denigration, with its emphasis on wit and its consequent appeal to the mind, to the use of prose as the appropriate vehicle for the voice of reason. So Brutus, anxious to allay the fears and doubts of the Roman citizenry and confident that the logic of his actions in killing the potential tyrant, Caesar, would find a logical response in the minds of his listeners, speaks a measured and balanced prose. Whereas Antony, anxious to let slip the dogs of war and fully aware of the emotional instability of his audience, inflames them with a blank verse

shrewdly calculated to arouse their feelings. And in an earlier Roman era (although in a later Shakespearean play), the
astute politician Menenius, speaking prose, seeks vainly to
give the counsel of reason to his perversely proud protégé,
Coriolanus, who constantly exposes his true feelings to the
mob in highly charged verse.

Reason suggests a cool tone. We are not surprised, then, to
find Shakespeare using prose for passages that are deliberately low keyed. The beginning of *King Lear* comes to mind.
Everyone who has read or seen the play recalls the powerful
and passionate blank verse that Shakespeare uses to convey
the sound and fury of the old king's wrath, directed first
against Cordelia because she will not flatter him ("Let it be
so, thy truth then be thy dower. . . . Here I disclaim all my
paternal care. . . . And as a stranger to my heart and me /
Hold thee from this forever.") and then against Kent because he has the decent courage to protest the outrage
("Peace, Kent! . . . . The bow is bent and drawn; make from
the shaft."). But many, recalling this high-pitched language
in which several characters talk at the top of their voices for
many lines, may forget the almost casual, low-keyed, seemingly back-of-the-hand remarks with which the play begins,
in a conversation between Gloucester, Kent, and Edmund.
Besides introducing us to these three important characters
and providing certain information (including the bastardy of
Edmund), this seemingly offhand prose serves to establish
in a rather subtle way the moral (more exactly, the immoral)
climate of the court, as Gloucester's youthful sexual pecca-
dillos are lightly mentioned and dismissed. Moreover—and
here we move to the core of the present concern—this relatively flat and monochromatic prose stands out in sharp
contrast to the high-flown verse that follows.

Then, at the scene's end, Shakespeare once again displays
linguistic cunning. He sweeps everyone (Lear, Gloucester,
Cordelia, the King of France, and the Duke of Burgundy) off
the stage—Kent has already been banished—and leaves only
the two cormorant daughters, Goneril and Regan. We have
just listened to these two vying with each other to see who
could best conceal her empty heart in bombastic and in-
flated verse.

Goneril   Sir, I love you more than word can wield the matter;
Dearer than eyesight, space, and liberty;
Beyond what can be valuèd, rich or rare. . . .

                                    (*I, i*, 55–57)

Regan   . . . I profess
Myself an enemy to all others joys
Which the most precious square of sense possesses,
And find I am alone felicitate
In your dear Highness' love.

                                    (*I, i*, 72–76)

Now, alone, they drop their masks and their voices and
speak a kind of cool prose that freezes our hearts and chills
our minds.

Goneril   You see how full of changes his age is. The observation we have made of it hath not been little. He always
loved our sister most, and with what poor judgment he
hath now cast her off appears too grossly.

                                    (*I, i*, 288–291)

Regan   'Tis the infirmity of his age; yet he hath ever but
slenderly known himself.   (*I, i*, 292–293)

Shakespeare has used a contrast in language to establish a
contrast in tone and mood.

This *principle of contrast* is Shakespeare's great discovery. It is to this we should look for any useful rationale that
underlies his choice of verse or prose. We will find the principle of dramatic contrast manifesting itself in a number of
ways. It will serve to point up a vivid contrast in
character—the tight-reined verse of the idealistic Hotspur
contrasting with the loose-reined prose of the realistic
Falstaff. It will serve to illuminate different aspects of the

same character—Hamlet mad and Hamlet in total control
speaks prose, but Hamlet tender or introspectively pensive
speaks verse. It will serve to distinguish point of view—
lovesick Orlando manufactures proper sentiments in
wooden verse, but Rosalind "wash[es] [his] liver as clean as
a sound sheep's heart" in a wonderfully earthy prose. It will
underscore a contrast in purpose—servants idling in a pan-
try engage in idle chatter in prose, but a servant "thrilled
with remorse" attempts in manly verse to stay the brutal
Cornwall from blinding old Gloucester even though doing
this costs him his own life.

Our final example permits us to clear up a common confusion. There is a widespread notion that class lines determine when prose and when verse is spoken in Elizabethan
drama. It is not hard to see how this notion came into being.
We have already indicated that much comic matter appears
in the medium of prose. And in a class society, very often
the "comics" are servants, country fellows, and others in
low estate. But once again Shakespeare slips through the net
of such easy formulas. A lower-class character, like
Cornwall's servant, speaks verse when the situation in
which he finds himself depicts human experience at a high
pitch. The poor groom who once attended to Richard II's
"roan Barbary" speaks dignified blank verse when, of all
Richard's sometime followers, he alone visits his master,
now in solitary confinement in Pomfret Castle. Conversely,
members of the upper classes adopt prose when they find
themselves in conversation with household servants and
familiars (Olivia speaks prose to Feste, Malvolio, and
Maria) or with tavern disreputables (Prince Hal speaks
prose to Falstaff and the Eastcheap gang and then sol-
iloquizes in blank verse after their departure from the
scene). More significantly, when Shakespeare wishes to
ventilate the conversations of his upper-class young lovers
with the fresh air of healthy humor, he gives them prose to
speak, as witness Beatrice and Benedick, who never speak
anything else to each other.

This brings us back full circle to our earlier assertion:

Shakespeare did not conceive of prose as a medium inferior to verse. He did not assume that the properties of verse and prose were foreign to each other. We suggested that the easy way in which we, as readers and listeners, move from verse (especially blank verse) to prose with no sense of disruption is the proof of Shakespeare's skill at using both of these language media so resourcefully that there is no invidious distinction between them. Further proof, if any is needed, may be found in the fact that the two characters universally acclaimed as the most eloquent of all Shakespeare's talkers—I refer to Hamlet and Falstaff—are both speakers of prose. Indeed, Falstaff speaks nothing else.

Our last word on the subject takes the form of something very like a paradox and attempts to realize the promise held out to the reader earlier in this section—that we would account for the lifelike quality of Shakespeare's prose. The paradox is this: Shakespeare's prose, while making use of every technique of metaphor and rhetoric found in his verse, yet remains conversational and idiomatic—qualities that we associate with the voices of living people. That he elected to use prose whenever his speakers were talking easily, unaffectedly, without self-conscious strain seems to be part of the secret. One wants to say that he caught the English people's natural language on the wing. But then one wants to add that the flights of words he netted in his prose were skimming close to the earth, not soaring into the empyrean. Efforts at general description are futile. Samples from Shakespeare are called for, and the best of these must come from Hamlet and Falstaff.

Here is Hamlet responding to the weary dutifulness of Polonius who, in answer to Hamlet's request "Will you see the players well bestowed?" has replied, "My lord, I will use them according to their desert."

> God's bodkin, man, much better! Use every man
> after his desert, and who shall scape whipping?
> Use them after your own honor and dignity. The
> less they deserve, the more merit is in your
> bounty. Take them in.   (*II, ii, 516–520*)

And here is Hamlet replying to Osric, who has conveyed the treacherous invitation to the fencing bout:

> Sir, I will walk here in the hall. If it please his
> majesty, it is the breathing time of day with me.
> Let the foils he brought, the gentleman willing,
> and the king hold his purpose, I will win for him
> an I can; if not, I will gain nothing but my shame
> and the odd hits.   *(V, ii, 167–171)*

And here is Hamlet's contemptuous response to Guilden-stern, who has confessed to having no skill in playing the recorder although he has been trying to play on an instrument of much greater complexity—Hamlet's mind:

> Why, look you now, how unworthy a thing you
> make of me! You would play upon me, you would
> seem to know my stops, you would pluck out the
> heart of my mystery, you would sound me from
> my lowest note to the top of my compass; and
> there is much music, excellent voice in this little
> organ, yet cannot you make it speak. 'Sblood, do
> you think I am easier to be played on than a pipe?
> Call me what instrument you will, though you
> can fret me, you cannot play upon me.
>   *(III, ii, 349–357)*

This easy way with language of a peerless prince can be—and is—equalled by "an old fat man," albeit in a very different style when, in response to Prince Hal's goading questions, "How long is't ago . . . since thou sawest thine own knee?" he replies:

> My own knee? When I was about thy years, Hal, I
> was not an eagle's talent in the waist; I could have
> crept into any alderman's thumb-ring. A plague
> of sighing and grief! It blows a man up like a
> bladder.   *(1 Henry IV, II, iv, 313–316)*

Falstaff is inexhaustible when it comes to inventing variations on the theme of his own appearance and qualities.

> My lord, I was born about three of the clock in the afternoon, with a white head and something a round belly. For my voice, I have lost it with halloing and singing of anthems. To approve my youth further, I will not. The truth is, I am only old in judgment and understanding. . . .
>
> *(2 Henry IV, I, ii, 177–182)*

And the depth of his real derelictions is only equaled by the height of his invented valor.

> But look you pray, all you that kiss my lady Peace at home, that our armies join not in a hot day, for, by the Lord, I take but two shirts out with me, and I mean not to sweat extraordinarily. If it be a hot day, and I brandish anything but a bottle, I would I might never spit white again. There is not a dangerous action can peep out his head but I am thrust upon it. Well, I cannot last ever. But it was always yet the trick of our English nation, if they have a good thing, to make it too common.
>
> *(2 Henry IV, I, ii, 194–203)*

Because Shakespeare did not regard prose as a medium inferior to verse, he could do more things with it than did his contemporaries. Thus, his achievement with prose is unique. Its excellence may be found always in its simplicity, ease, vigor, and colloquial naturalness. It may be found, moreover, in the care and accuracy with which he could tailor a particular prose style to suit a particular character. Hamlet's prose style is galvanic: the distance between the inciting force of his words and the reader-spectator's shock of recognition is short. Falstaff's prose style is relaxed: the distance between the stimulus and response is much longer. The distinction is nearly as sharp as that between an angry blow and a playful nudge. But the communication is equally clear and vivid. Language cannot do more than this.

9
PLAYHOUSE AND PLATFORM

A. PLAYHOUSE

> . . . Within this wooden O . . .
> *(Henry V, Prologue, 13)*

When Shakespeare inserted into the speech he gave the Prologue in *Henry V* the metaphor "Within this wooden O," he was presumably describing the kind of playhouse he and his audiences were accustomed to. He may even have been referring to the Globe Theater. It is natural to want to think so, for both the letter *O* and the theater's name, the *Globe,* suggest the same spherical structure. And it is also pleasantly fitting to think so, for *Henry V* was first performed in 1599, the very year in which this most famous playhouse in the English-speaking world was constructed.

Natural, but not inevitable; pleasant, but not quite likely. For the weight of historical evidence suggests that *Henry V* was played early in 1599, whereas the Globe, it appears, was not completed and ready for use until late August or early September of that year. And "this wooden O" might just as easily have described The Theatre or The Curtain (one authority is sure it is a reference to the latter),[1] two older theaters situated north of the city of London where Shakespeare's company performed for several years before they built the Globe. In short, Shakespeare's famous metaphor may aptly describe a typical, rather than a unique, Elizabethan public playhouse.

This is, perhaps, as it should be, for it reflects the necessarily conjectural state of much of our information about these Elizabethan and early Jacobean playhouses and their stages. It is not that we do not know some things, and those fairly exactly. We do possess two extant builders' contracts for the construction of two theaters, and these give us quite exact information about building materials and specifications. And we do have one contemporary drawing of the *stage* of a rival theater, the Swan; some near-contemporary panoramic drawings of London that depict theater *exteriors;* and, of course, such allusions from several playscripts as the one just quoted from Shakespeare. Moreover, we possess the invaluable diary of Philip Henslowe, one of the most successful theater owners of the time. His diary is a storehouse of information concerning such various matters as Elizabethan stage properties, a repertory company's schedule of performances, and box-office receipts. But the hard facts we have do not permit us fully and exactly to reconstruct any one theater down to its last details or to pinpoint with absolute certainty those details that any, or every, Elizabethan playhouse and stage had in common.

This is not an unhappy state of affairs. We need not be incontrovertibly certain of the precise shape of any specific Elizabethan public playhouse to arrive at a good understanding of the effects this kind of playhouse had on the plays Shakespeare wrote to be performed there. (We may *surmise* that the exterior of the Globe was round, we *know* that the Fortune was square, and we have reason to *believe* that some other theaters were polygonal or hexagonal.) Whatever their exact exterior shapes, these playhouses had much in common. And we know what they had in common. A representative English public theater of Shakespeare's time was a three-storied amphitheater surrounding an unroofed yard. The triple-tiered galleries surrounding the yard were roofed. Perhaps 12 feet deep, these galleries varied slightly in height, the ground-level gallery in one known instance measuring 12 feet, the second 11 feet, and the topmost 9 feet. Some portions of these encircling galleries appear to have been partitioned, thus affording *private rooms* that contained the most expensive seats.

The yard that the galleries surrounded was not very wide, 55 feet across in the instance of the Fortune, whose construction contract survives. Since this contract contained a clause to the effect that its stage should be "contrived and fashioned like unto" the Globe, we may assume that the dimensions of the latter's yard, as well as its stage, were similar to those of the Fortune. More important for our understanding than the exact arithmetic of these specifications is the realization that the diameter of these theaters—probably about 80 feet from one exterior wall to its opposite—was not great. When to this insight is added the knowledge that the great platform stage on which almost all the action of Shakespeare's plays took place projected halfway (or about 27 feet) into the yard, and that many in the audience stood in that yard surrounding the stage on three sides while the seated spectators were probably never farther away from the actors than 50 feet, with most of them much closer, then we are in a position to realize that the two all-important components of a Shakespearean play performed in a public theater were the actors and the lines the playwright gave them to speak. Clearly this was an actors' theater and a playwright's theater.

The Elizabethan metaphors for the yard—the *pit*—and for those who stood in it to watch the plays—the *groundlings*—prove instructive. The yard was called the pit because the platform stage was elevated 5 or 6 feet above the ground; and so, viewed from the perspective of the elevated actors, these earthbound spectators were indeed groundlings. Conversely, "these, our actors," dazzlingly costumed always, may well have appeared outsized to the spectators who stared up at them from below as they strutted and fretted "their hour upon the stage."

Not all of Shakespeare's audiences would be looking up, of

course. Those who had paid an extra penny for a seat in the first-floor gallery would look straight at the players, while those who had paid still more for the privilege would be looking down on them from their vantage points in the second and third galleries, somewhat as we do from our modern balconies and loges. Occasionally, some few gallants, wanting to be seen as well as see, might be seated on stools arranged around the periphery of the platform stage, but this presumably was not an everyday arrangement and appears to be a late development influenced by the adoption of this practice in the indoor or *private* theaters, as they were called.

Standing or seated, the audience was very proximate to the actors—far more so than we are today in our box-set theaters (although our arena theaters, or *theaters-in-the-round*, as they are known, produce a proximity and an effect that parallel those achieved in Shakespeare's theater). In Shakespeare's theater, illusion depended on the actor's ability to cast a spell over the audience, and for this purpose his most powerful charms were the playwright's words. No lights, no projections on a screen, no elaborate sets dictated to the audience what it should see. It saw with its mind's eye the images created by the words of the playwright delivered eloquently through the mouths of the gesticulating actors. "Let us . . . on your imaginary forces work," Shakespeare once said directly to the audience gathered to witness *Henry V.*

Since the Globe plays were performed in the afternoon, unaided by artificial light, in a country of cloudy skies and moist, foggy weather, one is compelled to conclude that this proximity of spectator to actor was an invention born of necessity. Even so, theater historians differ as to whether or not the *sight lines* (the visibility of the actor to the spectator from various angles of vision) were uniformly good. It seems certain that they were good for any action played on the forward part of the platform stage, and this supports the conclusion that by far the greatest portion of the action in Shakespearean plays took place there. Concerning other playing areas, wittily referred to by one scholar as the *sub-*

urbs of the central staging area, we will momentarily postpone discussion while directing our attention to still another feature of this playhouse considered as an entire structure.

If there appears to be some argument concerning the quality of the sight lines in this playhouse, there is none about the quality of the acoustics. In this connection, it would not be misleading to suggest that if you have never seen a plausible drawing of the exterior of an Elizabethan theater, you should imagine a kind of squat tower or, more fancifully but not unreasonably, a gigantic drum or cylinder. You will then more easily understand why one student of the period has likened the sound of the human voice projected in this theater to the sound of words spoken in a huge padded well, with the vocal sounds resonating audibly to the farthest reaches.[2]

This visual and auditory proximity of actor to audience has inspired some well-intentioned but dubious conjectures. Among these is the notion that discovers here the kind of intimacy that restores to a secular theater the spirit of ritual drama whose origins are in religion. A moment's reflection on one's own experiences in our modern theater-in-the-round is enough to arouse skepticism. Although it is true that the earliest English drama had its origins in religious ritual, those liturgical plays were pretty far removed in time from Shakespeare and his London audiences. Moreover our knowledge of Elizabethan Londoners persuades us that their reactions must have been more like ours than either sort is like that of the audiences that assembled in cathedrals to witness medieval tropes and dramas. It seems quite enough to assert the more demonstrable thesis that the Elizabethan theater helped to rivet audience attention on the actor and the lines he was given to speak. With little or nothing in the way of scenic illusion, and with only minimal stage properties to distract them, the members of Shakespeare's audiences were able to give their undivided attention to his words and to the actions of the actors who spoke them. This was a theater with no competition from set designers, lighting experts, production specialists, or egotistical directors anxious to place their own stamp on the author's play. When under these circumstances are introduced the greatest stage lines ever composed in English, spoken by a company of veteran actors uniformly reputed to be the best of their day, we have all the magic that such a conjunction of talent and circumstances ought to be asked to yield.

In fact, mundane matters may often afford more insight than do such abstract speculations. For instance, the seating capacity of Elizabethan playhouses is not without significance. Historians of later ages than our own will doubtless gauge the popularity of football from the size of our stadiums. So we can gauge the popularity of Elizabethan drama from the size of London's public theaters. During the height of Shakespeare's popularity, the decade from 1599 to 1609, there were several public theaters in pretty regular operation. Their seating capacities have been variously estimated, but apparently the largest could hold up to 3,000 spectators.[3] A figure in excess of 1,000 has been confidently advanced to represent the *average* attendance at an Elizabethan play.[4] This figure, there is evidence to show, was more than doubled for performances of hit plays. The London population that supported this entertainment is variously estimated at from 125,000 to 160,000 in round numbers, depending on whether the calculator is figuring the population within the walls of the city proper or is including in the total those who lived in the immediate environs.[5]

The special significance of all this for our inquiry is that a company of actors drawing such audiences will prosper, a prosperous company will be able to attract and hold the best actors and playwrights, and the combination will ensure the kind of continuity and longevity that can—and with Shakespeare's company did—elevate craftsmanship to artistry.

A homely economic note is relevant here. Shakespeare's plays were performed at popular prices. One penny (it has been estimated to have been worth about one-twelfth of a skilled craftsman's daily wage)[6] admitted a person through the single large entranceway opposite the stage to standing room in the yard; a second penny paid to a *gatherer* at an inner door or stairway secured a seat in the gallery; a third penny, a better seat and a cushion; and there were a few sixpenny and twelvepenny *rooms,* inevitably called *gentlemen's rooms*, close to the stage for the affluent.

Shakespeare's audience was truly representative of the London citizenry—a popular, not a coterie, audience. That fact determined Shakespeare to write plays of universal appeal. If he had not done so, we should not be reading them today. And so this popular audience found its way daily in clement weather to this popular theater. The best modern analogy is with our motion picture theaters: both they and Shakespeare's playhouse, by being accessible to nearly everyone, could be patronized by nearly everyone. Cynics notwithstanding, substantial segments of popular audiences will go for the best, so long as the best is pitched in a popular key. Good movies that hit the right note are preferred to poor movies. So Shakespeare's plays were preferred to the run-of-the-mill productions offered up in the public playhouses of Elizabethan London.

Where did the Globe audiences come from, and what did they see before them when they arrived to enjoy a play? The great majority of them came from the north side of the Thames, from the city proper, where they lived and worked. The Globe, like several other popular public theaters, was situated on the south side of the Thames. More precisely, it was in the borough of Southwark, the district of Bankside, and, significantly, within the *liberty* of the Clink, which kept it out of the censorious jurisdiction of the City. A flag waving from *the hut,* the topmost structure of the theater, announced *Play Today* for all those in London who cared to see. And they came across the Thames, ferried by hundreds of small boats or walking over London bridge. Those already on the southside of the Thames walked or rode horseback.

Once inside the Globe, they saw opposite the passage they had just entered the huge platform stage, elevated 5 or 6 feet off the ground and projecting straight out from that portion of the ground-level gallery given over to the actors to serve as their *tiring room* (dressing room, or, in today's parlance, *greenroom*). The space between the platform and the ground might be covered with wood palings or draped with cloth, black if the play to be performed was a tragedy, of lighter material if a comedy. Beneath the stage, the audience knew, was enough space to lower a trap in the floor of the platform, which might then serve as "Ophelia's grave" or as "the cellarage" to which the ghost of Hamlet's father was consigned or, yet again, might house the cauldron that served as the dreadful mixing bowl of the three witches in *Macbeth*. The tiring room would have two pairs of doors at either extreme of the backstage wall for the players' entrances and exits. On the second level, as an intrinsic part of the second-level gallery, was a place that could serve as a playing area if the play called for any scenes *above* or *aloft* or as a place for favored spectators if the play did not demand its use as an upper stage. Immediately below it, and between the stage doors, was a curtained-off recessed area or possibly a temporary structure protruding from the stage wall, either one of which could serve as the place where Claudius and Polonius hid behind the arras to listen to Hamlet talk to Ophelia; where, later, Polonius, again in hiding, would receive the deadly thrust from Hamlet's sword; or where the drunken Falstaff would be "discovered" asleep after the sheriff, who had been demanding knowledge of his whereabouts from Prince Hal, departed the Eastcheap Inn. Possibly a third-level gallery in the facade of the stage wall would be given over to the musicians, who might accompany songs during a performance, play during interludes between scenes of a performance, or perform after the play was over, when the principal comedian might entertain the audience with songs and jigs, much after the fashion of a London music hall or American burlesque performer. From either the top of the second-level gallery or from the third-level gallery would project a canopy or *shadow* extending about halfway over the platform stage, possibly supported by two sturdy pillars at its outer extremity. From this structure, special apparatus and even, in rare instances, performers could be lowered, if the play called for such exotic effects as a god descending from the heavens or some similar astonishment. Finally, at the top of the playhouse, were one or more huts, superstructures looking like small A-frames, in which stage machinery (including thunder machines) and devices for special effects were stored. From atop the uppermost hut flew the flag that announced the performance, and from a window in one of these huts sounded the trumpet that notified all within earshot that "the play is beginning."

Sir Philip Sidney once spoke of the peculiar power of a good story to hold old men from their firesides and children from their play. Something of this mesmerizing effect must have been exercised over his audiences by Shakespeare, for we have the astonishing testimony of an eyewitness how, during a performance of one of Shakespeare's least esteemed plays, *Henry VIII,* the Globe Theater caught fire and in a few minutes burned to the ground without anyone's being sufficiently aware of the danger, during the first few moments, to put out the fire or set in motion those who might have. Happily, this incident, in which life competed with art as a source of high drama, resulted in no fatalities. The details have been preserved in a contemporary account. On June 29, 1613, we are told, during a performance of *Henry VIII,* the Globe was burned to the ground by a fire that started when some wadding from a cannon used for special effects landed on the thatch roof of the upper galleries, whereupon "being thought at first but an idle smoke, and their eyes more attentive to the show, it kindled inwardly, and ran round like a train, consuming within less than an hour the whole house to the ground." [7] As in many Shakespearean plays, comedy competed with high drama: although no lives were lost, "one man had his breeches set on fire, that would perhaps have boiled him, if he had not by the benefit of a provident wit put it out with a bottle of ale." [8] The Globe was rebuilt the following year of the brick, timber, and mortar that were the common building materials of the theaters of the day, but this time the topmost gallery was roofed with stone tile.

B. PLATFORM

> . . . On this unworthy scaffold . . .
> *(Henry V, Prologue, 10)*

In referring to his theater as "this wooden O," Shakespeare was probably reporting a fact. When, however, in that same Prologue to *Henry V,* he referred to the platform stage on which his plays were performed as "this unworthy scaffold," he appears to have been rendering a judgment. Was Shakespeare in fact displeased with his stage? Did he feel that he and his fellow actors were made poor by the limitations of this nearly bare platform that could not "hold / The vasty fields of France" or contain the glorious English army "that did affright the air at Agincourt"?

There is no good reason to think so. Prologues are highly conventional utterances, and one of their conventions is a mildly self-deprecatory tone—a kind of oral genuflection before the audience one is struggling to please. Given his hero—England's favorite king—and his subject—that hero's famous victories over the despised French—and given the predictable expectations of his strongly nationalistic audience, it is little wonder that Shakespeare thought it wise to remind his listeners that a truly panoramic spectacle could be reproduced only in the theater of the mind ("Let us . . . on your imaginary forces work"). Nearly three and one-half centuries would have to pass before Laurence Olivier, aided by all the resources of modern motion picture technology, would produce a version of *Henry V* in which the dullest spectator could see "A kingdom for a stage, princes to act, / And monarchs to behold the swelling scene." Even so, it remains a moot question among imaginative lovers of Shakespeare whether the eye-filling sequences provided by the cameras and projectors of the modern movie are equal to the ear-pleasing lines supplied by a handful of actors declaiming from the platform stage of the Globe.

What was this stage like when actors were performing plays there? Since you are urged to try to stage Shakespearean plays in your mind's eye, it is proper at this point to provide you with a succession of clear examples of precisely how Shakespeare used all the playing areas his theater afforded him. So as to prevent your "inner eye" from jumping around, and to eliminate unnecessary confusion, we will proceed systematically to focus on each of these playing areas from the ground upward, pausing to discuss each in turn. In every instance, we will provide one or more examples of how Shakespeare actually used that particular stage or part of the stage. Whenever it seems necessary or desirable, we will take time to reconstruct the context of the scene to which we are alluding, and often we will accompany our reference by illuminating lines from the Shakespearean text.

Starting with the place beneath the elevated stage, variously referred to as *the cellarage* and *the hell,* we can scarcely do better than to recall bits of the dialogue between Hamlet and Horatio and the two soldiers, Marcellus and Bernardo, immediately after the ghost of his father has appeared to Hamlet. The ghost, having revealed to his son the circumstances of his foul murder and charged him to revenge that act, has departed with the final admonition, "Remember me." Thereafter, joined by Horatio and the two guardsmen, Hamlet seeks to swear them to secrecy concerning the night's events. At this point, we are told by means of Hamlet's speeches, by an explicit stage direction, and by two remarks made by the unseen ghost itself that this "perturbèd spirit" is working out his prescribed penance in a subterranean purgatory—the space beneath the stage. Here is the essential evidence excerpted from the longer scene:

Hamlet	Upon my sword.
Marcellus	We have sworn, my lord, already.
Hamlet	Indeed, upon my sword, indeed.
	Ghost cries under the stage.
Ghost	Swear.
Hamlet	Ha, ha, boy, says't thou so? Art thou there truepenny?
	Come on. You hear this fellow in the cellarage.

Consent to swear.

....

Ghost   Swear by his sword.
Hamlet   Well said, old mole! Cans't work i' th' earth so fast?
(I, v, 147–152, 161–162)

Unlike many contemporary playwrights who seek to maintain the illusion of "reality," Shakespeare provides Hamlet
with a phrase, "the cellarage," that reminds his audience
that they are witnessing a play. This was a nonillusionistic
theater in which the pitch of emotion was far more important than the degree of representational fidelity.

By logical progression, we move now from the place beneath the stage to the trapdoor (there may well have been
more than one) that gave access to that place from the platform stage above it. Again we draw on *Hamlet* for our illustration. This time, the evidence is confined to the dialogue,
there being preserved no explicit stage direction calling attention to this device. This omission need not disturb us
since it is consistent with Shakespeare's regular practice. So
clearly did he embed most of his stage directions in his
dialogue that he appears to have made very sparing use of
explicit and separate stage directions. He did not need
them.

Our scene is the burial ground of Elsinore. Hamlet and
Horatio have been philosophizing on the nature of life and
death, their conversation punctuated by the quips of the
grimly humorous gravedigger, when they notice a funeral
procession approaching. We know what Hamlet does not:
it is the funeral of the pathetically lovely Ophelia; and, as
this portion of the scene begins, her brother, Laertes,
remonstrates with the priest over her "maimèd rites"—the
limited service permitted by a church official really reluctant to permit any service at all because he regards her
death as "questionable," the circumstances of it suggesting
a suicide. In the course of the following dialogue, we discover the clues to the action. At one moment, Laertes jumps
into the half-open grave into which Ophelia's coffin has
been lowered, and a few seconds later, Hamlet leaps in after
him—and they grapple!

Laertes	Hold off the earth awhile,
	Till I have caught her once more in my arms.
	Now pile your dust upon the quick and dead....

....

Hamlet	What is he whose grief
	Bears such an emphasis?

....

	This is I,
	Hamlet, the Dane.
Laertes	The devil take thy soul!
Hamlet	Thou prays't not well
	I prithee take thy fingers from my throat

....

King	Pluck them asunder.

(V, i, 236–238, 241–242, 244–247, 251)

How a trapdoor could be used as a place through which to lower Ophelia's coffin and as the grave into which Laertes and Hamlet successively leap is so clear as to make the inference that it was so employed well nigh irresistible. But if this example retains a vestige of the speculative about it, the line from *Macbeth,* "Why sinks that cauldron?" (IV, i, 106) would appear to admit of no other construction. Nor would the fishing of a suit of rusty armor out of the sea (*Pericles,* II, i, 112–115) or the excavating of Yorick's skull from yet another grave (*Hamlet,* V, i, 161–169). Still, Shakespeare appears to have made rather sparing use of this device.

Since the overwhelming majority of scenes and parts of scenes in Shakespeare were played on the large platform stage that was the umbilicus of the entire theater, we face an embarrassment of riches when we are asked to select appropriate illustrations of its use. The solution, clearly, is to point out the range of scenes that were played there. We may start with a scene involving a single speaker, and he standing at the forward reaches of this huge platform talking directly to the members of the audience, who are gathered all about him. The opening lines of *Richard III* come to mind at once.

Richard   Now is the winter of our discontent
            Made glorious summer by this son of York. . . .
                                        (I, i, 1–2)

Whereupon we are treated to a witty disquisition on the reasons why "this weak piping time of peace" is not suitable to a deformed monster who will make war on all mankind. His threat is made explicit.

And therefore, since I cannot prove a lover
To entertain these fair well-spoken days,
I am determinèd to prove a villain. . . .
                                        (I, i, 28–30)

From solos, we may move through duets (Romeo meeting Juliet), trios (Hamlet exposing the clumsy subterfuges of Rosencrantz and Guildenstern), quartets (Macbeth ruminating rapturously over the witches' cryptic prophecies while Banquo, Ross, and Angus provide the counterpoint of the free speech of men with clear consciences), sextets (Caesar engaged in rapid colloquy with five Roman senators who are, unbeknownst to him, about to terminate his life as they terminate their conversation), octets (the four foolish lords of *Love's Labor's Lost* fencing maladroitly with four frivolous ladies whose verbal thrusts they cannot parry), and, by this declension, to numerous crowd scenes (the masked ball at the Capulets', the susceptible commoners whose feelings are manipulated by Antony's demagoguery, the courtiers who are "but mutes or audience" to the multiple murders that lead up to Hamlet's death).

These are enough to illustrate both the range and the variety of action on the platform stage. But there remain some curiosities, of which at least two are worth citing for the light they throw on the stage conventions of Shakespeare's day. Toward the end of *Richard III*, on the eve of the conclusive battle that will see Richard defeated and slain, Shakespeare adapts a piece of medieval stagecraft suitable to his needs. He wishes to have a succession of ghosts of the persons Richard has slain appear alternately to curse evil

Richard and to bless godly Richmond, the opponents in the next day's battle. To do this, he boldly employs the non-illusionistic device of the medieval stage: he places side by side on this stage the two tents that belong to Richard and Richmond, respectively, and that ostensibly are miles apart on the far reaches of Bosworth Field. The ghosts then enter while the two adversaries lie asleep and alternately bestow maledictions on the one and benedictions on the other, which both receive as in a dream. The ghosts departed, Shakespeare then has Richard awaken first, attempt to digest his dreams, talk over their effects with his henchman, Ratcliffe, and exit; whereupon Richmond awakens, describes his favorable dreams to his attendant lords, addresses his troops, and exits in turn. Richard enters once more, speaks to two of his henchmen, addresses his troops before battle, and the stage is finally cleared (V, ii, 118—352).

Another nonillusionistic staging device appears in *Romeo and Juliet*. Romeo and his friends, among them Mercutio and Benvolio, are dressed as *maskers* to attend the supper party being given by Old Capulet, a by no means unusual or unwelcome custom of the time, even though, technically, the maskers have not been invited. As they set out for the party, we discover a curious stage direction.

> *They march about the stage, and Servingmen come forth with napkins.*
>
> *(I, v, s.d.)*

With the advent of the servingmen, the stage, which has been a street in Verona, automatically becomes Capulet's dining room. There is nothing unusual in this: as we have pointed out previously, place follows persons on the Shakespearean stage. What is unusual is the distinct possibility—indeed, the likelihood—that the maskers do not ever leave the stage, since the "marching about" would itself signal a forthcoming change in locale. This is still one more illustration—if another is needed—of the great fluidity of Shakespeare's stage, an instrument of many resources which he learned to exploit freely and easily.

Surely the most hotly disputed of the playing places centers in the area between the two stage doors at either extreme of the rear wall that divided the platform stage from the tiring room. Today, most scholars of the theater refuse to employ the term *inner stage,* as it was once popularly known, to designate this place. Inner stage suggests a kind of permanence, a kind of formality, a kind of complexity such as might be found in an alcove—an architectural feature whose existence these scholars are now inclined to deny. We need not concern ourselves with these scholarly disputes but can, instead, content ourselves with envisioning some area or portable structure or both curtained off from the main stage. These curtains could be employed, at times, for concealment, as when Claudius and Polonius engage to act as "lawful espials" overhearing Hamlet's conversation with Ophelia so as to determine whether or not he is mad. At other times, the curtains could be drawn back to disclose a brief scene that in the Elizabethan theater went by the somewhat quaint name *discovery*. To cite one of the best-known examples, I quote the actual stage direction:

> *Here Prospero discovers Ferdinand and Miranda playing chess.*
>
> (*The Tempest, V, i, s.d., after 171*)

Or, more conjecturally, when the Nurse comes to try to wake Juliet from her drug-induced sleep, we may infer from her remarks that she first speaks to a Juliet hidden from view by bed curtains and discovers the young girl fully dressed only when she draws those curtains (IV, v, 1–16).

The most important thing to suggest about this controverted playing area is not the precise nature of this stage or its furniture or even the question of whether any specific scene was played there, but, rather, the certainty that any action beginning there would almost inevitably be drawn out onto the full platform stage as quickly as the playwright could manage it. No practical theater man, as Shakespeare was so manifestly, was going to risk obscuring or muffling any of his scenes from any portion of his audience.

If there has been dispute concerning both the nature and

the extent of Shakespeare's use of this curtained area, there is little concerning his use of an upper area, almost certainly the second gallery immediately above the rear stage wall. Once again, we may draw on some explicit stage directions as well as on the evidence found in Shakespeare's dialogue.

The most famous example involves the lovers, Romeo and Juliet. And here the evidence of both kinds—explicit stage directions and cues provided by the dialogue—is abundant. The following passages are presented in the order in which Shakespeare introduced them into his play. The first is the most celebrated.

Romeo   But soft! What light through yonder window breaks?
It is the East, and Juliet is the sun!   (*II, ii, 2–3*)

Parenthetically, it should be noted that the word *balcony* never appears, although a stage tradition has resulted in the world's thinking of a balcony, not a window, as the setting for the wooing scene. Shakespeare's next reference is to a stage property.

Romeo   Within this hour my man shall be with thee
And bring thee cords made like a tackled stair....
                                                     (*II, iv, 177–178*)

Thus Romeo arranges to deliver a rope ladder to the Nurse. She later confirms this plan in her remark to Juliet.

Nurse   Hie you to church; I must another way,
To fetch a ladder, by the which your love
Must climb a bird's nest soon when it is dark.
                                                     (*II, v, 72–74*)

Then, still later, when Juliet is impatiently waiting for Romeo to join her on their wedding night, we read this stage direction:

> *Enter Nurse, with cords.*   (*III, ii, s.d., after 31*)

The Friar aids the lovers. At one point he actively furthers their rendezvous.

Friar   Go get thee to thy love, as was decreed,
           Ascend her chamber, hence and comfort her.
                                    (*III, iii, 146–147*)

Following their wedding night together, Act III, Scene v begins with this stage direction:

> *Enter Romeo and Juliet aloft*

At once ecstatic in their consummated love and dismayed at their enforced parting, they make ready to take their reluctant leave of each other.

Juliet   Then, window, let day in, and let life out.
Romeo   Farewell, farewell! One kiss, and I'll descend.
                                    (*III, v, 41–42*)

The last piece of evidence is the saddest and most ominous. Romeo has descended from the window to the orchard below. Juliet stares down at him, exclaiming:

> O God, I have an ill-divining soul!
> Methinks I see thee, now thou art so low,
> As one dead in the bottom of a tomb.
>   (*III, v, 54–56*)

Not surprisingly, two other famous instances of the use of this stage area also involve lovers. The first is from *Antony and Cleopatra*. Antony, having already lost a world for love, now learns, by a false report, that Cleopatra has killed herself. In a final spasm of despair, he attempts a Roman suicide, falling on his sword. Ironically, he bungles the job and while he is suffering learns that Cleopatra and her maids have hidden in her "monument," her large and elaborate tomb. He bids retainers carry him to her. Act IV, Scene xv begins with this stage direction:

> *Enter Cleopatra and her Maids aloft, with Charmian and Iras.*

Antony is brought before the towering tomb, and he and Cleopatra begin their last conversation. She wishes to enfold him once more in her arms and orders her women to help draw him up. In what must have been one of the trickiest pieces of stage business in all Shakespeare, they do so. This action is reflected in the terse stage direction,

> *They heave Antony aloft to Cleopatra.*
> (*IV, xv, s.d., after 37*)

Incidentally, Shakespeare pursues his habit of wordplay relentlessly, when he has the retainers exclaim in chorus,

> A heavy sight! (*IV, xv, 40*)

Another example, this time from *The Merchant of Venice*, is lighter in every way. You will recall that Shylock's daughter, Jessica, in the time-honored romantic tradition of the beautiful daughter escaping from the clutches of her hateful father, arranges to elope with a young Venetian gallant, Lorenzo. The elopement scene makes use of the upper stage. Under the cover of another masque—this time it sounds like a sort of Venetian Mardi Gras—Jessica disguises herself as a boy, takes freely from her father's wealth in the absence of a formal dowry, and holds herself in readiness against the arrival of the masked Lorenzo and his reveling friends. Lorenzo, knowing Shylock is away, boldly approaches the house and hails Jessica. We read the stage direction,

> *Jessica above*   (*II, vi, s.d., after 25*)

and in a moment hear her call down to her lover:

> Here, catch this casket; it is worth the pains.
> (*II, vi, 33*)

Whereupon after she has spoken a few more words, Lorenzo replies:

> Descend, for you must be my torchbearer.
> (*II, vi, 40*)

The scene ends with a little flurry of wordplay about being *light* and with jokes about Jessica's disguise as a boy—a favorite joke with Elizabethan audiences because of the double play involved in the convention of the boy actor playing the girl disguised as a boy.

It is not surprising that the upper stage was also used to represent the parapets of castle walls from which Richard II would wail "Down, down, I come, like glist'ring Phaeton"; or along which Richard III might be seen *"Aloft, between two Bishops"* as he assumes a demeanor of false piety while waiting for the Mayor and the citizens of London, urged on by Buckingham, to persuade him to take the crown; or, again, to represent the town walls of Harfleur from which the besieged French parley with the victorious Henry V for terms of surrender. Indeed, some speculative "reconstructions" of the Globe propose a stage wall painted to simulate a city or castle wall or some design that would serve both purposes.

More likely, such decoration as this stage wall (or any other surface of the stage) presented was ornamental and not scenic, although, like the painted mask of comedy and mask of tragedy familiarly adorning our stage curtains or proscenium arches or pilasters, some of the ornamental effects could have had broad symbolic suggestiveness.

These, then, were the principal resources of Shakespeare's stage. All that remain unmentioned are minor and speculative ones. It is not known with certainty if the canopy over the stage was supported by two pillars, as it appears was true of the Swan Theater, or, assuming that these pillars existed, if they were levied on to serve as trees (for Orlando to hang his verses on) or, as seems quite likely, for concealment (for the three murderers to waylay Banquo). Nor is it certain if the Globe boasted a musicians' gallery directly above the second gallery we have been discussing and, if so, whether this was occasionally used as a playing area, as when Cassius bids Pindarus to climb a mountain top to report on the movement of the enemy. But these seldom-used resources do not require protracted discussion. It is possible that they existed, and it does not demand excessive ingenuity to determine how they were used if they were available. But they would not be essential to produce the playscripts of Shakespeare that we have.

Our purpose from the outset has been to come to as clear an understanding as possible of Shakespeare's habitual ways of composing his plays and performing them. We will not go wrong if we visualize nearly all of the action as taking place on a remarkably bare stage employing a minimum of furniture. We should not conclude from this, however, that the effect was mean or beggarly. Shakespeare's players were armed with a language so rich in imagery that no painted set could hope to compete with its resources. These same players, moreover, were richly—even gorgeously—costumed when the occasion demanded. Most of these costumes were Elizabethan, although Greek and Roman plays employed some costumes at least suggestive of those periods; and a few conventional characters, like ghosts and messengers, were painted white or wore the gowns or boots that identified their roles. Interestingly, one or two concessions to realism were made in this essentially nonillusionistic theater. Swordplay was thrillingly convincing, the duelists performing with professional skill. And bloodletting, by means of strategically placed animal bladders that could be pricked by sword or dagger, would seem real enough to satisfy the most avid lover of sensationalism.

Nor was the appeal of spectacle scanted. The music and the dancing that graced the Capulet ball where Romeo first met Juliet would simultaneously woo the ear and eye. The parade of apparitions and kings that greeted the amazed stare of Macbeth would rivet the attention of the audience, the aristocrat no less than the apprentice. And the company of Venetian senators who listened spellbound to the reminiscences of Othello would vie in richly costumed splendor with those other Venetian nobles who marveled at the learning of the "young doctor of Rome" as "he" outwitted the envenomed Shylock in their legal battle for a pound of flesh.

In a word, this was not an unworthy scaffold with no means of gratifying the basic appeals of spectacle and pageantry that we associate with the word *theatrical*. But it was a stage free from the clutter of properties, sets, and heavy trappings that could fatally divert attention away from passion to pelf, from perception to pomp, from feelings to furniture. It was a stage that placed great demands on the actor, but one that freed him to meet those demands. Relieved of both the support and the smother of an enshrouding set, he was on his own, permitted, if he was able, to create his own ambience, aided by the matchless language of Shakespeare.

And he needed the rich resources of this language for, more than the modern actor, he depended almost entirely on words. There were no phones to answer, cigarettes to light, drinks to mix and pour, lamps to turn on and off. True, his words and gestures were occasionally punctuated by some *business* (more often than not musical), and there was some horseplay and some fighting; but by and large, he and his fellows simply talked and talked and talked. And they did so in close proximity to their audience. Is it any wonder that such a theater and such a stage gave rise to the greatest blank verse line in English drama? The circumstances demanded it. It has often been observed that some of our best movies are those made with the smallest budgets. The same principle is at work here: Remove the possibility of depending on hardware, and the dramatic artist must fall back on his imagination. What is left are the essentials: people speaking to one another.

We began this discussion by asking if Shakespeare really thought his platform stage an unworthy scaffold. We have argued that he did not. We conclude by citing the similar judgment made more than 300 years later by England's second greatest playwright. George Bernard Shaw, weary of both the plays and the playhouses that characterized the theater in Victorian and Edwardian England, declared emphatically, "In the new theater the stage must be . . . a tribune [platform], and not a ridiculous peep show with painted canvas profiles pretending to be natural scenery." He added, "The old formula of two trestles, four boards, and a passion still holds, and will hold until we grow out of playgoing altogether."[9]

10
ACTOR AND
AUDIENCE

A. ACTOR

These our actors . . .
(The Tempest, IV, i, 148)

There exists a considerable body of lore concerning the repertory company Shakespeare wrote for, acted in, and partially controlled; the actors who made up this company; and the audiences who, for a quarter of a century during his professional lifetime, went to see his plays. Much of this lore possesses great intrinsic interest, but only bits of it contribute very directly to a modern reader's and playgoer's understanding of Shakespeare's plays. It is with these bits that we are concerned in this chapter.

The evidence that no English writer has ever been more totally immersed in the professional theater than Shakespeare is writ large all over his plays. We have already explored the principal elements of these plays and have discovered some of the habitual ways Shakespeare worked to compose them. There remains a practical side to which we have not yet directed our full attention—the extent to which the actors for whom Shakespeare wrote the major and minor roles in his long succession of plays, in interesting if largely unconscious ways, may have determined the parts he wrote for them. Examining the successive dramatis personae of the thirty-seven plays commonly attributed to Shakespeare, we discover some curious patterns from which we may draw interesting—and sometimes amusing—inferences concerning the probable effects on these plays of the acting company for which they were written.

Shakespeare's company (known as the Lord Chamberlain's Men, 1594–1603, and as the King's Men, 1603–1616, the date of Shakespeare's death, and for many years after) like its competitors was a repertory company. It put on a different play each day for as long as a fortnight, and there was no such thing as any single play's enjoying a long consecutive run. This meant that Shakespeare as a playwright had constantly to provide new plays with new roles for all the permanent members of his company. From these circumstances one might expect that certain patterns—patterns of roles and casting rooted in the practical requirements of the workaday theater—would emerge. They do, and from these patterns we may draw some plausible conclusions.

A survey of the dramatis personae discloses, for instance, that there are relatively few female roles—often only two and almost never more than four *named* women—in any of his plays. Knowing, as we do, that most female roles were played by boy actors in his day, we may safely conclude that in his company at any given period only a very limited number of boy actors were capable of playing major roles. This emphatically does not mean that boy actors as a group were inferior performers. Contemporary testimony, including the loving "Epitaph on Salomon Pavy," composed by Ben Jonson on the occasion of the death of a boy actor, persuades us that some of them were very good indeed.

The significance for us, rather, is that circumstances like these may have determined what Shakespeare could and could not do in his plays. For example, blessed with two first-rate boy actors during the period 1594–1601, he wrote for them a succession of unforgettable female roles in his five best romantic comedies. More than that. We know that one of these boys was tall and the other short, for the dialogue of several of these plays tells us this about the comic heroines they portrayed. Here is the honor roll of these favorite heroines, with the first-named in every instance being the taller of the two: Helena and Hermia in *A Midsummer Night's Dream*, Portia and Nerissa in *The Merchant of Venice*, Beatrice and Hero in *Much Ado About Nothing*, Rosalind and Celia in *As You Like It* (amusingly, Shakespeare confused their heights in one careless passage in this play), and Viola and Olivia in *Twelfth Night*. Since boy actors might join an adult acting company as apprentices at the tender age of six or eight (recall Lady Macduff's little son and the younger of the two little princes put to death by Richard III) and might remain in that capacity until their voices changed (recall Hamlet's "Pray God, your voice, like a piece of uncurrent gold, be not cracked within the ring"), we may conclude that our talented duo simply outgrew their parts after this seven-year period. In any event, nothing quite like them appears in the plays Shakespeare wrote and produced either before or after this time. Of course, no one is proposing that any *effect* as remarkable as this cluster of incomparable romantic comedies has as its *single cause* the presence in the acting company of two boy actors, but that their presence is one of the determinants of the plan and shape of these plays seems unarguable. And the presence of such practical determinants in the working plans of a dramatic genius does much to humanize both him and the products of his pen.

Naive persons who have deplored Shakespeare's handicap in having to use boy actors to play his women's roles not only underestimate the skill of the boy actors but also disclose a superficial reading of the plays. Shakespeare's good sense apparently told him that he need not stage scenes between men and women that emphasized heavy breathing sexual passion. This restriction did not leave him, as it might some modern writers, with nothing to stage. With unerring taste and inexhaustible invention, he created relationships between men and women which represent a very wide range of human behavior: witty banter (Beatrice and

Benedick), rollicking horseplay (Petruchio and Kate), injured innocence (Ophelia and Hamlet), cold hate (Goneril and Regan with Lear), earthy humor (Doll Tearsheet and Falstaff), stupefying shock (Desdemona and Othello); and the instances could be multiplied. Moreover, the so-called exceptions prove, on examination, not to be exceptional. Even Cleopatra's fabled sexual allure is more talked about than demonstrated, although she and Antony do exchange kisses, as do Troilus and Cressida when they first meet. But body contact is everywhere subordinated to the contact of two minds or souls or psyches. And this latter contact is established by the magic of words.

Despite all this, everyone who reads Shakespeare's plays remembers his major heroines as full-bodied women. There is no contradiction here. What we have is the evidence of the remarkable connotative qualities of the words—words that confer on their speakers a three-dimensional character that is the wonder and despair of would-be imitators. But note, the life is in the language. Contemporary actresses who essay to play the roles Shakespeare wrote for his talented boy apprentices would do well to recall Hamlet's advice to the players: "Suit the action to the word, the word to the action, with this special observance, that you o'er step not the modesty of nature."

If Shakespeare was compelled by circumstances to limit the number of female roles in his plays, he could be lavish with the parts he wrote for the adult male actors. Again, the dramatis personae of almost any of his plays yields proof of this. Consider, as a single example, that *1 Henry IV* provides such choice roles as Falstaff, Hotspur, Prince Hal, King Henry, and Glendower, to say nothing of Worcester, Mortimer, Northumberland, Douglas, Vernon, and the like. His plays continually reveal these multiple opportunities, not only for the leading actors (who might be *patented members,* their names appearing in royal patents issued to his company by Queen Elizabeth and later by King James, or *sharers,* who collected the fees and shared the box-office profits, or both) but also for secondary actors (called *hired men*) who often doubled in roles when the plots called for a very large cast. (These minor actors also served as prompters, doorkeepers, musicians, and stagehands when they were not acting on the stage.)

We have suggested that this disproportion between the relatively large number of adult male actors—sometimes as many as twelve in a prosperous company like Shakespeare's—and the small number of boy actors reflects a practical situation that determined in one obvious way the casting possibilities and practices in Shakespeare's plays. Because he had to take into account this disparity between the number of male and female roles he could conveniently cast, Shakespeare created an inordinately large number of widowers, of whom Polonius, Shylock, Lear, and Prospero are among the best known. That he totally surmounted this practical exigency, successfully disguising the practice to which he was driven by necessity, is attested to by the fact that none of us ever feels the need to even conceive of the existence of any mesdames Polonius, Shylock, Lear, or Prospero. We never inquire about them because we never miss them. This is perhaps a homely example of how a great artist transcends his everyday working conditions, but it is surely an instructive one.

The existence of this cluster of widowers suggests that other clusters of characters may be discovered in Shakespeare's play. These other clusters do in fact exist. One of the most interesting is that succession of old men, usually garrulous, unconsciously comic, and frequently irascible, who strongly suggest either parts written for the same actor or a character type with a strong appeal to Shakespeare or, most likely, both. Beginning perhaps with Gremio in *The Taming of the Shrew,* developing certainly with Old Capulet in *Romeo and Juliet* and York in *Richard II,* continuing possibly with Antonio in *Much Ado About Nothing* and certainly with Polonius in *Hamlet* and Brabantio in *Othello,* this character appears as late as Gloucester in *King Lear,* Menenius in *Coriolanus,* and Gonzalo in *The Tempest.* The inference that these roles were played by one actor has led to the surmise that this actor was none other than John Heminge, Shakespeare's lifelong colleague in the theater and one of the two men responsible for collecting, editing, and publishing his plays posthumously in the First Folio of 1623. Be that as it may, readers (and playgoers) who perceive this similarity in roles have learned something useful about Shakespeare's working habits, have obtained yet another insight into the practical economics necessary to a repertory company, and—perhaps more important—by seeing the gross similarities among a number of characters have been invited to refine their ability to perceive also the distinctions that individualize them, and thus to sharpen their critical ability.

This ability to see similarities where others see only differences and, conversely, differences where others see only similarities is one of the marks of a critical intelligence. Not surprisingly, it is a form of critical intelligence that Shakespeare himself manifested frequently and never more clearly than when he drew on the *character types* of an evolving dramatic tradition and fashioned from these types a series of remarkable individuals. We may instance some of the old men we have just been talking about. The irascible old man, usually a father, was a stock character in Roman comedy; he was just as much at home in British comedy as the ogre father of romantic fiction. When one sees what Shakespeare was able to do with this type in modeling Capulet and again, and very differently, in drawing Desdemona's angry father, Brabantio, one is provided with yet another reminder of how genius at once depends on and transcends convention. It is not unfair to recall in this connection the immense skill of the actor—if, indeed, a single man played these successive roles—who understood Shakespeare's intent in endowing these types with the idiosyncrasies that individualize them and succeeded in projecting these unique qualities on the stage of the Globe. Other stock characters on which Shakespeare drew freely from Roman comedy or Continental and British sources include the witty servant, beginning with the twin Dromios in *The Comedy of Errors* and progressing through Tranio and Grumio of *The Taming of the Shrew* and on to Fabian in *Twelfth Night;* the shrewish wife, who appears in both of the early farces just named; the braggart warrior, who receives a broad and parodistic treatment in Ancient Pistol of *2 Henry IV,* and *Henry V* and a much more interesting transmogrification in the ineffable Falstaff; and the malcontent who is projected in interestingly different ways in Malvolio in *Twelfth Night* and Jaques in *As You Like It.*

You may grow alert to other patterns or clusters, some of which again invite the conclusion that Shakespeare may have had a particular actor in mind when he created them. For example, there are the young lions—Tybalt, Hotspur, Laertes, and Macduff—and their counterparts, those sober, good young men—Benvolio, Sebastian, and Horatio. Without needing to engage in the guessing game that has attributed the former roles to William Slye and the latter to Henry Condell (Heminge's collaborator on the First Folio), it is enough for us to suggest that there are such patterns and to realize that where these patterns exist, there may well be others. There is no swifter way to achieve an insight into the artistry of a dramatist than to recognize the patterns that both the bent of his mind and the circumstances under which he worked led him to favor. Expressed another way, it is a fair if somewhat cryptic judgment that says "Shakespeare is his own best critic" if by this we mean that Shakespeare, like every artist, falls into habitual ways of doing things and that a recognition of these ways will illuminate his plays.

Yet another piece of lore revealing the intimate relationship between the actors in Shakespeare's company and the roles they led him to create concerns two of the best comedians of his day—Will Kempe and Robert Armin. These men, although both of their names appear on the list of "The Names of the Principall Actors / in all these Players," printed on one of the opening pages of the First Folio, were not members of the company at the same time. And thereby hangs a tale.

Will Kempe was the kind of funnyman who got his laughs by exaggerated behavior and overstatement. He appeared in plays written before 1599, in such roles as the clownish Peter in *Romeo and Juliet,* Bully Bottom in *A Midsummer Night's Dream,* Launcelot Gobbo in *The Merchant of Venice,* and that immortal ass, Dogberry, in *Much Ado About Nothing.* In addition, as an accomplished dancer, he also regularly appeared in the jigs—comic afterpieces, featuring both dance and ad lib patter, which were tacked on to the end of dramatic performances in the public theaters. Jigs invited comic improvisation; so, too, might some of the smaller parts Shakespeare appears to have written for this major clown. Whether or not it was Kempe whom Shakespeare had in mind when he wrote Hamlet's attack on comic improvisation:

> And let those that play your clowns speak no more than is set down for them, for there be of them that will themselves laugh, to set on some quantity of barren spectators to laugh too, though in the mean time some necessary question of the play be then to be considered. That's villainous, and shows the most pitiful ambition in the fool that uses it . . .   (*III, ii, 36–42*)

we know that Kempe left Shakespeare's company in 1599. He was replaced by Robert Armin, the kind of funnyman who got his laughs by means of sly, satiric sallies and comic understatement. With this change in comedians there was a commensurate change in the comic roles Shakespeare devised for them. The Dogberrys, Bottoms, and Gobbos now disappeared, to be replaced by a succession of witty fools, of whom Touchstone in *As You Like It,* Feste in *Twelfth Night,* and the nameless Fool in *King Lear* are the immortal prototypes. The reader or playgoer quickly discerns that these "fools" are really the wise men of their respective plays: given the license of their traditional cap and bells, they systematically expose the folly of their betters, in contrast with the earlier clowns, who are used primarily to intensify the comic situation.[1]

There are other curiosities of this kind which throw a revealing light on the plays. One more at least deserves mention here. Shakespearean actors were required to be most versatile: ideally, they were dexterous dancers, skillful swordsmen, tuneful singers, even agile acrobats. (Accounts of contemporary travelers reveal that the "English comedians" were celebrated throughout Western Europe for their skill in all the arts of the theater.) But then as now, a towering talent could more than compensate for some deficiency. And so it was with Richard Burbage, the star of Shakespeare's company and generally reckoned the paramount actor of his day. Burbage, it seems, could not sing. We have documentary evidence that Burbage played Hamlet, Richard III, Othello, and Lear; and no one doubts that he played most of Shakespeare's major heroes—Romeo, Brutus, Prince Hal, Benedick, Macbeth, Orlando, Antony, Coriolanus, and others. Significantly, none of these roles has songs written for it unless we except Benedick, who, however, sings only four lines and then breaks off, apologizing for his bad voice.

This oddity escapes triviality when we consider the role of music in Shakespeare. To Shakespeare, a love of music was an infallible index to good character; conversely, "The man that hath no music in himself, / Nor is not moved with concord of sweet sounds, / Is fit for treasons, stratagems, and spoils." The playwright who could write these lines and many others expressing the same sentiments, to say nothing of the delightful songs that he scattered through his plays, surely might be expected to let his major heroes sing occasionally. That instead he reduced them to approving auditors of the singing of others compels the conclusion that Burbage could not sing: one more reminder of the practical contingencies that Shakespeare cheerfully, so far as we know, observed.

But it was not only Shakespeare's fellow actors whose presence shaped and conditioned the plays he tailored to their requirements. His audience, too—as audiences always must—exercised a determining influence on the plays he offered for their pleasure.

B. AUDIENCES

> . . . as you are known
> The first and happiest hearers of the town. . . .
> *(Henry VIII, Prologue, 23–24)*

Any discussion of Shakespeare's audience had better begin by setting right some popular misconceptions. Prompted partly by the slanders hurled by the Puritan critics of the theater in Shakespeare's own day and partly by a curious combination of bardolatry and prudery on the part of influential nineteenth-century commentators, a popular notion has established itself that Shakespeare's audiences were a rowdy lot, a colorful gang of blackguards with more than their share of light women, idle apprentices, roaring bullyboys, and the like. And the corollary of this caricature is the apologetic explanation that the great Shakespeare was compelled to introduce bawdy lines and scenes of crude horseplay to cater to the low tastes of this coarse-grained crew. Ironically, this false picture reveals more about the Victorians who conceived it than about the Elizabethans it was supposed to portray. Made myopic by their too limited view of the proper subject matter and tone of literature, these nineteenth-century commentators tried to make over Shakespeare in their own image, explaining away as necessary concessions to the groundlings those robust lines and scenes that a healthier criticism sees as an indispensable part of the total fabric of the plays.

But the significant truth, partially obscured by this faulty legend, is that Shakespeare's audience was truly a popular one. When we say this, we are referring to the persons who came to the great public theaters like the Globe. On occasions, Shakespeare's company was commissioned to give a special performance before the royal court and, less frequently, before a particular audience, such as a company of law students at one of the *Inns of Court,* as the law schools were called. Even this momentary shift in audiences, however, did not result in a shift in scenarios: Shakespeare's practice of writing something for everybody ensured the success of almost all of his plays before any late Elizabethan or early Jacobean audience.

To return to the popular audience of the public theaters, it was remarkably representative of the London of his day: noblemen and their ladies, merchants and their wives, lawyers and doctors, foreign tourists, visiting country gentry, artisans of every kind and their apprentices, soldiers and sailors, housemaids and hostlers, and presumably the usual complement of whores, pickpockets, and "sturdy beggars." All of these people found their inexpensive standing room or more expensive seats according to the depth of their purses and not the length of their pedigrees.

This universal audience by demanding plays of universal appeal motivated Shakespeare, at least in his most successful efforts, to strike the popular note that has ensured the appeal of his plays down to our own day. Shakespeare the playwright was lucky in his audiences. Had he written his plays for the same audience of young noblemen for whom he supplied the mannered rhetoric and conventional figures of his two long narrative poems, *Venus and Adonis* and *The Rape of Lucrece,* perhaps he would today be recalled only by literary antiquarians.

Even as it is, Shakespeare did not entirely escape this danger. Toward the end of his career, his company purchased an indoor theater known as Blackfriars (because the land on which it was situated and the building itself were originally part of a Dominican priory). The audiences of Blackfriars were for the most part a coterie of sophisticates, with a disproportionate number of aristocrats represented. Their tastes ran to the novel, and the novelties they liked emphasized the ornate and the fantastic. For them Shakespeare composed his four symbolic romances: *Pericles, Cymbeline, The Winter's Tale,* and *The Tempest.* Now, despite the distinctive merits of these romances and the relative fame of the latter two, it flies in the face of reality to claim for them anything like the broad appeal of the major comedies, tragedies, and histories. Even a most sympathetic reading of *The Tempest,* to name the best known of the four, compels the conclusion that we are treading here on a singularly artificial turf, breathing a somewhat rarefied air, observing a most mannered form of behavior. It is a very skillfully wrought piece of its kind, but like the shepherdess Phebe, it is not for all markets. These are not the qualifications we feel the need to assert when we see or read *Julius Caesar* or *Macbeth* or *Twelfth Night* or *1 Henry IV* or *Hamlet* or *Richard III,* to cite only a half-dozen of Shakespeare's most popular plays.

But having asserted the equation that popular audiences will promote popular plays, we must do more. Popular audiences are, by definition, socially heterogeneous. What *homogeneous* qualities permitted Shakespeare to play on this representative audience as though it were a unified sounding board? The answers to this question are several, and they disclose much about Shakespearean plays as well as about those Renaissance Londoners who went to see and hear them.

Shakespeare's Londoners were, first of all, nationalistic. In this respect they reflected Renaissance rather than medieval values. Never, perhaps, has a people been more acutely conscious of its national language. The truth is that Londoners in Shakespeare's day were more than a little word drunk. New words, new word combinations, extravagant figures of speech were in the air. Even men of learning asserted the right of English to take its place with Latin as the proper medium to express the best that is known and thought in the world. Shakespeare was the fortunate beneficiary of this great linguistic groundswell in addition to being its chiefest ornament.

Linguistic nationalism is doubtless a subtle manifestation; political nationalism is more gross. Shakespeare's Londoners were self-conscious political nationals: they were proud of their growing naval power, climaxed by the defeat of the Spanish Armada; a majority of them adhered to their recently evolved state religion, the Church of England brand of Protestantism; they shared with their queen a fear of factionalism and a suspicion of foreign plots that sought to promote divisiveness; they were ready to respond, with that kind of passionate pride that lies at the root of all nationalism, to symbolical and rhetorical reminders of what it means to be an Englishman. Shakespeare appears to have shared these sentiments. John of Gaunt's dying apostrophe to England may be the most stirring hymn of national praise ever written. The rhetoric of Henry V urging on his ragged troops to their great victory at Agincourt is well-nigh irresistible to even a pacifist. And we are told that audiences wept openly at the scene of the death of Talbot, the great opponent of Joan of Arc, who, as the leader of the despised French, seemed appropriately villainous to Shakespeare's auditors.

But more than these heroics and histrionics is sounded in Shakespeare's history plays: running through these plays like a refrain is the insistence on the need for civil order, for national unity, for political stability. The heroine of Shakespeare's English histories is England herself. And Shakespeare, like Englishmen after him, not only thrilled to the notion that Britannia ruled the waves but also regularly prescribed the course of action that he thought would ensure her eminence.

Perhaps even more important than the conscious attitudes of a people are their unconscious ones—that cluster of unexamined assumptions that underlies their codes of individual and social behavior. Obviously, these attitudes will be reflected in plays that are selective mirrors of the society for which they are written. Although it is impossible to catalogue, let alone discuss, all the attitudes that conditioned the behavior of Shakespeare's audiences, even a brief mention of three or four will assist the modern reader or viewer of his plays.

Adherents of the Women's Liberation movement will not take a favorable view of Portia's glad surrender to Bassanio:

> Happiest of all, is that her gentle spirit
> Commits itself to yours to be directed,
> As from her lord, her governor, her king.
> (*The Merchant of Venice, III, ii, 163–165*)

But willy nilly, it accurately reflects the view of Renaissance Englishmen that marriage was the only recognized vocation for women. This does not mean that women then, anymore than now, were mute and static pawns of men, or that Shakespeare thought so. Shakespeare's women, and especially his comic heroines, are sufficient reminder of the folly of underestimating the power of women. After all, it is this selfsame Portia who outwits Shylock, rescues Antonio, and lovingly manipulates her husband, Bassanio. But it does mean that modern readers must expect to watch these women move within the circle of a widely accepted convention. This adjustment should be no more difficult than the one that requires us to remember that Roman togas, medieval armor, or doublet and hose do not alter the universal human qualities of the men who wear them.

More difficult to grasp, because it strikes at the roots of our own unconscious assumptions, is the antiromantic view of marriage characteristic of the period. Both in life and in literature, the material aspects of marriage were often of paramount importance. Shakespeare's audience, for example, did not look on the impecunious Bassanio as some vulgar fortune hunter. To cite another instance of this antiromantic viewpoint, Juliet's reservations about marrying young Paris after Old Capulet has made all the arrangements strike him as outrageous. And so they would have seemed to most affluent Elizabethan fathers. The marriages of convenience arranged by Shakespeare's kings and gentry would not have shocked his audiences. Nor would the curious legality of a marriage consummated after only a secular *contract* and before a church wedding. Shakespeare's own marriage to Anne Hathaway precisely illustrates this old custom. More to our purpose, it helps to clarify the situation of another (and pregnant) Juliet and her Claudio in *Measure for Measure;* and it does much to explain Shakespeare's use of "the bed trick" (the posting off to the bed of a man, a woman who is, viewed this way, already his lawful wife), as with Mariana and Angelo in the same play. In a word, certain actions that have puzzled and even offended some of

Shakespeare's readers have their origins in the conventions of his day as well as in the plots of the prose and verse romances from which he lifted them.

It might be fairly said that the model Elizabethan home was a microcosm of the model Elizabethan state: a father-centered family was the counterpart of a monarch-centered nation. Both institutions, family and state, traced their origins to the same conceptual source—an ideal of permanent order suggested by a favorite metaphor—"the great chain of being." The idea behind the metaphor was a fixed tradition in Shakespeare's day. Everything in the universe, from earthly dust to heavenly God, was arranged according to a fixed and permanent system of ascending values called *degrees*. This principle of hierarchical organization was discovered in all human institutions. Hence, in a kingdom, the monarch was God's steward, and all groups, ranks, and classes in society owed him unswerving allegiance. What the king was to his nation the father was to his family. And the order in the universe had to serve as the model for the order that every right-thinking person sought to impose on his own conduct.

Now, whereas it is true that these models and abstractions did not have a one-to-one correspondence with any actual kings or fathers or other individuals, nevertheless they reflected deeply held ideals and as such they both motivated and conditioned people's actual behavior. (Any contemporary American who experiences difficulty grasping this concept need only consider for a moment the role of such ideals as "democracy" and "democratic behavior" in our own society to understand it at once: we all live by means of myth as well as reality.)

Readers and viewers of Shakespeare's plays will see this principle of order operating most vividly in his tragedies, where Shakespeare makes constant use of the correspondence he discovers between microcosm and macrocosm. Thus an "insurrection" in the breast of an individual man (Brutus) can result in "havoc" in the state (the assassination of Caesar and the ensuing civil war) and both can be accompanied by "civil strife in heaven" (the numerous

omens and portents that signal nature's displeasure with
human behavior in *Julius Caesar*). The same processes are
carried out on an even more massive and frightening scale in
both *King Lear* and *Macbeth*. And they have their smaller,
comic counterparts in the discords and errors that mark
Shakespeare's comedies. In all of these disruptions, mas-
sively tragic or dwarfishly comic, the premise is the same:
as creatures endowed with reason, human beings can set
their will against the order of things, but they do so at their
own risk.

If one were to conclude from the foregoing that Shakespeare's views of society was not a democratic one, he would
be right. At this point the modern reader should be willing
to substitute a sense of history for sentimentality. Shakespeare was a poet, not a prophet. It is enough that as a poet he
could discover worth in any person, regardless of class. (We
may recall the common soldier, Michael Williams in *Henry
V,* or Cornwall's nameless servant in *King Lear,* who could
not stand by and watch his master torture the defenseless
Gloucester.) Even so, Shakespeare did not frequently assign to commoners the virtues that mattered most to
Elizabethans. Certainly we must not expect him to anticipate universal suffrage and education and thus discover the
possibility of political wisdom in the common man. His
strictures against the "mob," whether led by Roman
tribunes or by Jack Cade, are unsparing.

Another attribute of Shakespeare's audiences that contributed to their homogeneity has been less frequently re-
marked on. By an amusing coincidence, it is a quality shared
by a modern American audience. I refer to the passion for
self-improvement. Perhaps no society besides our own has
been inundated by such a flood of "how-to-do" and "how-
to-become" literature. An Elizabethan could learn from
these printed sources how to cook and how to write love
letters, how to remove spots from velvet and how to behave
like a gentleman. What has this to do with plays? The public
theater was regarded by Elizabethans as a source of edification as well as entertainment. Renaissance writers and their
audiences were often unabashedly didactic. Shakespeare's

plays contain many *set pieces,* moral homilies that in a few lines distill popular wisdom. Although it is true that some of the most famous of these, including Polonius's farewell to Laertes and Iago's remarks on "a good name," are inserted for ironic effect, since in both instances their speakers are cynical immoralists, this is by no means true of them all. (We have already alluded to Portia's speech giving herself to Bassanio, and we may add Malcolm's catechism on the qualities of a good king in *Macbeth.*) Truth to tell, a careful search of the complete Shakespearean canon would yield matter for a little textbook of the received truths of his age.

But Shakespeare and his fellow playwrights offered more than moral edification. To the curious, their plays sometimes served as a source of news—delayed news, to be sure; but at a time when no newspapers existed, topicality was a relative matter. None of Shakespeare's plays, it is true, sought to exploit some very recent event—a battle, murder, spy plot, hanging, or the like—as did some of the plays of his day. But scholars seeking evidence by means of which to date his plays have discovered and recorded a number of topical references salted away in the lines of these plays. In *The Tempest,* for example, Shakespeare's storm at sea, and also a few details of his magic isle, appear to have their immediate sources in passages from contemporary pamphlets describing Atlantic voyages, including, notably, the description of a shipwreck in the Bermudas. And the earthquake mentioned by Juliet's Nurse in her first speech may refer to any one of several tremors that shook England in the eighties.

On the whole, though, Shakespeare's "news" is the universal news of poetry. And its appeal is universal, too. We are not surprised to learn from a contemporary writer, John Marston, of a young gallant who, wishing to appear impressive before his friends and especially before his beloved, went to the theater armed with a notebook and came away with so much verbal plunder that for days, in Marston's words, from his lips "doth flow / Naught but pure Juliet and her Romeo."

As foolish as this young man may sound in Marston's satiric anecdote, he illustrates what is the most significant of all the attributes that Shakespeare's audiences appear to have enjoyed in common—a marvelous ear for both the language of music and the music of language. Elizabethan England has been called a nest of singing birds. The compliment is deserved. Historians rank this period as the high-water mark of English music. With the return of the recorder to popularity today and the revival of many of the ballads and madrigals of the period, and when every teen-ager can hum or sing "Greensleeves," it is not so difficult to imagine the pleasure with which Shakespeare's audiences listened to such songs as "It was a lover and his lass" or "Take, O take those lips away" or "Fear no more the heat o' the sun." And there are at least twenty other songs that his contemporary listeners, and many modern readers as well, would rank with these. Perhaps a time like ours, when every third young person seems able to pluck a tune from a guitar, is peculiarly fit to understand a time like his, when, we are told, Londoners would find citterns strapped to pegs on the wall of their barbershops ready to be taken down and strummed while the customer was waiting for his haircut.

That there is some carryover between this kind of musical literacy and the kind of aural literacy displayed by those who listen to spoken poetry with pleasure and understanding seems indisputable. It has often been assumed that the rate of literacy—as that term is normally defined—was not high in Shakespeare's London in the absence of universal education. But scholarship chastens our glibness about such matters. Lately, we have learned that school attendance in Shakespeare's London was much more common than we had assumed and that the dissemination of simple reading manuals for home instruction was far more widespread than we had supposed.

However that may be, the degree and extent of the special kind of aural literacy we are interested in must have been extraordinary. The popularity of Shakespeare's plays proves this beyond cavil. People in his day did not suffer from the disadvantage of knowing that Shakespeare was a peerless genius or that attendance at his plays certified one's cultural superiority. They simply discovered that they liked his plays better than anyone else's. That in doing so they were responding with delight to the best in Shakespeare seems unarguable. And such a response, it may be agreed, depends on a high degree of aural literacy.

If this aural literacy was extraordinary, the reasons for it seem ordinary enough. That we find extraordinary the notion of a large, popular audience being easy with some of the richest poetry ever composed is a commentary on the shifts in emphasis that mark our own time. For most of us, alas, poetry has become the possession of the few. But if we had been fond of the theater; if we had been accustomed to hearing there a poetic stage line all of our theatergoing lives (the tradition of verse in drama was established long before Shakespeare); if part-songs and catches and madrigals were as natural and casual a source of domestic entertainment as cards and cassette music are to us; if the educated among us were accustomed to reading even our history in verse; if the sermons we heard at St. Paul's and other leading churches, and even the final words of those who died on the gallows at Tyburn, were alike embellished with rhetorical patterns of great rhythmic and even poetic power; if we were, in a word, no more self-conscious about verse and poetry than we are about prose and documentary film, then we, too, would have taken our place in the Globe or some other London public theater and listened to a flow of blank verse and rimed verse, and prose as eloquent as much of that verse, with something like the comfortable comprehension we must attribute to the audiences whom the plays of Shakespeare delighted.

But since we are not Elizabethan playgoers, we have to make some adjustments. Precisely what we need to do to compensate for the changes that have taken place between Shakespeare's time and our own in order to ensure something like an Elizabethan comprehension of his accomplishment has been the subject of the preceding chapters. As we contemplate the distance between Shakespeare and ourselves, it is nonetheless reassuring to recall that England's greatest poetic dramatist wrote for a popular—if not exactly a mass—audience and that this audience understood him so well that it filled the theaters where his plays were shown and sent him back to Stratford a relatively rich man before he was fifty.

Since that day, and to an extent unprecedented in the history of any literature, Shakespeare's reputation has steadily grown, until now it is sometimes difficult to see the playwright for the reputation. It has been the purpose of this book to invite an understanding of his achievement that will convert an attitude of awe or fear or unacknowledged boredom, befitting a reputation, to one of ease and delight and aroused curiosity, befitting—in Wordsworth's memorable phrase—a man speaking to men.

EPILOGUE

> ... And did you speak to him again?
> How strange it seems and new!

The first two lines of Browning's "Memorabilia" suggested the title for this book. The next two lines, reproduced above, declare obliquely, as poetry does, the book's purpose: to assist you to achieve what Melville called "the shock of recognition," in this instance an electric awareness that you are standing confidently with those who feel easy in the presence of Shakespeare.

To achieve this confidence, you have had to clear away from your view of Shakespeare's plays some obstructions—obstructions imposed by changes in language, in time and circumstance, and in literary technique. The test of your success is simple: when you have removed these obstructions, you will find yourself exclaiming, with something like Browning's admiring wonder, "How strange it seems and new!"

The writer, too, must meet a test. *Have* his readers come to see Shakespeare plain? And have they done so with increased pleasure? I must hope so, "or else," to echo Shakespeare for the last time, "my project fails, / Which was to please."

FURTHER READING

A. IN SHAKESPEARE

Turning to this section, you doubtless expect to find a list of more books *about* Shakespeare. And you will find a few. But first you will find a carefully composed list of "books" *by* Shakespeare. And this is as it should be. Books like *Shakespeare Plain* are at best what Shylock said of cats, "harmless, necessary things." But the plays of Shakespeare are "the thing itself."

Still, even readers attracted to Shakespeare, facing some thirty-seven plays, do not always know just where to begin—or begin again. To ensure the greatest pleasure with the greatest understanding, they should read the best plays in the best order.

Fortunately, the verdict of nearly 400 years of history is in: we know which are the best plays. Less certainly, but nevertheless with great confidence, we can determine the best order. Experienced teachers know which plays—and not only individual plays, but also entire clusters of plays of the same kind—are most accessible to modern readers.

For Shakespeare's plays should be read in logical clusters. Read that way, Shakespeare becomes his own best interpreter. Readers discover that they can learn more—and more pleasurably—about a single Shakespearean tragedy by immediately reading two or three other Shakespearean tragedies than they are likely to learn from books that discuss these tragedies. Only after they have read many plays are they in a position to judge the worth of the help offered them by critics and commentators.

Shakespeare wrote several kinds of plays—principally tragedies, romantic comedies, histories, farces, and symbolic romances. There follows, then, a guide to the best plays of Shakespeare arranged in clusters and in the order in which they can be read with the greatest immediate pleasure and understanding. Because brevity is indispensable in a list, I must ask readers to excuse the tone: it is impossible to be brief without sounding dogmatic.

The great tragedies should be read first. So far from being intimidated by their awesome reputation, you will find encouragement in the realization that they are the most famous Shakespearean plays precisely because they are the most accessible. The tragedies have survived the sea change of travel better than have any other kinds of Shakespearean plays: they translate more readily than the others into foreign languages and thus are received more enthusiastically in foreign theaters. What is true of the foreign playhouse is equally true of the native classroom: the tragedies are at once the most popular and the most "teachable" of the plays.

The three most accessible tragedies are *Hamlet, Othello,* and *Julius Caesar.* They may be read in any order. *Hamlet* tells the story of the best-loved hero in dramatic literature and presents astonishing variety with no diminution of interest: there are no poor scenes in *Hamlet. Othello* gains by its concentration: of all the tragedies it has the simplest plot, the fewest characters, the sharpest focus. This makes it, in some important ways, the easiest to follow. *Julius Caesar* employs the simplest language. Almost all of the characters—and these include such memorable figures as Caesar, Brutus, Cassius, and Mark Antony—speak remarkably alike, in a kind of clear, public rhetoric. The absence of linguistic variety in *Julius Caesar* makes for easier reading.

Three other major tragedies may now be undertaken. Dark, mysterious and disturbing, and characterized by poetry of great power and some obscurity are *Macbeth* and

King Lear. As the shorter, swifter, more tightly focused of the two, *Macbeth* should be read before *Lear*. After these two, read *Antony and Cleopatra*. Although as a historical narrative it follows hard on the action in *Julius Caesar,* it should probably be read last in this set of six great tragedies. The scope and magnitude of its action, the number and variety of its scenes, the complexities of its ironies, and the sophistication of its themes all make it a candidate for a later reading.

Romeo and Juliet is a law unto itself. The great range and variety of its language styles present some difficulties, and there is a decided falling off of the intensity of interest past the midpoint—the *fourth-act lull,* as it has been called. But the play has been a universal favorite on the stage. And a pleasant reminder of its popularity with readers, especially young readers, is the report that the pages detailing the so-called balcony scene were the most commonly read passages in the copy of the First Folio that was once kept chained to a desk in the library of Oxford University. Read it in any order of the tragedies that pleases you.

The best of the history plays should be read next. Beginners sometimes complain that they get lost amidst the numerous characters of these plays, especially when Shakespeare employs the practice of later Russian novelists in assigning two or more names to some of his characters. But the three plays I shall nominate forestall that problem because each of them features principal characters of such brilliance that they cannot be confused with anyone else.

Richard III, the first history play one should read, is, in the best sense of the term, a one-man play. Despite its length, the episodic quality of its plot, and the oddity of one or two subordinate characters, like old Queen Margaret, *Richard III* is brilliantly focused on its central character, who is never long off the stage and whose amazing eloquence mesmerizes not only all the other characters but finally the readers and playgoers as well. Richard, of course, is a villain; but because he is such a melodramatic villain, we are always aware that he is a stage figure and so can revel in his wit and wickedness without forfeiting our own claim to common decency.

Once familiar with the pomp and panoply, the march and

countermarch of an English history play, you can turn at once to Shakespeare's masterpiece in this genre: *Henry IV, Parts 1 and 2,* which may be considered one play. Part 1 has the better story and introduces all the major characters, including the greatest of Shakespeare's comic figures, Falstaff, and one of the most eloquent and endearing of his romantic figures, Hotspur. Part 2 is for those who simply cannot get enough of Falstaff.

Then you should turn to *Richard II.* You will immediately feel at home with the story stuff, recognizing this play as the forerunner of the *Henry IV* plays you have just read. And Chapter 3 of *Shakespeare Plain* has acclimatized you to the *world* of this play. But above all, you will wish to read it for its matchless lyrics: the impassioned outpourings in the play's second half of Richard II who, in the process of losing a crown, a kingdom, and finally his life, remains king of his griefs and, for all of us who can be seduced by language, king of our hearts.

I suspect that the choices I have made so far will excite little controversy. But my next suggested cluster might. Although Shakespeare's romantic comedies are universally ranked among his greatest achievements, they appear relatively inaccessible to many college students and to many older adults as well. For one thing, high comedy is more intellectual than tragedy: it speaks to the head more than to the heart. For another, it is tied much more closely to the conventions of a particular age than is tragedy. Ben Jonson said of Shakespeare, "He was not of an age but for all time." But Shakespeare's romantic comedies partake more of the age for which they were written than do his tragedies. Therefore, my advice to you is to sample first that form of comedy that is most familiar—the farce. Less dependent on poetry and polished wit than is high comedy, possessed of more primitive appeals, speaking to human situations so fundamental as to be truly universal, farce proves more immediately accessible to modern audiences than does that special brand of Shakespearean comedy that has come to be designated *romantic.* Even if this statement is debatable as it applies to the classroom, it is incontrovertible when applied to the stage.

There is another advantage to reading Shakespearean comedy in this suggested order. *The Comedy of Errors* and *The Taming of the Shrew,* the two farces I am recommending here, contain in embryonic or nascent form many of the characters and devices that Shakespeare developed more fully later. Petruchio and Kate are rough, knockabout studies for Benedick and Beatrice to come. The twin Dromios of *Errors* anticipate such clowns as Lancelot Gobbo in *The Merchant of Venice* and Bully Bottom in *A Midsummer Night's Dream.* The darkly threatening aspect of the fate of old Aegon in *Errors* foreshadows the more complex and interesting variations on the threat to comic happiness projected by Shylock in *The Merchant of Venice* and by Malvolio in *Twelfth Night.* In a word, many of the techniques Shakespeare later refined and complicated are seen plain in the farces. In saying this, there is no intention to be patronizing about farce. One can take in a cottage more readily than a palace, but this does not mean that once admitted to the palace, one renounces cottages forever. Indeed, one may sometimes return to them with relief.

The great romantic comedies are five in number: *A Midsummer Night's Dream, The Merchant of Venice, As You Like It, Twelfth Night,* and *Much Ado About Nothing.* I list them in the order I would read them. They demonstrate very well the validity of my thesis that Shakespeare is his own best commentator. They have a common subject—love. And they have a common viewpoint that may be epitomized in the image of a mask. All the principal characters are set the task of ridding themselves of their masks of delusion (of many different kinds of delusion, of course) concerning love. When they succeed, they view love, and themselves in love, through the clear eyes of comic sanity. The heroes and heroines of these comedies win through; the villains and misfits never see straight. Four of these five plays have glorious heroines who combine great beauty with matchless sense and sensibility. All of the plays are constructed with two or more plots which, by means of ironic juxtaposition, serve as mirrors for their common themes and thus illuminate and enrich those themes. In short, each of these plays throws light on all of the others; and read in succession, they tell the reader most of what he needs to know about Shakespeare's way with this kind of play.

My final cluster comprises four plays now commonly referred to as the *symbolic romances: The Tempest, The Winter's Tale, Cymbeline,* and *Pericles.* I have listed them in the *reverse* order of their composition, and I advise reading them that way. Indeed, the last two, distinctly inferior to the first pair, may be skipped altogether; or they may be read after the first two so as to disclose in rough form the common ingredients that characterize all four—ingredients so skillfully woven into the textures of the first two as to render them less immediately apparent to the untrained eye. Although by now readers of *Shakespeare Plain* are well aware that Shakespeare's plays do not pretend in any literal sense to "hold the mirror up to nature"—that they are not, in fine, attempting either photographic or phonographic fidelity to everyday life—it is well to warn you that in these four fantasies, you must be prepared to encounter persons and events never seen on land or sea. But although you must accept the premises of fantasy if you are to comprehend the characters and actions, you will find yourself very much at home with the ideas and moral values. The themes are vintage Shakespeare.

Readers who have missed the mention so far of such current classroom favorites as *Measure for Measure, Love's Labor's Lost, Troilus and Cressida,* and *Coriolanus* may wonder why. For one thing, the first three of these four plays do not lend themselves very precisely to any classification. For another, each of them is attended by special problems of interpretation. It may be the challenge of these problems that attracts so many college teachers to them. But it is a challenge they would do well to resist until their students have read and comprehended the more accessible plays. I confess I am impatient with teachers who insist on taking captive audiences on spelunking expeditions into labyrinths when these same audiences have never yet climbed a mountain peak or crossed a broad savannah. There is world enough and time for these difficult plays as well as for others I have left unmentioned.

B. ABOUT SHAKESPEARE

I begin my list of books *about* Shakespeare by citing a title that makes it almost unnecessary to list any others. Ronald Berman's annotated bibliography, *A Reader's Guide to Shakespeare's Plays,* revised edition (1973), comprises some 3,000 entries that among them comprehend almost every important aspect of every play of Shakespeare.

I list next the books that I found most generally useful while writing *Shakespeare Plain.* The operative word here is *generally.* From some of these books I did not draw a single datum, quote a single statement, or—at least consciously— glean any concrete idea. But I drew continuous nourishment from them all. In alphabetical order of their author's names they are

Bernard Beckerman, *Shakespeare at the Globe* (1962)
Eric Bentley, *The Life of the Drama* (1946)
S. L. Bethell, *Shakespeare and the Popular Dramatic Tradition* (1944)
Marchette Chute, *Shakespeare of London* (1949)
Leonard Dean (editor,) *Shakespeare: Modern Essays in Criticism* (1967)
Henri Fluchère, *Shakespeare & The Elizabethans* (1964)
Harley Granville-Barker, *Prefaces to Shakespeare,* 2 vols. (1946–1947)
Alfred Harbage, *William Shakespeare: A Reader's Guide* (1963)
Alvin Kernan, *Character and Conflict* (1969)
Theodore Spencer, *Shakespeare and the Nature of Man* (1942)
Mark Van Doren, *Shakespeare* (1939)

There are books and short pieces (including some in the foregoing list) to which I am consciously indebted for both statements and ideas. Sources of specific quotations and allusions are recorded in the "Notes." For help with ideas, I turned to some of the following books and essays. Occasionally I list books I read *after* writing my own. I do so because they offer help, to readers who may wish to pursue in greater detail a particular line of inquiry. For this reason too I have arranged all of the titles under the heading of the chapter with which they are most closely associated.

CHAPTER 1. PLAYSCRIPT AND PERFORMANCE

In addition to the indirect light that the books of Bentley, Harbage, and Kernan throw on the concerns of this chapter, perhaps the most direct illumination will be found in the recently published *Shakespeare in Performance* (1976), edited by John Russell Brown. In this book the texts of six plays (*Romeo and Juliet, 1 Henry IV, Twelfth Night, Othello, King Lear, The Tempest*) are accompanied by a marginal running commentary which—aided by photographs of recent productions—calls attention to many of the significant components of an actual stage performance: physical actions that support or contrast with words; the effects of silences; the movements and groupings of actors; the changing tempos of exits and entrances; vocal climaxes; the use made of costume changes, stage properties, sound effects, music; and how the shape of the Elizabethan theater contributed to the action of the plays.

Roger Manvell provides a sensible and quiet-toned treatment of the problems that attend the filming of Shakespeare's plays in his *Shakespeare and the Film* (1971). The radical differences between a Shakespearean play and a Shakespearean film, to which I allude, receive the most incisive analysis I have read in an interview between Manvell and the eminent Shakespearean director, Peter Hall, reproduced on pages 120–127 of Manvell's book.

CHAPTER 2. PERSON AND CHARACTER

The literature on Shakespeare's characters is vast. Paradoxically, but not, I think, perversely, I have not found most of it useful. This is because the older pieces, beginning in the last quarter of the eighteenth century and carrying up to the first decade of the twentieth, embrace the critical heresy that Shakespeare's fictive characters are "real persons." And much of what has been written since on the subject, in an effort to eradicate this heresy, explains Shakespeare's characters as manifestations of traditional *types* (e.g., Falstaff is a variation of *the braggart warrior* of Roman comedy) or dramatic conventions (e.g., Othello is easily duped by Iago because Shakespeare is adopting the convention of *the calumniator believed*). Neither of these critical positions seems tenable to me: the older one simply turns its back on the achievement of art and blurs it with "life"; the newer, while appearing to be scholarly and "historical," does not correspond to the experience of most readers and playgoers whose imaginations have been engaged by the plays.

For better or for worse, I have had to find my own way helped by the almost parenthetical insights of fine commentators, four of whom are acknowledged in my "Notes." As *Shakespeare Plain* was being readied for the press, I came across two pieces that had previously escaped my attention. L. C. Knights, in a lecture entitled appropriately "The Question of Character in Shakespeare," reproduced as the final essay in *Further Explorations* (1965), has placed all of us in his debt by providing at once a lucid summary of the problems and a sweet-tempered survey of the proposed solutions. And Arthur Sewell's *Character and Society in Shakespeare* (1951) is a steady flow of *aperçus* that add up to what is easily the best book on the subject I have read.

CHAPTER 3. SETTING AND WORLD

Here again, much of my indebtedness is subliminal, although readers of A. C. Bradley's first lecture on *Macbeth,* in his *Shakespearean Tragedy* (1904; reissued in several editions since) and Mark Van Doren's complementary echoing of Bradley in the chapter on *Macbeth* from his book, *Shakespeare* (1939), will recognize the sources for much of what I say about the world of *Macbeth.* Maynard Mack's "The World of *Hamlet*," originally appearing in *The Yale Review,* XLI (1952) and reprinted in Dean's anthology cited above, defines the metaphor *world* memorably and provides a model of the kinds of insights that the exploration of the world of any play can afford the close reader. And in the "Introduction" to his *Shakespeare,* Mark Van Doren provides a brief, but characteristically eloquent, statement of the paradox that informs each of the worlds of Shakespeare's plays: "internally consistent, immediately knowable, and—at the same time it is familiar—permanently fresh and strange."

CHAPTER 4. STRUCTURE AND CONVENTION

Two books that squarely address themselves to the problem of act division in Shakespearean texts are those of W. T. Jewkes, *Act Division in Elizabethan and Jacobean Plays* (1958) and Henry L. Snuggs, *Shakespeare and Five Acts* (1960). The best book on Shakespearean dramaturgy is Bernard Beckerman's *Shakespeare at the Globe* (1962). Shakespearean dramatic *conventions* are treated in many books, but the general reader will find very readable and helpful the dicussions in the book by Henri Fluchère cited in the general list above and the essay by Harley Granville-Barker cited in the "Notes." And, brief as it is, Thornton Wilder's "Preface" to his edition of *Three Plays* (1957) says more about the artistic gains achieved by Shakespeare's handling of the conventions of time and place than do many pages printed elsewhere.

CHAPTER 5. STORY AND PLOT

Here again, the law of parsimony seems to apply. Much of the very considerable wordage addressed to this subject is misleading or relatively useless because the writers are relying on theoretical principles that do not fit Shakespearean playscripts. My heavy dependence on Bernard Beckerman's book, just cited, is my testimony to the soundness of his analyses of Shakespearean plot structures. The second part of an older book by Richard Moulton, *Shakespeare as a Dramatic Artist,* 3rd edition (1893), although excessively abstract is, nonetheless, full of useful insights.

CHAPTER 6. THEME AND MEANING

Anyone attempting to write on this subject must echo Vernon Louis Parrington who, when describing his attempt to chart a course through an equally difficult field of inquiry, spoke of himself as one of "those who like Merlin pursue the light of their hopes where it flickers above the treacherous marshlands." In my efforts to find my way, I have found help in various places, notably from Theodore Spencer's *Shakespeare and the Nature of Man* (1942), from Alfred Harbage's *As They Liked It* (1947, reissued in paperback in 1961), and from Brents Stirling's *Unity in Shakespearean Tragedy* (1956). Three books I would have benefited from had I encountered them earlier are Geoffrey Bush's *Shakespeare and the Natural Condition* (1956), A. P. Rossiter's *Angel with Horns* (1961), and Norman Rabkin's *Shakespeare and the Common Understanding* (1967).

CHAPTER 7. STYLE AND IMAGE

Wolfgang Clemen's *The Development of Shakespeare's Imagery* (1951) is the best full treatment of this subject that has so occupied twentiety-century critics. Although never explicitly making this claim, *Shakespeare* (1939) by Mark Van Doren is at once the most astute and most delightful treatment of Shakespeare's language I have encountered. In his little book, Van Doren looks at everything Shakespeare wrote through the filter of language. The results are wonderfully revealing. Using a more formal and direct approach, Alfred Harbage provides equal rewards in the essays he devotes to "Words" and "Lines" in the early portion of his *William Shakespeare: A Reader's Guide* (1963). These two essays, and their companion essay called "The Script," combine to make up what one can only call a tour de force of commentary on Shakespearean technique.

CHAPTER 8. VERSE AND PROSE

F. W. Ness's *The Use of Rhyme in Shakespeare's Plays* (1941) and Milton Crane's *Shakespeare's Prose* (1951) are the

standard works on their respective subjects. Brian Vickers'
The Artistry of Shakespeare's Prose (1968), as its title suggests,
refines some of Crane's insights. Nothing comparable has
been written on Shakespeare's blank verse, probably because
of its protean character: no commentator or critic can quite
pin it down. The Van Doren and Harbage books just mentioned can be helpful here nonetheless. Eric Bentley has
some interesting and even audacious things to say about the
language of drama under the heading "Dialogue" in his *The
Life of the Drama* (1964).

CHAPTER 9. PLAYHOUSE AND PLATFORM

C. Walter Hodges in *The Globe Restored* (1956) writes the
clearest account of the prevailing view of Elizabethan stage
facilities. An additional dividend for the readers of his book
are the many illustrations drawn by the author, a skilled
artist as well as a fine historian of English drama. A. M.
Nagler's *Shakespeare's Stage* (1958) offers a good, relatively
terse account. One of Professor Harbage's less well-known
books, *Theatre for Shakespeare* (1955), provides splendid insights under the guise of a polemic for "a Shakespearean
theater for out times." In this book, originally composed as a
set of public lectures, one can take additional delight in
hearing the voice of a witty and polished speaker.

CHAPTER 10. ACTOR AND AUDIENCE

Alfred Harbage's *Shakespeare's Audience* (1941) is the
definitive work on that subject. T. W. Baldwin's *The Organization and Personnel of the Shakespearean Company* (1927)
is the standard book on his subject, but the general reader
will probably wish to use it mainly as a reference work.
Brief, readable accounts of Shakespeare's company may be
found here and there in the pages of Marchette Chute's
Shakespeare of London (1949).

Truly sophisticated readers, who have discovered how much learning, albeit worn very lightly, can be transmitted through the pages of a book written for children by an accomplished writer, will wish to read any or all of these three books: Marchette Chute's *An Introduction to Shakespeare* (1953), C. Walter Hodges's *Shakespeare's Theatre* (1964), and Hodges's *Shakespeare and the Players* (1968). Like the unscrupulous reader of detective fiction who "peeks at the end" and thereafter "foots it featly" through the most complicated plot, those of you have peeked at the end of this section before reading any other books *about* Shakespeare may become the delighted beneficiaries of your own "immoralism." If you read first what is here mentioned last, you will be off to a swift and smooth start on the road to seeing Shakespeare plain.

CHRONOLOGY

The chronology that begins on the next page is a highly selective list of dates. The principle of selection was simply what is deemed to be most immediately useful to readers of this book. The historical and biographical dates, with the exception of the date assigned to Shakespeare's arrival in London, are certain. Many of the dates of play productions are, however, necessarily conjectural. Still, these conjectures represent a consensus of current scholarly opinion, and in no case will they seriously mislead the reader.

YEAR	IMPORTANT HISTORICAL EVENTS	BIOGRAPHICAL EVENTS: SHAKESPEARE AND HIS FAMILY	PRODUCTIONS OF SHAKESPEARE'S PLAYS
1558	Accession of Queen Elizabeth		
1564		Birth of Shakespeare	
1576	First permanent play-house, The Theatre, built		
1580	Sir Francis Drake circumnavigates the earth		
1582		Shakespeare's marriage	
1583		Shakespeare's daughter, Susanna, born	
1585		Shakespeare's twins, Hamnet and Judith, born	
1588	Defeat of the Spanish Armada	Shakespeare probably in London	

YEAR	IMPORTANT HISTORICAL EVENTS	BIOGRAPHICAL EVENTS: SHAKESPEARE AND HIS FAMILY	PRODUCTIONS OF SHAKESPEARE'S PLAYS
1590		Shakespeare variously employed as actor and writer	*The Comedy of Errors*
1590–1592			*1 Henry VI* *2 Henry VI* *3 Henry VI*
1592–1593	Plague closes London theatres at intervals	*Venus and Adonis* published (1593)	*Richard III* *Titus Andronicus*
1594		The Lord Chamberlain's Men (Shakespeare's long-time company) formed	*The Two Gentlemen of Verona* *The Taming of the Shrew*
1594–1595		*The Rape of Lucrece* published (1594)	*Love's Labor's Lost* *King John*
1595–1596		Application for grant of a coat of arms to Shakespeare's father (1595) Death of Shakespeare's son, Hamnet (1596)	*A Midsummer Night's Dream* *Richard II* *Romeo and Juliet*

Year			Plays
1597	Shakespeare buys New Place in Stratford		*The Merchant of Venice* *1 Henry IV*
1598			*2 Henry IV* *As You Like It*
1599	The Globe built		*Henry V* *Julius Caesar* *Much Ado About Nothing*
1600			*Twelfth Night* *The Merry Wives of Windsor*
1601		Insurrection and execution of Essex	*Hamlet*
1602			*Troilus and Cressida*
1603	The Lord Chamberlain's Men become the King's Men	Death of Queen Elizabeth and accession of James VI of Scotland as James I of England	*All's Well That Ends Well*
1604		Treaty of peace with Spain	*Othello* *Measure for Measure*
1605	Shakespeare purchases more land in Stratford	The Gunpowder Plot	*King Lear*

YEAR	IMPORTANT HISTORICAL EVENTS	BIOGRAPHICAL EVENTS: SHAKESPEARE AND HIS FAMILY	PRODUCTIONS OF SHAKESPEARE'S PLAYS
1606	Charter for Virginia		Macbeth
1606–1607		Susanna Shakespeare marries Dr. John Hall (1607)	Antony and Cleopatra
1607–1608		Burbage leases the Blackfriars for indoor performances (1608)	Timon of Athens Coriolanus Pericles
1609		The King's Men begin to play in Blackfriars Theater as well as the Globe	Cymbeline
1610			The Winter's Tale
1611	Authorized version of the Bible published		The Tempest
1613		The Globe destroyed by fire	Henry VIII
1614		The Globe rebuilt	

280

1616   Judith Shakespeare marries
       Shakespeare dies

1623   First Folio published

NOTES

CHAPTER TWO. PERSON AND CHARACTER

1. Mark Schorer, *The Story,* Prentice-Hall, Inc., Englewood Cliffs, N.J. (1950), p. 4, quoting the British novelist Ivy Compton-Burnett.
2. Alvin B. Kernan, *Character and Conflict,* 2d. edition, Harcourt, Brace & World, Inc., New York (1969), p. 22.
3. Brents Stirling, "Introduction," *The Merchant of Venice,* The Pelican Shakespeare, Penguin Books, Inc., Baltimore (1959), p. 23.
4. Alfred Harbage, "Shakespeare's Technique," in the "General Introduction" to *William Shakespeare: The Complete Works,* The Pelican Text Revised, Penguin Books, Inc., Baltimore (1969), pp. 34–35.

CHAPTER THREE. SETTING AND WORLD

1. Thornton Wilder, "Preface," *Three Plays,* Harper & Row, Inc., New York (1957), p. xi.
2. Sir Kenneth Clark, *Civilization,* Harper & Row, Inc., New York (1969), p. 70.
3. Herman Melville, *Billy Budd Sailor,* edited by Harrison Hayford and Merton M. Sealts, Jr., University of Chicago Press, Chicago (1962), p. 111.

CHAPTER FOUR. STRUCTURE AND CONVENTION

1. Mark Van Doren, *Shakespeare,* Henry Holt & Company, Inc., New York (1939), pp. 163–166.

2. Harley Granville-Barker, "Shakespeare's Dramatic Art," from *A Companion to Shakespeare Studies,* edited by H. Granville-Barker and G. B. Harrison (paperback Anchor Book), Doubleday & Company, Inc., Garden City, N.Y. (1960), p. 66.

3. Thornton Wilder, "Preface," *Three Plays,* Harper & Row, Inc., New York (1957), p. xi.

CHAPTER FIVE. STORY AND PLOT

1. E. M. Forster, *Aspects of the Novel* (paperback Harvest Book), Harcourt, Brace & World, Inc., New York (1954), p. 86.

2. *Aristotle on the Art of Poetry,* translated by Ingram Bywater, The Clarendon Press, Oxford, England (1959), *passim.*

3. Walter Raleigh (editor), *Johnson on Shakespeare,* Oxford University Press, London (1952), p. 180. Also in W. K. Wimsatt (editor), *Samuel Johnson on Shakespeare,* Hill & Wang, New York (1960), p. 107.

4. T. S. Eliot, "Shakespeare and the Stoicism of Seneca," *Elizabethan Essays,* Faber & Faber, Ltd., London (1934), p. 33.

CHAPTER SIX. THEME AND MEANING

1. Alfred Harbage, *As They Liked It,* Harper Torchbooks, New York (1961), p. 6; originally published by The Macmillan Company, New York (1947).

2. Theodore Spencer, *Shakespeare and the Nature of Man,* (Macmillan Paperbacks Edition), The Macmillan Company, New York (1961), pp. 29–45.

CHAPTER SEVEN. STYLE AND IMAGE

1. Mark Van Doren, *Shakespeare,* Henry Holt & Company, Inc., New York (1939), p. xiii.

2. *Aristotle on the Art of Poetry,* translated by Ingram Bywater, The Clarendon Press, Oxford, England (1959), p. 78.

3. Alfred Longueil, Emeritus Professor of English, University of California at Los Angeles, in a letter to the author dated August 14, 1974.

4. Caroline Spurgeon, *Shakespeare's Imagery and What It Tells Us* (paperback edition), Beacon Press, Boston (1958); originally published by The University Press, Cambridge, England (1935).

5. W. H. Clemen, *The Development of Shakespeare's Imagery*, Harvard University Press, Cambridge, Mass. (1951).

6. Henry James, "The Figure in the Carpet," Macmillan and Company (1896); frequently reprinted in collections of James's short stories and novellas, including F. O. Matthiessen (editor), *Henry James: Stories of Artists and Writers* (paperback), New Directions Publishing Corp., New York (1944).

CHAPTER EIGHT. VERSE AND PROSE

1. Eric Bentley, *The Life of the Drama*, Atheneum Publishers, New York (1964), p. 86.

CHAPTER NINE. PLAYHOUSE AND PLATFORM

1. John Dover Wilson, "Introduction" and "Notes," *King Henry V*, The New Shakespeare, The University Press, Cambridge, England (1947), footnote 2, p. x and Note 13, p. 122.

2. Marchette Chute, *Shakespeare of London* (paperback edition), E. P. Dutton & Co., Inc., New York (1950), p. 27.

3. A. M. Nagler, *Shakespeare's Stage*, Yale University Press, New Haven, Conn. (1958), pp. 9–10.

4. Alfred Harbage, *Shakespeare's Audience*, Columbia University Press, New York (1941), pp. 30–33.

5. Ibid., pp. 40–41.

6. Alfred Harbage, *Shakespeare and The Rival Traditions*, Barnes & Noble, Inc., New York (1968), p. 16; originally published by The Macmillan Company, New York (1952).

7. Joseph Quincy Adams, *A Life of William Shakespeare*, Houghton Mifflin Company, Boston (1923), pp. 436–437, quoting the original account in a letter by Sir Henry Wotton, from *Reliquiae Wottonianae*, 1672 edition, p. 425.

8. Ibid.

9. E. J. West (editor) "Playhouses and Plays," *Shaw on Theatre*, Hill & Wang, New York (1958), p. 181.

CHAPTER TEN. ACTOR AND AUDIENCE

1. A. M. Nagler, *Shakespeare's Stage,* Yale University Press, New Haven, Conn. (1958), pp. 72–75; this account draws on the speculations of T. W. Baldwin, *The Organization and Personnel of the Shakespearean Company,* Princeton University Press, Princeton (1927), 229–283.

INDEX

Catalog

If you are interested in a list of fine Paperback
books, covering a wide range of subjects
and interests, send your name and address,
requesting your free catalog, to:

McGraw-Hill Paperbacks
1221 Avenue of Americas
New York, N.Y. 10020